SPADINA

James Austin (1813-1897) of *Spadina*.

SPADINA

A Story of Old Toronto

AUSTIN SETON THOMPSON

Pagurian Press Limited
TORONTO

ISBN 0-88932-004-7

Printed and Bound in Canada

Preface

Few houses in Toronto have had such an interesting history as *Spadina,*
standing on Davenport Hill east of *Casa Loma.* The first house on the site
was built in 1818 by Dr. William Warren Baldwin. This two-storey frame
building burned down in 1835, and a smaller house was built by Baldwin in
the same year. In 1866 it was bought from Baldwin's grandson by James
Austin, who tore it down and built another which is still standing and still
lived in by a member of the Austin family. Thus for over 150 years the
property has been occupied by only two families.

These families had much in common. William Warren Baldwin and James
Austin were both Irish immigrants with extraordinary ability. Baldwin came
to York in 1799 when he was twenty-four years old. He was already a doctor, but the infant colony did not provide sufficient scope for his profession
and he became a lawyer. He and his son, the Honourable Robert Baldwin,
were increasingly active in the political reform movement and evolved the
principle of Responsible Government with which their names will always be
associated. James Austin was only sixteen when he came to Canada in 1829
and was apprenticed to William Lyon Mackenzie to learn the printing trade.
In the 1840's he began a very successful career in the wholesale grocery
business, and in 1871 he became one of the founders and first president of
The Dominion Bank, a position later held by his son, Albert William Austin.

Both Baldwin and Austin became rich — Baldwin by inherited land,
Austin by trade. Both had the Irish feeling for close family relationships and
for the importance of a family estate. To each *Spadina* was not just a house,
but a symbol of family stability and permanence. Other members of their
families built houses near *Spadina:* Baldwin's brother built *Russell Hill* and
his son built *Mashquoteh,* while Austin's son-in-law built *Ravenswood.* Later
more large houses were built on Davenport Hill — Samuel Nordheimer's
Glenedyth, Sir John Eaton's *Ardwold,* and finally Sir Henry Pellatt's magnificent folly, *Casa Loma.* All but *Spadina* and *Casa Loma* have been demolished, and only *Spadina* remains the family home it has been for generations.

Life at *Spadina* was always leisurely. Money and servants were generally
plentiful, and pleasant rituals and habits developed in both families. There
were always a great many visitors. Although the Baldwins usually used their
town house on Front Street for formal parties, many famous Canadians
passed through the door which is still preserved in the present *Spadina.* The
Austins also entertained extensively — one Sunday afternoon the Archbishop
of Canterbury and J. Pierpont Morgan came to tea. An even greater lion,

however, escaped; in 1919 when the Prince of Wales also climbed the Hill, his motorcade only had enough time to pause at the entrance to *Spadina* for a "brief exchange of pleasantries" with Albert Austin and his neighbour Sir John Eaton.

Baldwins and Austins were born and married and died at *Spadina*. The Baldwins had a private cemetery, St. Martin's Rood, on the *Spadina* grounds, and it was here on a blustery December day in 1858 that the Honourable Robert Baldwin was buried, near the house where he had lived since his retirement in 1851. As he had requested, his coffin was chained to that of his long-dead wife. It was at *Spadina* also that the wedding breakfast for James Austin's youngest daughter Margaret was held in 1869. Margaret Austin married a British army officer, the regimental band played, and it was a great social occasion. The twenty-year-old bride accompanied her husband to England, only to return to *Spadina* to die, little more than two years later.

In 1818 when *Spadina* was first built, it was a country house some distance from the town. Metropolitan Toronto has swept past the property, leaving it an anachronistic oasis in the heart of a changing city. Its very existence has been threatened in the past, and it is certainly not now immune from future attack by the planner and developer. It remains, however, a rare survival of a former age, wearing its years with grace and dignity. Its story, and the story of those who lived there, is part of the history of Toronto.

February 26, 1975

EDITH G. FIRTH
Baldwin Room
Metropolitan Toronto
Central Library

Contents

List of Illustrations xi

Acknowledgments 13

A Table of Baldwin Family Relationships 16

A Table of Austin Family Relationships 17

PART I   The Dynasts (1793-1865) 19

1.   The King's Bounty 21

2.   The Baldwins Arrive in Upper Canada 37

3.   Dr. Baldwin Moves to York 45

4.   A House of Modest Aspect 52

5.   The Death of the Honourable Peter Russell 59

6.   1812 Overture 66

7.   Dr. Baldwin Builds Spadina 74

8.   The End of an Era 82

     Notes to Part I 99

PART II   The Golden Key (1866-1936) 105

9.   King Street Auction 107

10.   James Austin Builds a New Spadina 112

11.   The Men of Montreal 128

12.   A Railroad Saga 137

13.   A Time to Sow 143

14. Manitoba Fever 152

15. A Bird of Ill Omen 162

16. The Death of James Austin 170

17. Pomp and Circumstance 188

18. Only Yesterday 199

    Notes to Part II 214

    Index 219

List of Illustrations

James Austin (1813-1897) .... Frontispiece

Map of *Spadina* and Environs, 1819 .... 24, 25

The Honourable Peter Russell (1733-1808) 28

Elizabeth Russell (1754-1822) 31

William Willcocks (1736-1813) 32

Russell Abbey 34

Dr. William Warren Baldwin (1775-1844) 44

The original *Spadina* (1818-1835) 78

Russell Hill (1819-1871) 79

The second *Spadina* (1836-1866) 85

Davenport 87

The Honourable Robert Baldwin (1804-1858) 94

William Willcocks Baldwin (1830-1893) 97

James Austin's *Spadina,* built in 1866 113

Dr. Baldwin's front door 114

The reception room, *Spadina* 116

The drawing room, *Spadina* 117

A cast-iron radiator, *Spadina* 118

Detail of radiator, *Spadina* 119

Ravenswood 120

A view of the "Battery," Davenport Hill 121

A view of Toronto from the Bathurst Street Hill (1875) 122

A view of Toronto from the *Spadina* farmlands 123

Susan Bright Austin (1817-1907) 124

A rustic bridge spanning the Castle Frank stream 130

A carriage drive on the *Spadina* property 132

Glenedyth 138

The head-office building of The Dominion Bank (1878) 148

Plaster head of James Austin 150

Albert William Austin's Winnipeg Street Railway 157

E. S. Shrapnel's sketch of James Henry Austin 158

Susan Bright Austin's *Spadina* parlour 178

The billiard room, *Spadina* 179

Albert William Austin (1857-1934) 180

Mary Richmond Kerr Austin (1860-1942) 182

The Lambton Golf and Country Club (1904) 184

Building permit for *Casa Loma* 191

A view from the tower of the *Casa Loma* stables 192, 193

Vegetable garden and stables, *Casa Loma* 195

James Austin, Sir Frank Smith, and Sir Edmund B. Osler 200

Ardwold 203

The lawn south of Ravenswood (1905) 204

Ardwold's classical Italian garden 205

Oil sketch, "Top of Hill, Spadina Avenue, Toronto, 1909,"
    painted by Lawren Harris 207

Spadina after its 1907 renovation 208

Acknowledgments

The early chapters of this book are mainly concerned with episodes in the lives of four pioneer residents of the Town of York: Receiver General Peter Russell and his half-sister, Elizabeth, their cousin William Willcocks, and Dr. William Warren Baldwin who married Willcocks' daughter, Phoebe. At the time of the settlement of York and the surrounding district, Russell and Willcocks were the first owners of a tract of land that for convenience may be called the Spadina Enclave—a corridor of real estate, extending north from the present Queen Street to Eglinton Avenue, through which Spadina Avenue and part of Spadina Road now pass. It was in the centre of this enclave, on the crest of the Davenport Hill, that Dr. Baldwin built the first *Spadina* house in 1818 on land he had inherited from his father-in-law, William Willcocks.

An Irish doctor turned lawyer, Dr. William Warren Baldwin was active in the cause of political reform in Upper Canada until his death in 1844. His son, the Honourable Robert Baldwin, carried his father's beliefs to the national forum, and with the Honourable Louis-Hippolyte LaFontaine of Lower Canada, played a prominent role in attaining acceptance of the principles of responsible government in Canada. The Honourable Robert Baldwin died at *Spadina* in 1858 and, like his father, was buried in the Baldwins' private cemetery on the Davenport Hill, near his *Spadina* house.

William Willcocks Baldwin, the Honourable Robert Baldwin's eldest son, inherited his father's *Spadina* house with 80 acres of land around it. After mortgaging it heavily, he sold it at public auction in February, 1866. The auctioneer's hammer that fell that month in a crowded room on King Street East, knelled the passing of a family tie with the *Spadina* farmlands that reached back to colonial times. It also heralded the arrival on the scene of a new owner, James Austin, one of a number of capitalists who were then becoming prominent in the life of mid-Victorian Toronto. Austin, who as a boy had emigrated to York from Northern Ireland in 1829, lost no time in demolishing the frame and stucco Baldwin dwelling, and raising a new *Spadina* of solid brick on the site. His pre-Confederation house still stands today.

In order to draw an accurate picture of the way in which the extensive Russell and Willcocks land holdings fell into the hands of Dr. Baldwin's family, thereby providing him and his son, the Honourable Robert Baldwin, with a secure financial base from which to launch their famous battle for

xiii

political reform, it was necessary to examine in detail many early deeds, wills, and registered plans. The same techniques were used to verify the material contained in the later chapters of this book as well. For his invaluable assistance in all these inquiries, I record with sadness my indebtedness to the late Stanley Armour, Q.C. who for over a year, indeed to the day of his death, helped me unravel many of the mysteries relating to the property transactions described in this work. My thanks are also due Mr. Joseph Haughey, Deputy Registrar of the City Registry Office, for the cheerful help he unfailingly gave Mr. Armour and myself. When the trail appeared lost, his expert knowledge was always available to guide us on to our destination. In the same vein, I offer my thanks to Mr. Scott James of the City of Toronto Archives.

I also acknowledge my gratitude to Miss Edith G. Firth, head of the Canadiana & Manuscript Section of the Metropolitan Toronto Central Library, for her patient help and practical counsel at an early stage in the preparation of this work. I have drawn as well on the documents she has assembled and edited in *The Town of York* (Volumes I and II). They were a veritable life-raft for a layman historian embarking upon a voyage of this kind. I also direct my thanks to Mr. Henry E. Guest in Winnipeg for allowing me to borrow freely from his valued thesis, written for the Faculty of Graduate Studies of the University of Manitoba, on the life of Dr. William Warren Baldwin.

I am indebted to a great many other people who have provided me with material for the later chapters of this book which record the principal events in the lives of James Austin of *Spadina* and his son, Albert William. In particular, I thank Miss M. Geary of the Consumers' Gas Company for making available to me historical information relating to the long period of James Austin's association with that company as its president. As my narrative reached out to Winnipeg, where Albert Austin established the Winnipeg Street Railway in 1882, I was fortunate in being introduced to Mr. Herbert W. Blake who placed at my disposal his extensive knowledge of the history of Winnipeg's transportation system. I am happy to acknowledge his assistance.

For permission to reproduce paintings and photographs in their possession, I also thank Air Commodore A. Dwight Ross, G.C., C.B.E., C.D., the Nordheimer family, Mrs. E. Llewellyn G. Smith who is a great, great granddaughter of James Austin, Mr. Howard K. Harris of Vancouver, The Toronto-Dominion Bank, Eaton's Archives, the Management of *Casa Loma,* and, of course, the custodians of the John Ross Robertson Collection and the Public Archives of Ontario. For assistance of a technical nature, I am indebted to Mr. Langton G. Baker, and for advice concerning the manuscript, to Mr. Walter Bowker.

I also record my appreciation of my mother's contribution to this work by submitting to prolonged questioning about her childhood days at *Spadina* on the Davenport Hill—the days before Sir Henry Pellatt built *Casa Loma* on part of the old *Spadina* farmlands, and Sir John Eaton's splendid villa, *Ardwold,* rose on the site of her aunt's neighbouring *Ravenswood.* As the only surviving grandchild of James Austin, Kathleen Austin Thompson's recollections of the days when the *Spadina* house she still occupies was a lonely place, on the outskirts of Toronto, have been essential to this narrative.

Finally, my special thanks are due my son Evan who devoted a good part of several summer holidays from school to burrowing in the Central Library and the Ontario Archives on behalf of this narrative, which he, his younger brother Jamie, and my wife Joan, by their unflagging patience made it possible for me to write.

Toronto   A.S.T.

November 10, 1974

A TABLE OF BALDWIN FAMILY RELATIONSHIPS

Robert Baldwin (the EMIGRANT) m. (1769) Barbara Spread
1741-1816   1748-1791

Four of their sixteen children were:

Barbara m. (1797) Daniel Sullivan
1770-1853   1742?-1822

Two of their eight children were:

Daniel (clerk in Dr. Baldwin's
Law Office in *Russell Abbey*)
1798-1821

Augusta Elizabeth
(married her first cousin,
Robert Baldwin, in 1827)

William Warren m. (1803) Phoebe Willcocks
1775-1844   1771-1851
(Dr. Baldwin of *Spadina*) (daughter of William
                            and Phoebe Willcocks
                            of York)

Robert m. (1827) Augusta Elizabeth Sullivan
1804-1858   1809-1836
(The Hon.)

William Willcocks (married twice
1830-1893   in 1854 and 1856)
(Sold *Spadina* at auction in 1866)

Phoebe Maria
1828-1860

Augustus William ("Little Billy")
1805-1806

Henry
1807-1820

William Augustus (married twice
1808-1883   in 1834 and 1852)
(Baldwin of *Mashquoteh*)

Quetton St. George
1810-1829

Augustus Warren m. (1827) Augusta Jackson
1776-1866
(Captain Baldwin of *Russell Hill*)

Augusta Elizabeth
b. 1831 m. (1851)
Hon. John Ross
1818-1871

John Spread m. (1822) Anne Shaw
1787-1843   1798-1870
One of their nine children was:

Henrietta Eugenia m. (1841) Henry Scadding
1823-1843   1813-1901

Robert (married twice in
1834-1885 1859 and 1877)

A TABLE OF AUSTIN FAMILY RELATIONSHIPS

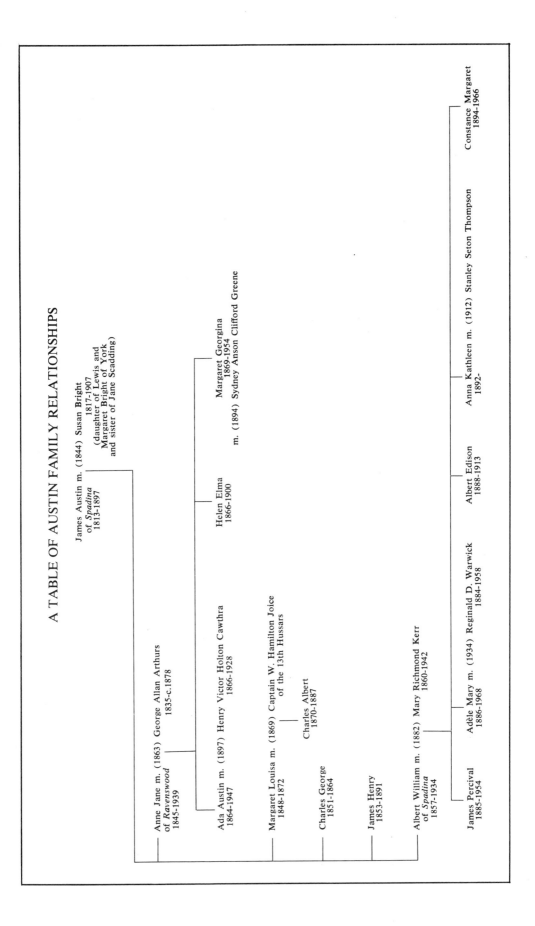

James Austin m. (1844) Susan Bright
of *Spadina*   1817-1907
1813-1897   (daughter of Lewis and
                    Margaret Bright of York
                    and sister of Jane Scadding)

Anne Jane m. (1863) George Allan Arthurs
of *Ravenswood*
1845-1939   1835-c.1878

Ada Austin m. (1897) Henry Victor Holton Cawthra
1864-1947   1866-1928

Margaret Louisa m. (1869) Captain W. Hamilton Joice
1848-1872   of the 13th Hussars

Charles Albert
1870-1887

Charles George
1851-1864

James Henry
1853-1891

Albert William m. (1882) Mary Richmond Kerr
of *Spadina*   1860-1942
1857-1934

Helen Elma
1866-1900

Margaret Georgina
1869-1954
m. (1894) Sydney Anson Clifford Greene

James Percival
1885-1954

Adèle Mary m. (1934) Reginald D. Warwick
1886-1968   1884-1958

Albert Edison
1888-1913

Anna Kathleen m. (1912) Stanley Seton Thompson
1892-

Constance Margaret
1894-1966

Part I

The Dynasts (1793-1865)

Chapter 1

The King's Bounty

His Excellency, Colonel John Graves Simcoe, lieutenant-governor of the Province of Upper Canada, had ordered his Executive Council to meet with him on Monday, September 2, 1793, at the new townsite of York on Lake Ontario. He wished to deal with the large number of petitions for land that had accumulated during the summer, not only for lots in the Town of York, which was now ready for settlement at the eastern end of the Toronto Bay, but also for the more generous park and farm lots which had just been surveyed in the adjoining Township of York.

The governor had set up his camp a month earlier on a grassy knoll overlooking the entrance to the Toronto Bay, at the foot of the present Bathurst Street. The site he had chosen was some distance to the west of the town he was establishing, but with a soldier's eye he had placed his encampment opposite the western tip of the low-lying peninsula, or Toronto Island as it is now, so that he could better direct the construction of the defences needed to guard the entrance to the Harbour of York. At that moment, he was more interested in developing a defensible naval station within the sheltered bay, at a comfortable distance from the Americans on the other side of Lake Ontario, than he was in immersing himself in the tedious details of founding a town. The security of the colony was uppermost in his mind.

Simcoe's campsite, which is unmarked today, consisted simply of a "Canvas house" to which was attached an arbour for dining and a tent for Council meetings which could accommodate only a table and three chairs. With soldierly foresight he had purchased his "Canvas house" in London before leaving for British North America. It had belonged to the late Captain James Cook, the famous explorer of the South Pacific, who had served under his father, Captain John Simcoe of the Royal Navy, in General Wolfe's expedition against Quebec in 1759. This large tent provided the governor and his wife with a bedroom, which also served as a reception room during the day, and an additional room for their nurse and infant children.

Behind the governor's compound, stretching north to the steep ridge several miles from the bay, now the Davenport Hill, lay only a wilderness of silent forests and dark ravines. While some settlers had recently appeared in the district, the area about to be settled was still largely the haunt of a few roving bands of Indians. Despite the primitive setting, it was not out of character for Brigade Major Littlehales, Simcoe's military secretary, to record grandly that the meeting was held in the "Council Chamber" at York. The British, always effective colonizers, had a remarkable aptitude for investing

21

the simplest colonial proceedings with the aura of Westminster. Indeed, only a few days before, Simcoe had changed the name of the locality from the Indian word Toronto to the English name of York. The formal proclamation had been accompanied by a flag-raising ceremony and a salute of guns from the ships at anchor in the bay. Simcoe missed no opportunity of casting the Imperial light into the darkest corners of the colony. Earlier, he had renamed Niagara "Newark," now Niagara-on-the-Lake, and preferred the name Kingston to Cataraqui. On a long, tedious march from Detroit with his soldiers and Indian guides, he had startled the Indians who were lolling around the campfire by insisting that the entire party, before retiring for the night, scramble to their feet and sing "God Save the King."

He was now determined to imbue the American immigrants to Upper Canada with a proper reverence for British institutions and traditions. As commanding officer of the renowned Queen's Rangers, he had fought in the Revolutionary War against American republicanism, which he hated even more now the virus had spread across the Atlantic to France with whom England was at war.

When Simcoe had been proclaimed lieutenant-governor of the new province of Upper Canada in Kingston the year before, three members of His Excellency's Executive Council had also been sworn into office. They were William Osgoode, James Baby, and Peter Russell. Simcoe's royal instructions, however, called for the appointment of five individuals to form his Council; the remaining nominees were William Robertson, who was absent from the province, and Alexander Grant, who turned up a few days after the ceremonies. Of these men, only Simcoe, Osgoode, and Russell were present at the first land-granting meetings held in infant York. William Osgoode, the chief justice of Upper Canada, and Peter Russell, the receiver general, had been living at Newark, on the Niagara River, for only a little over a year. Notwithstanding that the viceregal throne had been transferred to York, Simcoe having decided to spend the winter there in his "Canvas house," the seat of government was to remain in Newark until dwellings for the public officials could be built in the new town. Despite the constant "beat of drums & crash of falling Trees," as Mrs. Simcoe put it, Russell and Osgoode managed to endure the discomforts of the governor's encampment with patience and equanimity. Their visit was only for a few days.

In addition to the three members of the Council, Littlehales was present as secretary, together with Alexander Aitkin, the deputy surveyor, who had spent the summer surveying the area. He produced his maps and surveys which the secretary carefully noted "were ordered to be laid on the Table." The historic meeting was subject to a number of annoying distractions. To begin with, a strong wind was rising on the lake which made it difficult for Littlehales to secure the maps which the honourable members, with growing impatience, were attempting to examine. The tent or "Council Chamber" itself was creaking ominously under the force of the wind, and the waves could be heard clearly as they broke against the shore. Not far distant, in the vicinity of the later Fort York, a detachment of the Queen's Rangers were noisily at work felling trees and building huts in preparation for their winter sojourn. Adding to the commotion and bustle were the cries of the governor's children, who were playing in their canvas dwelling nearby.

Despite the cramped and noisy quarters, the Council handled a large volume of business with commendable dispatch. And the principle of *noblesse oblige* was meticulously applied. That is to say, the petitions before it that

Monday related mainly to minor officials of government, a few Loyalists, and a number of other settlers. The more important allocations, namely to themselves, the other senior officials, and military officers, were held over for a second meeting the following Wednesday.

Among those favoured by the Council's first dispensations were John Scadding, Simcoe's clerk and father of the Reverend Henry Scadding, D.D., a later Toronto historian; Christopher Robinson, a Loyalist and father of John Beverley Robinson, a later chief justice of Upper Canada; and William Willcocks and his son Charles who were Irish relatives of the Honourable Peter Russell.[1] The provisional grants of wild lands to the Willcocks' are of special interest because they encompassed the lands upon which both the future *Spadina* property and Spadina Avenue were later to be developed.

At the end of the meeting, the deputy surveyor was asked to point out the lots granted, and to acquaint the grantees with the requirement that they be "immediately located." In the case of Willcocks and his son, this direction could not possibly have been carried out, as the Council well knew. William Willcocks at that moment was in Ireland serving a term as mayor of Cork while attempting to recruit emigrants for a grandiose scheme he was promoting for the settlement of the Township of Whitby, some distance to the east of the Bay of Toronto. Willcocks was a first cousin of the Honourable Peter Russell, who, upon his appointment in 1792 as Simcoe's receiver general, stimulated Willcocks' interest in emigrating to Upper Canada. Willcocks, a merchant of Cork, visited the new province briefly that year and then hurried back to Ireland to organize a group of settlers. With Irish logic the voters of his city saw nothing inconsistent in electing Willcocks mayor while he was trying to organize an exodus from their district.

The minutes of the Council meeting in Simcoe's tent on September 2, 1793 included the following entries relating to William and Charles Willcocks:

> Mr. William Willcocks praying for a Front Town Lot. Granted, and No. 15 first Concession, 100 acres, and half No. 24 second Concession, with his son — Mr. Charles Willcocks praying for a Front Town Lot. Granted, and No. 13 first Concession, 100 acres, and half No. 24 Second Concession with his Father (they having an Order of Council for the same).[2]

The front town lots referred to lay within the Town of York as conceived by Simcoe and surveyed by Alexander Aitkin. The townsite consisted of ten blocks bounded by the present George, Duke, Berkeley, and Front streets. The Don River lay just to the east.

The First Concession lots, known as park lots, had a frontage of 660 feet on Lot Street (now Queen Street) and extended north 6,600 feet to what is now Bloor Street. They were numbered from east to west, and each contained 100 acres. The Second Concession lots were called farm lots, and they each consisted of 200 acres. They were also numbered from east to west, but their frontage on Bloor Street was 1,320 feet. They extended north to what is now St. Clair Avenue, a distance of 6,600 feet. All these lots were within the original Township of York.

The 100-acre park lots were granted by Simcoe as "douceurs" to compensate his officials for uprooting themselves in Newark and moving across the lake to York. The word "park" implies an estate with sweeping lawns and carriage drives encircling an impressive manor house—and perhaps

SPADINA AND ENVIRONS

A.D. 1819

TOWNSHIP OF YORK
PROVINCE OF UPPER CANADA

HOUSES:

A	"DAVENPORT"-	LIEUT. JOHN McGILL
B	"SPADINA" -	DR. W.W. BALDWIN
C	"RUSSELL HILL"-	CAPT. A.W. BALDWIN
D	"PETERSFIELD"-	ELIZABETH RUSSELL
E	"THE GRANGE"-	D'ARCY BOULTON JR.

ORIGINAL CROWN GRANTS

PARK LOTS (FIRST CON. - 100 ACRES EACH)

13	ROBERT ISAAC DEY GRAY	MAY 1, 1798
14	HON. PETER RUSSELL,	MARCH 23, 1798
15	WILLIAM WILLCOCKS ESQ.,	DEC 22, 1798
16	HON. JAMES BABY	DEC 21, 1798

FARM LOTS (SECOND CON. - 200 ACRES EACH)

23	HON PETER RUSSELL,	MAY 6, 1796
24	WILLIAM WILLCOCKS ESQ.,	DEC 22, 1798
25	LIEUT JOHN McGILL	MAR 26, 1798
	(ADJUTANT, QUEEN'S RANGERS)	

FARM LOTS (THIRD CON. - 200 ACRES EACH)

22	HON. PETER RUSSELL	JULY 17, 1797
23	HON PETER RUSSELL	MAY 6, 1796

SCALE IN FEET

'I CHAIN EQUALS 66 FEET

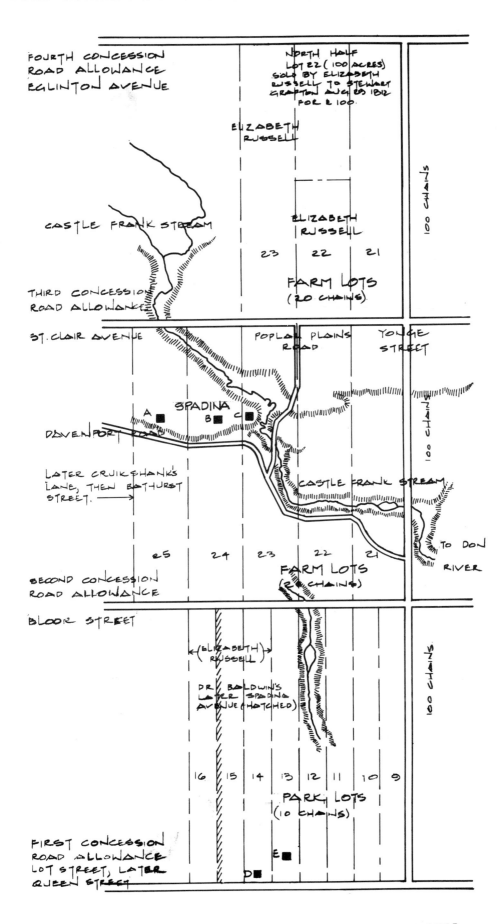

FOURTH CONCESSION
ROAD ALLOWANCE
EGLINTON AVENUE

NORTH HALF
LOT 22 (100 ACRES)
SOLD BY ELIZABETH
RUSSELL TO STEWART
GRAFTON AUG 25 1812
FOR £ 100.

ELIZABETH
RUSSELL

CASTLE FRANK STREAM

ELIZABETH
RUSSELL

23 | 22 | 21

FARM LOTS
(20 CHAINS)

THIRD CONCESSION
ROAD ALLOWANCE

100 CHAINS

ST. CLAIR AVENUE

POPLAR PLAINS
ROAD

YONGE
STREET

A   SPADINA
B   C

DAVENPORT ROAD

LATER CRUIKSHANK'S
LANE, THEN BATHURST
STREET.

CASTLE FRANK STREAM

100 CHAINS

25 | 24 | 23 | 22 | 21

TO DON
RIVER

FARM LOTS
(20 CHAINS)

SECOND CONCESSION
ROAD ALLOWANCE

BLOOR STREET

(ELIZABETH
RUSSELL)

DR. BALDWIN'S
LATER SPADINA
AVENUE (HATCHED)

100 CHAINS

16 | 15 | 14 | 13 | 12 | 11 | 10 | 9

PARK LOTS
(10 CHAINS)

E

FIRST CONCESSION
ROAD ALLOWANCE
LOT STREET, LATER
QUEEN STREET

D

Simcoe, who dreamed of establishing an aristocratic society in Upper Canada, chose the name to gratify the pretensions of his officials. But few, if any, of the early park lots were to be developed in this way. While a small number of original recipients lived on them, generally in modest dwellings, most preferred to live in town and sell or lease their properties to other settlers.

In an instruction to a Committee of his Executive Council in 1796, Simcoe asked them to consider

> what period in the opinion of the Committee ought to be allotted to each Officer of the Government for the construction of a House, in the front Lots of the Town of York, agreeably to a Plan that shall be recommended by the Committee to His Excellency provided such Officers receive one hundred Acres of Land respectively in the first Concession of the Township of York, and adjacent to the Town, in aid of the expense necessary to the Erection of such a House conformably to the original principal.

Clearly, Simcoe anticipated that at least some recipients of park lots would sell or lease them as required to help defray the cost of building their houses in the new Town of York.

The 200-acre farm lots, as their name implied, were intended to provide agricultural support for the inhabitants of the new community. The settlement at first was entirely dependent upon water-borne supplies from Newark and Kingston. Simcoe, his eye warily on the Americans across the lake, was anxious that the Town of York become self-sufficient as quickly as possible in the matter of its essential food supplies.

The provisional grant of Lot No. 15, First Concession (through which Spadina Avenue now passes), together with Lot No. 24, Second Concession (the later *Spadina* property), provided the mayor of Cork with a corridor of real estate extending north from the present Queen Street to St. Clair Avenue along the line of modern-day Spadina Avenue.

On Wednesday, September 4, 1793, the Executive Council met again to deal chiefly with the land petitions of the senior government and military officials. At this meeting the Honourable Peter Russell was granted a front town lot in the Town of York, as well as Lot No. 14, First Concession (100 acres), and Lot No. 23, Second Concession (200 acres). He also received Lot No. 23 (200 acres) in the Third Concession. It will be seen that these provisional grants offered Russell a personal land corridor extending from Queen Street to the present Eglinton Avenue, amounting to 500 acres. Moreover, his Park Lot 14, First Concession, adjoined William Willcocks' Lot 15 which lay to the west. Similarly, the receiver general's Farm Lot 23 in the Second Concession, extending from Bloor Street to St. Clair Avenue, was adjacent to Willcocks' Lot 24. (See pages 24 and 25.)

The question naturally arises as to why the two cousins made these particular selections when, in 1793, the area about to be settled was virtually in a state of wilderness. Indeed, it is doubtful that they had even ventured into the rough terrain to reconnoitre it. It was a condition of the granting of the petitions that settlement work be done on the lands affected. Only then could a formal deed from the Crown be obtained. Understandably, if these adjoining lands were to be developed by Russell and Willcocks there would be mutual advantages in the matter of clearing and building on them. But there was a further advantage inherent in the land spread now available to the two men. Along the foot of the hill that flings itself across the north-central part of the present city of Toronto, later called by geologists the Davenport Ridge or the Lake Iroquois Escarpment, lay an important and well-travelled trail, which had been used by the Indians long before European settlement occurred. It led west from the Don River to the famous route by the Humber River over which the Indians and early fur traders portaged north from Lake Ontario to the Holland River, Lake Simcoe, and Georgian Bay. In later times this ancient trail was to become the Davenport Road. In 1793 it offered Russell and Willcocks, as well as the other petitioners whose lands were astride it, the obvious advantage of an open approach to the heart of their land holdings. In addition, it could be developed easily into a useful road, particularly since the trail passed just north of the townsite of York at the eastern end of the Toronto Bay.

Aside from their town lots, most of the public officials received only 100 acres in York Township. The main reason for these relatively modest grants was that most of them had already choice land elsewhere, offering natural mill sites or better soil, and since they were not convinced in 1793 that the seat of government would be moved from Newark to York, they were satisfied to accept a minor stake in the first round of land allocations. Even so, the grant of a front town lot and 300 acres of township land to William Willcocks, *in absentia,* was generous.

It was a matter of clearly defined policy that petitioners with military service or a Loyalist background were entitled to extra land: Captain Shank of the Queen's Rangers, for example, Simcoe's second-in-command, received 500 acres, as did Captain Aeneas Shaw. Ensign and Adjutant John McGill was granted the 200-acre Farm Lot No. 25, in the Second Concession, which adjoined the Willcocks farm lot and likewise extended from the present Bloor Street to St. Clair Avenue. The west limit of the McGill property was formed by the later Bathurst Street. The faithful George Playter, a Loyalist who had first settled in Kingston and then removed to York, was recognized with a generous 500-acre grant; and Thomas Ridout, who had been captured by the Indians in 1787 and brought to Canada, received a 200-acre farm lot in the Third Concession. Chief Justice William Osgoode was also granted a 200-acre farm lot in the more remote Third Concession, together with a 100-acre park lot in the First Concession, a total of 300 acres, the same as the absent Mayor of Cork.

On the face of it, Willcocks' liberal share of the King's Bounty must have owed much to Receiver General Peter Russell's influence with Simcoe and his Council. Willcocks enjoyed neither the preferred status of a government official, nor that of a Loyalist. He had no connection with the Queen's Rangers. He and his associates already held in their pockets a provisional grant of the whole of Whitby Township. The land given him in the York settlement area was simply frosting on the cake. Admittedly, Simcoe was doing everything in his power to attract desirable immigrants to the new province, and Willcocks' recruiting efforts in Ireland, although they finally ended in failure, would not have escaped the governor's notice. This fact alone probably induced Simcoe to accede to the receiver general's request that he and his cousin be granted adjoining properties in York Township.

Their business concluded, Chief Justice Osgoode and Receiver General Russell were glad to sail back across Lake Ontario to their comfortable houses in Newark. William Osgoode was subsequently appointed to the more lucrative post of chief justice of Lower Canada, and left the province the following year. The Honourable Peter Russell, despite Governor Simcoe's

The Honourable Peter Russell (1733-1808), receiver general of the Province of Upper Canada from 1792 to 1808. He also served as president of the Executive Council and administrator of the province from 1796 to 1799 following Governor Simcoe's return to England. He acquired thousands of acres of land in Upper Canada which he left to his half-sister Elizabeth Russell. His 900-acre farm, *Petersfield*, extended from Queen Street to Eglinton Avenue. Spadina Avenue was later laid out on part of this property.

—attributed to William Berczy
(Public Archives of Ontario)

proddings on numerous occasions, did not move to York until late in 1797, a year after Simcoe had returned to England. The main reason for the delay was the difficulty he encountered, in common with the other government officials, in having a suitable house built in the new town. There was an acute shortage of labour for both public and private projects which Russell blamed on the withdrawal of troops from Upper Canada. He certainly approved without reservation the selection of the York townsite as an alternative seat of government to Newark. He wrote on his return from York to his friend John Gray of Montreal:

> I have now the pleasure to tell you that I am charmed with the Situation of the proposed City of York in the Bay of Toronto, & the fertility of the Country round it—Both which for Beauty, safety & Convenience, exceeds every thing the most partial and prejudicial wishes can form.[3]

The Honourable Peter Russell was a bachelor. He was born in Cork, Ireland in 1733, and attended St. John's College, Cambridge. He originally intended to prepare himself for the church, but that lofty goal had to be abandoned when his gambling debts forced him to leave the university. Like his father, Captain Richard Russell, he decided to follow a military career. He bought a commission as an ensign, and went on to serve with the British Army for twenty-six years, finally attaining the rank of captain.

Like Simcoe, Peter Russell had taken part in the American Revolutionary War. He held the post of assistant secretary to Sir Henry Clinton, commander-in-chief of the British forces. It was a civilian appointment because shortly before sailing for America in 1776 he was under the painful necessity of selling his captaincy in the army in order to extricate his father from his debts and provide for his half-sister Elizabeth to whom he was deeply attached. He once complained of his Irish forebears that studying only to enjoy the present, they never thought of making provision for the future. Like others in the early days of York, who came to build their fortunes anew, the Honourable Peter Russell was no stranger to the processes of the bankruptcy court.[4]

Following the American war, Russell returned to England where he found himself without employment. Probably through the influence of Sir Henry Clinton, he finally succeeded in obtaining the position of receiver general of the newly formed province of Upper Canada. The appointment gave him a seat on Simcoe's Executive Council, entitling him to the use of the title "Honourable," membership in the Legislative Council, and the right to a grant of 6,000 acres of land.

Peter Russell was distantly related to the Duke of Bedford, the head of the Russell family in England which had its seat in the stately park of Woburn Abbey in Bedfordshire. In the sixteenth century, John Russell, the first Earl of Bedford, had laid the foundations for the later wealth and influence of the house of Russell by acquiring extensive lands in England. By the end of the nineteenth century, his descendant, the Duke of Bedford, held over 33,000 acres in Bedfordshire alone. In the wild domains of Upper Canada, responding wholeheartedly to the tradition of the English branch of his family, Peter Russell managed to do even better. At the time of his death in York in 1808, according to William Lyon Mackenzie's later assertion, he had built up a stock of real estate in excess of 50,000 acres.

The receiver general and his half-sister Elizabeth, as members of Governor Simcoe's official family, had settled at Newark in the summer of 1792.

The only accommodation they could find in the scattered village at the mouth of the Niagara River was a dilapidated log house with two dank and dismal rooms. By the summer of 1793, however, things had taken a turn for the better. Elizabeth Russell, who was then aged thirty-nine, described the improvement in their affairs in a letter to a friend in England:

> We are comfortably settled in our new House and have a nice little farm about us. We eat our own Mutton and Pork and Poultry. Last year we grew our own Buck wheat and Indian corn and have two Oxen got two cows with their calves with plenty of pigs and a mare and Sheep. We have not made Butter yet but hope soon to do so. I must act the part of dairy maid as I have not got a female servant yet.[5]

The Russells' new house was about three-quarters of a mile from Newark —a distance, Elizabeth Russell lamented, too great to allow her to attend the military balls in town. While she was never included in Mrs. Simcoe's inner circle of friends, in part at least because of the disparity in their ages, she naturally accompanied her brother to the occasional dinner party at the governor's place. Such occasions, however, seemed to bring only temporary relief from the pangs of loneliness and homesickness with which she and most of the other uprooted British settlers were afflicted. "I long to go to England," she wrote, "for I grow tired of this country so little comfort is there compared to what I have been accustomed to." And John White, the attorney general who was later killed in a duel in York, exclaimed bitterly in a letter from Newark: "Look at me—cut off from society that alone makes life desirous—the Society of those that we love. Banished—solitary—hopeless—planted in a desart (sic), surrounded by savages—disappointed—and without prospect."[6]

In the background, of course, was the awareness on the part of all the government officials that their existence in Newark was transitory. There was no incentive to sink their roots. To make matters worse, Simcoe was talking of the forthcoming move to York as temporary, to be followed by the establishment of a permanent provincial capital in the vicinity of the present London, Ontario. Finally, accentuating the feeling of instability in the struggling colony was the atmosphere of suspicion and hostility that permeated their relations with the restless, new republic across the Niagara River.

In 1795, when only twelve houses were standing in York, Peter Russell finally committed himself to purchase Christopher Robinson's newly built dwelling. It was situated close to the southwest corner of the present King and Princess streets, and cost 100 guineas which he complained to Simcoe he could "ill-afford." After protracted negotiations with local carpenters with a view to improving the modest structure, Samuel Marther, a builder, undertook to make the required additions in the fall of 1796. It was an ill-fated

---

project. To Russell's intense disappointment, a fire, which was attributed to the negligence of the carpenters, led to the total destruction of the house on a January night in 1797. Only the gaunt chimneys were left standing. The work was started afresh, on a site closer to the bay, at the northwest corner of today's Front and Princess streets, and this time the project was placed in the more competent hands of William von Moll Berczy. He was the leader of the German settlement in Markham Township, and a gifted artist, architect, and writer. His later death in New York in mysterious circumstances—his trunk in a shabby inn was found to have been rifled, and his exhumed coffin disclosed only a ballast of rocks—constitutes the most macabre episode in the early history of York.[7]

The receiver general's new dwelling, which commanded a view of the entire Harbour of York, was completed in the autumn of 1797 at a crushing cost of over £1000, which Russell's perquisites of office were strained to cover. The house was a U-shaped bungalow built in the neo-classical style, and was enclosed by a neat, low picket fence. The clapboard exterior was relieved by eleven large, shuttered windows, and a handsome panelled door imparted to the house an air of restrained elegance.*

When Governor Simcoe left Upper Canada for England in July 1796, his absence was thought to be only temporary. The Honourable Peter Russell, as the senior member of the Executive Council, became the chief representative of King George III in the province. In addition to continuing to act as receiver general, the titles and functions of president of the Council and administrator were also vested in Russell. As president, he officiated at the opening of the first meeting of the Parliament of Upper Canada to be held in York, on June 1, 1797. It was not until the following November 3, however, that he and his sister finally extricated themselves from Newark and took up their residence in their newly built *Russell Abbey*. It was with evident relief that he wrote to Governor Simcoe, on December 9, 1797, to inform him of this fact. His lengthy letter reveals his many concerns in York, and confirms the general expectation that Governor Simcoe would soon be returning to the province:

> I have the pleasure to inform your Excellency, that I arrived here on the 3d. Ultimo with my family and all my effects, which were with great difficulty & some damage got on Shore, as a Violent Storm of Wind, Rain, & Snow came on Immediately after, & has continued almost ever

---

*The Receiver General's house was popularly called *Russell Abbey* after his death in 1808, an affectionate nickname given the dwelling by Elizabeth Russell's circle of relatives. It was destroyed by fire in 1856.

The "Old Esquire," William Willcocks (1736-1813), whose daughter Phoebe married Dr. William Warren Baldwin in 1803. Willcocks was a cousin of the Honourable Peter Russell, and the first owner of the 200-acre farm lot, later known as the *Spadina* property, under a Crown Grant dated December 22nd, 1798. He left the farm to his son-in-law, Dr. Baldwin, who built the first *Spadina* house on it, atop the Davenport Hill, in 1818. Willcocks was the first postmaster of York, and resigned in 1800 when his accounts were questioned. He was an incorrigible land speculator, and acquired a number of large properties throughout the province. Lake Willcocks, which adjoined his 800-acre farm in the Township of Whitchurch, was named for him.

—Metropolitan Toronto Library Board

Russell Abbey was built for the Honourable Peter Russell by William Berczy in 1797. It was situated between Front and King Streets at Princess Street, and provided a fine view of the Toronto Bay. The *Abbey* was the principal residence of the Russells in York, Peter Russell dying there in 1808, and his half-sister Elizabeth in 1822. Following the War of 1812, Dr. William Baldwin and his family resided at *Russell Abbey* with Miss Russell. After he had built *Spadina* on the Davenport Hill in 1818, Dr. Baldwin maintained his law office in a couple of rooms in Miss Russell's house.

—Metropolitan Toronto Library Board

since with very little intermission accompanied by a most intense frost. So that our Harbor is now completely blocked up for the Winter, and I am not without apprehensions that our Inhabitants of this Settlement may suffer for want of flour, as their expected supplies of that Article have been cut off by this early visit of hard weather. Boards & scantling are likewise very scarce here and not to be procured now from the Mills. I am in consequence wholly uninclosed and without covering for my Horses, Oxen, or Poultry, and what is still worse my friend Mr. McGill has very unlike a friend neglected to lay in Hay for me altho' he was early requested to do so; And I cannot procure a Sufficiency for their Support at any price. The Attorney General and Mr. Smith have by very great exertions got themselves Housed the latter pretty comfortably. But Mr. Jarvis having not made the smallest effort for the removal of his Office remains still at Niagara and most probably means to do so until your Excellency's arrival. The Two Wings to the Government House are raised with Brick & completely covered in. The South One, being in the greatest forwardness I have directed to be fited up for a temporary Court House for the Kings Bench in the ensuing Term, and I hope they may both be in a condition to receive the Two Houses of Parliament in June next, I have not yet given directions for proceeding with the remainder of your Excellency's plan for the Government House, being alarmed at the magnitude of the expence which Captain Graham estimates at (£10,000) I shall however order a large Kiln of Bricks to be prepared in the Spring and burnt, (as they will readily sell for what they cost if Government does not want them) and Boards & Scantling may be cut and seasoned upon the same principle—But I sincerely hope to have the pleasure of seeing Your Excellency here before we shall have occasion to proceed further with the building.—

I have extended this Town Westward towards the Garrison, & to the North as far as the Base of Hundred Acre Lots, reserving between the part that was laid out by Your Excellency and this Addition, a large Space for public buildings (vizt. a Church, Court House, Jail, Market, Hospital, School House &c) most of the Lots have been already taken up, & about forty Houses erected & several more are beginning.

The Huts at the Garrison requiring considerable repair to render them Habitable in Winter, I have caused The Blockhouse (which Your Excellency originally intended to place on the Peninsula) to be raised on the Knoll on this Side the Garrison Creek & fited as a Barrack for 70 Men. On the Top of it is put a light House, which renders it a convenient & conspicuous object to guide Vessels into the Harbor. Upon the Whole I flatter myself Your Excellency will not be displeased with what I have done at this place.[8]

In the meantime, William Willcocks, having completed his term of office as Mayor of Cork, had returned to the colony in 1795. By 1797 he too was busy settling himself and his family into a new house. It was at the corner of Frederick and Duke Street, a short distance from his cousin Peter Russell. He now had with him his wife Phoebe, his son Charles, aged thirty-five, and his three daughters, Maria, Phoebe, and Eugenia. His plans for the settlement of the Township of Whitby having been frustrated owing to a change in government policy and his inability to produce sufficient settlers, Willcocks was now attempting to establish himself as a merchant in York. He had been appointed a magistrate in 1796, and the following year Peter Russell again used his influence to obtain for him the position of York's first postmaster. He still enjoyed the provisional ownership of the 300 acres of York Township lands that Simcoe's Council had awarded him at its meeting in 1793 (part of the later *Spadina* enclave), though issuance of his Crown Patents still awaited his attention to the necessary settlement work.

Simcoe's departure from the province in the summer of 1796 did not create a serious political vacuum. The fact that the office of lieutenant-governor was left vacant for three years can be taken as a tacit expression of confidence by the British Colonial Office in Russell's caretaker administration. After Simcoe's "whirlwind administration," as Edith G. Firth has called it, the colony needed the plodding virtues of a practical and careful man—and these qualities Russell was able to provide. During the summer of 1797, for example, while his new house was being readied in York, Russell became impatient with his secretary and registrar, William Jarvis. The process of issuing patents of land, which was Jarvis' responsibility, had fallen behind, and there was unmistakable evidence of inefficiency and confusion in his department. Russell set up a committee consisting of Chief Justice Elmsley and D. W. Smith, the surveyor general, to enquire into the registrar's administration and recommend suitable measures for its improvement. While such a step doubtless earned for Russell the enmity of Jarvis, it resulted in a smoothing out of that important part of the government's operations and the granting of Crown Patents was speeded up.

By the following year, Lieutenant John McGill, adjutant of the Queen's Rangers, was confirmed as the owner of the 200-acre farm lot known as Lot 25, Second Concession from the Bay, and William Willcocks received his Crown grant of Lot 24 in the same Concession, together with Lot 15 lying to the south. And Peter Russell also took formal title that year to Lot 14, First Concession from the Bay. The year before he had added the 200-acre Farm Lot 22 in the Third Concession to his land portfolio. His Crown grants covering Lots 23 in the Second and Third Concessions had been obtained from Governor Simcoe in May, 1796, just before the governor's departure from Upper Canada. Finally, the Honourable James Baby, a member of the Executive Council, was also confirmed in 1798 as the owner of the 100-acre park lot known as Lot 16 in the First Concession from the Bay. Baby's lot, of course, adjoined Willcocks' park lot and also extended from Queen Street to Bloor Street. The provisional grant of Park Lot 13 made to Charles Willcocks, William Willcocks' son, in 1793 was never confirmed. Instead, that 100-acre lot was granted by Crown Patent to the solicitor general, Robert Isaac Dey Gray, on May 1st, 1798. All these Crown grants are depicted on pages 24, 25.

While in York Peter Russell always resided at *Russell Abbey*. He did, however, build a substantial farm house on his Park Lot 14 which he called *Petersfield*. The house was set back from the present Queen Street, and was a few hundred yards east of Spadina Avenue at the head of the present Peter Street. He was one of the earliest settlers in York to develop his farm to the point of commercial profitability.

As the eighteenth century drew to a close, only two dwellings of note had been established on the lands shown on pages 24, 25: *Petersfield,* the hub of Russell's 700-acre farm, as it was then, stretching from today's Queen Street to Eglinton Avenue, and *Davenport,* Adjutant McGill's house, which he had built on the top of the hill overlooking part of his farm lot affording him an impressive view of the Town of York, whose smoking chimneys could be seen three miles to the southeast. Unlike McGill, Willcocks never lived on the farm lot granted him, but to satisfy the requirements for settlement and occupation, he built a small log dwelling on the present Davenport Hill just to the east of the *McGill* house. We may assume that Willcocks built his cabin on the later *Spadina* lands around 1797 in order to qualify for his Crown grant the following year, and before his interest shifted to more distant sections of the province for speculative land development. In any event, the dwelling was probably occupied by an early settler of York—possibly by his son Charles for a time, who would have farmed the 200-acre property "on shares" with William Willcocks. An old legend, transmitted through successive owners of the original Willcocks tract, has it that bands of Indians, wandering along the trail at the foot of the Davenport Hill, frequently paused to study their reflection in the glazed windows of the hilltop cabin. Its occupants, it is said, were often startled by the appearance at their window of a dark and grimacing face. Like a subterranean stream unexpectedly breaking through the surface of history, the early Willcocks' cabin comes to light again in this narrative, when its location is disclosed in a deed of land made in 1889, and its survival to that date is confirmed.[9]

Chapter 2

The Baldwins Arrive in Upper Canada

As the fall of 1798 approached, Peter Russell had reason to be pleased with the way things were developing in York. His mind was carried back to the autumn days of 1793 when he and William Osgoode had met in a tent on the Toronto Bay with Governor Simcoe and members of his Council to decide on the land grants to be made to the early settlers. On September 13, he was moved to write to his old colleague, Osgoode, in Quebec:

> You would be pleased to see this place now as it is really beautiful and makes a very different appearance from what it did when we were here together about this time six (sic) years ago. I have a very comfortable house near the Bay, from whence I see everything in the harbour & entering it, & Miss Russell has an extensive poultry yard which keeps her fully amused and contributes somewhat to her Health. I have about 700 Acres two miles from the Town, on which I have put a farmer on shares, in hopes of supplying my Table without searching the Country for Provisions.[1]

The latter reference is, of course, to his 700-acre network of farms based on *Petersfield* where John Denison with his wife Sophia was to reside for many years as manager of that portion of the Russell estate.*

While a few of the amenities of life were becoming available, York was still an isolated frontier town with only a little more than 400 people on its rolls. The pioneer community was still almost wholly dependent upon lake navigation. With the onset of winter, communication with the outside world was infrequent and unpredictable. The pressing need was for year-round roads, not just Simcoe's visionary Yonge Street leading to Lake Simcoe and the wilderness beyond, nor his overland route to the Thames River, but a clearly defined road back to civilization, to Kingston and the Bay of Quinte, to Cornwall and Montreal.

Russell was keenly aware of the urgent need of better road communications if the community of York was to attract more settlers and develop into a prosperous settlement. He gave road-building an important priority. He was responsible for the extension of Yonge Street below Queen Street to the

---

*John Denison (1755-1824), a Yorkshireman, was the founder of the Canadian military family of that name. He settled in Kingston in 1792 where he rented a brewery, moving to York in 1796. After managing *Petersfield* for a number of years, he retired to his own farm at Weston. Elizabeth Russell was godmother to his daughter, Elizabeth Sophia.

Bay, the development of the Dundas Highway from York to Burlington Bay at the head of Lake Ontario, and more important, he initiated the contract with Asa Danforth who began work on June 1, 1799, cutting a road from York to the Bay of Quinte. Russell came to regard the building of this historic road as his greatest achievement.

While planning these basic thoroughfares to link the Town of York with the outside world, Russell was by no means unmindful of his own local property interests and the economic advantages to be derived from improving access to them. Since his *Petersfield* farm, as we have seen, lay west of the present Yonge Street, it is not surprising to find him in 1799 trying to influence a diversion of Yonge Street south from Eglinton Avenue so it would pass through his property by way of what is today Poplar Plains Road, St. George Street, and Beverly Street to Queen Street.[2] Although this plan was not adopted, from the earliest days of *Petersfield,* a country lane was developed by Russell along this route.

As further evidence of Russell's interest in improving the road network in this area, early in 1799 William Chewett, the deputy surveyor general, reported to his superior, D. W. Smith, on the feasibility of developing a road from Simcoe's *Castle Frank* by the Don River to the Poplar Plains, the early name given to the tableland to which the present Poplar Plains Road now leads. Two negroes, he said, were prepared to undertake the project which they estimated could be completed within ten days at a cost of twenty-four dollars.[3] While it is not known how much work was done as a result of Chewett's report, the project confirms that the trail that became the Davenport Road was recognized from the earliest days of settlement as a potentially important east-west route north of the Town of York.

As the year 1799 progressed, it became clear that Governor Simcoe would not be returning as lieutenant-governor to Upper Canada. Rumours had been swirling around York for some time that he was to be appointed governor-general of Canada, succeeding General Prescott who was leaving the country for England. Upon being sounded out by the Duke of Portland with respect to such an appointment, however, Simcoe imposed a condition that was not acceptable. "A Peerage," he said, "is the object for which alone I would willingly spend five years in the King's American Dominions, colonizing, legislating, and establishing, I trust, on immovable foundations His Majesty's empire in Canada." In distant York, however, Peter Russell was convinced that the rumours of Simcoe's new appointment were true, and in May 1799, he wrote to Simcoe asking him to use his influence to help him secure the appointment of lieutenant-governor of Upper Canada.[4] He had already set the wheels in motion in other centres of influence as well. On April 10, 1799, Colonel W. H. Clinton, private secretary to the Duke of York, wrote to his friend Russell: "I am surprised that you have not been nominated to succeed General Simcoe. I cannot find out that there is even an intention to appoint anyone."

The uncertainty as to Simcoe's successor was resolved abruptly in June 1799, with the arrival at Quebec of His Excellency Peter Hunter, a Scottish professional soldier, who had been appointed not only lieutenant-governor of Upper Canada, but commander-in-chief of His Majesty's Forces in Lower and Upper Canada as well. With Hunter's arrival in Upper Canada the following August, while remaining a member of the Executive and Legislative Councils, Russell reverted to his former position of receiver general, after having enjoyed for three years the highest office in the province. He was then sixty-six years of age, and from that point on his influence began to wane.

While York was drowsing through the summer of 1799 awaiting with curiosity the arrival of the new lieutenant-governor, a family of Irish immigrants reached the town, on July 13, who were well known to William Willcocks and Peter Russell. The head of the family was Robert Baldwin, a widower fifty-eight years of age. With him were two of his sons and four of his daughters. The oldest was Dr. William Warren Baldwin, aged twenty-four, who was a recent graduate of the Medical School at Edinburgh University. The youngest son, John Spread Baldwin, was aged twelve, and the four girls ranged in age from eight to seventeen. The family had come from Knockmore, near Cork in Ireland, where Robert Baldwin had managed a farm. While they had set sail from the Cove of Cork in mid-October, 1798, through a series of misadventures, they were diverted to England where they were compelled to spend the winter. Late in the spring, they finally sailed from Falmouth in the *Grantham,* bound for Halifax and New York.

They chose to disembark at New York, and enter Upper Canada by way of the Hudson and Mohawk Rivers to Oswego on Lake Ontario. This route was favoured by immigrants of that time since it was shorter than the Canadian route, and avoided the formidable rapids of the St. Lawrence River. A schooner took the party to York from the American harbour, while their heavy baggage was freighted around the western shore of Lake Ontario in bateaux.

While in York, the Baldwin family stayed with William Willcocks and his family on Duke Street, just a short distance from *Russell Abbey.* During this time they were frequent visitors at the receiver general's house where Peter and Elizabeth Russell had been settled comfortably for nearly two years. To Robert Baldwin, after a journey of ten months, with its hardships and frustrations, the gracious house must have seemed like an oasis of tranquility and plenty. The Baldwins, doubtless, were taken along to *Petersfield* to see the Russell farm now under development, and they may have even strolled north along the meandering lane that led to the escarpment overlooking the Town of York upon which the young Dr. Baldwin was later to build his *Spadina* house. We may be sure the talk went on until late into the night in *Russell Abbey* as Russell, Willcocks, and Baldwin discussed conditions in the province, and in particular the prospects for Robert Baldwin and his family.

The conversation would have centered, of course, on the localities that were most desirable for settlement. Willcocks was becoming interested in the land now opening up in William von Moll Berczy's settlement in Markham Township, as well as in the area around Oak Ridges to the north where a band of French Royalists were trying to establish themselves. They had emigrated to Upper Canada from England under the leadership of the Comte de Puisaye in 1798. Russell was expansive on the subject of the road now being built by Danforth to the Bay of Quinte, and the benefits that the province would derive from it. But Baldwin's Irish friend, Richard Lovekin, had already settled in Clarke Township, near Newcastle, about fifty miles east of York, and he finally succeeded in influencing Baldwin to take up a tract of land in that district.

In the circle formed by Russell, Willcocks, and Baldwin as they sat in *Russell Abbey* sipping their port, was to be seen in microcosm the hopes and dreams that motivated almost all the immigrants who were now arriving in Upper Canada. They came to acquire cheap land. They came to repair their shattered fortunes. They came in search of a new life. For the three men gathered around the receiver general's table, this was indeed the case. Life in the Old World had yielded them a loaf of stone. In a financial sense, their careers had been little short of disastrous. William Willcocks had suffered a resounding bankruptcy as a merchant in Cork. Peter Russell's resources had been drained off rescuing his father from a sea of debt. And Robert Baldwin had become bankrupt in 1788 following an unsuccessful excursion into the field of journalism.[5] Thanks to a benevolent uncle, Sir Robert Warren, he was excused his debts and assisted to emigrate to British North America with his family. His son, Dr. William Warren Baldwin, later took the position that the chief reason for the Baldwin family emigrating to Upper Canada was the political ferment existing in Ireland. In a letter written in 1801 to his cousin in Cork, who hardly needed to be reminded of the fact, he said: "The horrors of domestic war conspired to drive us from our native country." Notwithstanding the doctor's dramatic assertion, the common goal of virtually all the immigrants arriving in Upper Canada at that time was to acquire cheap land. And it was to be had virtually for the asking. A few, like Dr. Baldwin, soon began to dream of founding family dynasties in Upper Canada, to be supported by great landed estates.

Robert Baldwin, whose concerns at the moment were more practical than dynastic, was anxious to proceed to the farm he had selected for settlement in the Township of Clarke on the north shore of Lake Ontario. While he was aware that only ten acres had been cleared to a point of permitting cultivation, and that it offered only a primitive settler's cabin for him and his six children, he was confident that the property could be brought to a point of profitable development before long. The trip to their new home was made by bateaux from York, and involved at least two October nights of camping on the heavily wooded shore of Lake Ontario. For the youngest children the excitement of the day must have yielded to a wakeful anxiousness at night as they listened to the howling of a distant wolf pack, or close by, to the lonely, haunting cry of a loon. Robert Baldwin and his son, William Warren, took turns maintaining a bright and reassuring campfire throughout the night.

Meanwhile, back in York, William Willcocks was pondering the opportunities for land speculation that were now presenting themselves in Markham and Whitchurch Townships. The area was opening up around Berczy's settlement, and as we have noted earlier, some French Royalists were attempting to settle themselves further up Yonge Street on lands granted them by the Crown in the Oak Ridges area. Before long, Willcocks had acquired a handsome farm for himself, which he called *Millbrook,* just to the north of the present Buttonville in Markham Township. He also obtained another property in Whitchurch Township to be called *Larchmere,* beside Lake Willcocks, which was named for him.

But his interest in land acquisition and development did not by any means occupy all of Willcocks' time. He had certain official duties of a minor nature to perform in York: he was a magistrate, and a judge of the Home District Court. He was also the town's first postmaster. But the fees he earned from these offices were only nominal, and could not begin to satisfy his appetite for money to buy more land, build mills, and develop roads.

Occasionally, the former Mayor of Cork thrust himself into the political

arena, drawing with advantage upon his previous experience in Irish municipal elections. In York's first election, in 1800, he decided to espouse the
cause of Judge Henry Allcock who was shortly to succeed John Elmsley as
chief justice of the province. The Judge was a candidate for a seat in the
Provincial Assembly representing the East Riding of the County of York.
As was the custom, the polls were open for several days, and the contest
narrowed down to Allcock, Samuel Heron, William Jarvis, and John Small,
who a few months earlier had killed John White, the attorney general, in a
duel. The *Upper Canada Gazette,* the official organ of the government,
noted dryly that "the election terminated sooner than was expected by consequence of a daring riot instigated by persons inimical to peace and good
order." An "Impartial Bystander" described the bizarre scene of that hot
July day more graphically:

> Mr. Jarvis appeared discouraged, and told some of his friends that they
> were at liberty to vote for mr. Alcock. At this time a body of soldiers
> were approaching the hustlings, who it was supposed would have voted
> for mr. Alcock:—A drunken fellow, who observed them, raised the
> *hue and cry,* and swore that no soldiers had a right to vote there;—his
> turbulence was noted by the magistrats present, who commanded the
> peace, and ordered the man into custody. It is said that mr. Wilcox
> jun. [Charles Willcocks] went to the man, shook his fists at him, and
> menaced him with the jail. The man, when in custody of the constables,
> promised to be peaceable; some of the people ran to him, rescued him
> from the constables, and one of them, armed with a cudgel, threatened
> to knock mr. Allen esq. down if he interposed. . . . The poll had been,
> at the beginning of these appearances, adjourned to the ensuing day.
> Mr. Weeks, seeing that mr. Alcock had at this juncture a majority,
> insisted that the poll should be closed, in which he was joined by
> mr. Alcock and the returning officer, seemingly intimidated and bewil-
> dered, complied, after having but a moment before adjourned it. The
> other candidates, except mr. Heron, were struck silent with this inconsis-
> tency, he made a verbal protest against it as being illegal. . . . The riot
> act was then read by William Wilcox, esq. and the people voluntarily
> dispersed.[6]

A petition was subsequently presented to Governor Hunter, and in due
course Judge Allcock was disqualified, and the proceedings were pronounced
void. In the enquiry by the House of Assembly that followed, many elements
of unfairness were found in the election not the least of which was the closing of the poll and the reading of the Riot Act by Magistrate William Willcocks, who was actively supporting Allcock, while over fifty people were
standing around waiting to vote.

The following September, in 1800, Willcocks approached John Gray of
Montreal for a loan to help him develop his land holdings. Gray, as we have
seen, was a friend of Peter Russell's, and had an important connection with
the North West Company, which at that time was considering using York
as a staging area for its fur trading activities. By using Simcoe's Yonge Street
that led to Lake Simcoe, the route to the northwest would be shorter and
the Niagara portage avoided. Gray was a man of considerable means and
influence, and was a frequent visitor to York at the time. He later served as
the first president of the Bank of Montreal, from 1817 to 1820.

John Gray was agreeable to Willcocks' proposal, and made £1500 available to him. But he insisted on security for his loan, and Willcocks was
obliged to execute a mortgage in his favour. Among the lands he mortgaged

to Gray was his 200-acre farm lot in the Second Concession from the Bay (the later *Spadina* property), as well as his 100-acre Queen Street park lot to the south upon which the greater part of Spadina Avenue is now located. It is probable that the proceeds of this loan were used for Willcocks' land development activities in Markham Township or in the Lake Willcocks area.

Willcocks' duties as postmaster of York had not been onerous, but neither did they produce the kind of money he needed for land speculation. Compared to the sum Gray had made available to him, which was later to give rise to ill-feeling between them, his stipend from the Post Office must have seemed like a mere pittance. And to make matters worse, the authorities questioned his accounts. A week before Christmas, in 1800, Willcocks inserted the following indignant notice in the *Upper Canada Gazette:*

> To prevent disappointment and trouble, the Public is requested to take notice, that some time ago Mr. Willcocks resigned his place of Post Master of York, his reasonable charges for the rent of an office, stationery, fire, candles, and a servant to attend, being disputed; although by his assiduity and attention, the revenue was productive beyond expectation, as appears by the accounts he rendered, and the money he remitted to the Post Master General at Quebec.

This incident is probably the first recorded case of an expense account being questioned in the history of Toronto.

In May 1802, wishing to lay his hands on additional capital, Willcocks approached Peter Russell with an offer to sell him his park lot No. 15 on today's Queen Street, which lay just to the west of Russell's *Petersfield* farm property. Russell was always interested in expanding his land holdings and accepted the offer, subject to the lot being released from John Gray's mortgage which had been registered against it two years before. This the Montreal merchant agreed to do against payment of £200.

Again in 1806, Russell had an opportunity to purchase the next park lot to the west on the present Queen Street (Lot 16) from the Honourable James Baby. With the completion of this transaction, Peter Russell enjoyed the absolute ownership of 300 acres of land between today's Queen and Bloor Streets on either side of and including the present Spadina Avenue, and 600 acres between Bloor Street and Eglinton Avenue to the east of Spadina Avenue. Willcocks, however, continued to cling to his 200-acre farm lot, the later *Spadina* property, which lay to the north of the land he sold to Russell in 1802.

Back in Clarke Township, the Baldwins were establishing themselves on their new farm. On their arrival in 1799, the family had been appalled to find that they had to make their home in a draughty cabin with a cedar-bark roof, the chinks between the rough-hewn logs stuffed with moss. It is to their credit that they persevered. The cabin consisted of one large room which was immediately partitioned. The Baldwin sons settled themselves as best they could in the loft which was reached by a ladder.

Gradually the place was put in order, and by 1802 Robert Baldwin was able to harvest his own wheat and Indian corn, and store it in an adequate barn. He had a flock of sheep, cattle, pigs, and a gaggle of noisy geese. But it was a Baldwin characteristic to want to get into things. Honours come easily to an educated man in the backwoods of a new country. In 1800, he was appointed lieutenant of the County of Durham. He was also a justice of the peace, and as a member of the Court of the Quarter Sessions, he had to make frequent trips through the woods to nearby Newcastle. As a lieutenant-colonel in the local militia, he was responsible for its training, and especially its annual muster. On at least one occasion, a large, hungry group of militiamen were instructed to gather at his farm house, and the Baldwin daughters were called upon to provide a country feast for their delectation. It is probable that Robert Baldwin enjoyed these opportunities of dignified and squire-like public service. It is certain that the young, ambitious Dr. Baldwin did not. While by no means indifferent to honours himself, he thought his father's offices were "all honour and little profit." It was inevitable that he would seek to escape from the drudgery of the farm at the earliest opportunity. His mood was expressed in a letter he wrote to his cousin, John Baldwin, Jr., in Ireland, in October, 1801:

> The only circumstance which gives this place any enjoyment for me is the steady and unaltered friendship of Mr. Russell—Whenever my father or myself are in town we live entirely at the Russells'—he has insisted on it and his sister's amiable manners render it easy and agreeable.

The Honourable Peter Russell was the colonial prototype of the educated, landed gentleman of the eighteenth century—the age of brilliant *salons,* and talented amateurs dabbling in architecture, botany, or chemistry. He liked to conduct metallurgical experiments in his private laboratory on the *Russell Abbey* property. He admired the writings of Johnathan Swift, his fellow countryman, and at night before a blazing fire enjoyed reading aloud from *Gulliver's Travels.* Following the American Revolutionary War, Russell had even tried his hand at writing. In collaboration with Sir Henry Clinton, he produced a history of that struggle, which Edward Gibbon is said to have read with approval.

On his visits to York, Dr. Baldwin fitted easily and amiably into the congenial life of *Russell Abbey*. He played his flute in the evening, and drawing on his medical training at Edinburgh, helped the receiver general with his amateur scientific experiments. As a guest of the Russells, he was included in their picnic outings up the Don River to Simcoe's *Castle Frank,* and on one occasion, in September 1800, accompanied the portly Russell on a long walk from his *Petersfield* farm house to "Sugar Loaf Hill," the beauty of which touched him deeply. A reference to the Russells' "old sugar loaf lot" in a much later letter from Dr. Baldwin identifies the site they visited as being on the top of the Davenport Hill.[7] The young doctor could not have imagined that he and his brother, Captain Augustus Warren Baldwin, would later build their *Spadina* and *Russell Hill* houses on the promontory he visited that summer afternoon with the ageing received general.

Dr. William Warren Baldwin (1775-1844) emigrated to Upper Canada from Ireland in 1799 with his father, brother, and four sisters. He practiced medicine and law in York, conducted a school for boys, and was a leader in the later reform movement. His marriage to Phoebe Willcocks led to his two surviving sons, the Honourable Robert Baldwin and William Augustus Baldwin, inheriting thousands of acres of land throughout Upper Canada which had been acquired earlier by the Honourable Peter Russell and his cousin William Willcocks. Dr. Baldwin built the first *Spadina* house in 1818, and later laid out the broad Spadina Avenue, from Queen Street to Bloor Street, on the land which his wife and sister-in-law had inherited from Elizabeth Russell.

—Metropolitan Toronto Library Board

Chapter 3

Dr. Baldwin Moves to York

In the spring of 1802, Dr. William Warren Baldwin finally decided to leave the family farm in Clarke Township and seek his fortune in York. He took a room at William Willcocks' place on Duke Street, and let it be known that his services as a medical practitioner were now available. It did not take him long to discover, however, that there were simply too few prospective patients in the struggling little town to enable him to support himself solely from the practice of medicine. He had to find some additional means of making a livelihood. He finally settled upon the idea of starting a school, and it was launched with a notice in the *Upper Canada Gazette:*

> Dr. Baldwin understanding that some of the gentlemen of this Town have expressed some anxiety for the establishment of a Classical School, begs leave to inform them and the public that he intends on Monday the first day of January next, to open a School in which he will instruct Twelve Boys in Writing, Reading, and Classics and Arithmetic. The terms are, for each boy, eight guineas per annum, to be paid quarterly or half-yearly; one guinea entrance and one cord of wood to be supplied by each of the boys on opening the School. N.B.—Mr. Baldwin will meet his pupils at Mr. Willcocks' house on Duke Street   York, December 18th, 1802.

It was at this time that Dr. Baldwin's friendship with the astute trader Laurent Quetton de St. George was formed. St. George was then conducting his business in York from Mr. Willcocks' house, and was a leading member of the French Royalist group. He owned property in their settlement area in the Oak Ridges, and was one of the few Royalists to prosper in Canada. He expanded his York business into a chain of stores in Kingston, Amherstburg, Orillia, and Niagara. It is said that he assumed the name of St. George because he had landed in England on St. George's Day, a fugitive from the terror of the French Revolution. He finally returned to France with the fall of Napoleon in 1815, and died there in 1821. Dr. Baldwin corresponded with him regularly after 1815, and upon his death acted as the Canadian executor of his varied interests in Canada. Dr. Baldwin's younger brother, John Spread Baldwin, while a lad in his teens, left the family farm in Clarke Township a few years after his brother and was taken into St. George's growing business in York. St. George Street, once one of Toronto's most im-

pressive addresses, was named for Quetton de St. George. It was laid out
on what was originally part of Receiver General Peter Russell's *Petersfield*
farm property.

Dr. Baldwin began his classes in January 1803, but his was not the only
school in Upper Canada to open its doors that year. To the east, in distant
Cornwall, a United Empire Loyalist-founded village by the St. Lawrence
River, the Reverend John Strachan was also building a schoolhouse near
his new parish church, which was to become more celebrated in the annals
of Upper Canada than Baldwin's make-shift project in York.

Strachan had emigrated to Upper Canada in 1799, the same year as the
Baldwin family had arrived in York. He was then twenty-one years of age.
His father had been the manager of a granite quarry in Aberdeen, and with
his death as a result of an eye injury suffered in the quarry, when Strachan
was just sixteen, the young Scot was thrown on his own resources. Doggedly,
he taught at various schools in Scotland, and earned enough money to put
himself through King's College, Aberdeen, from which he was graduated
Master of Arts in 1796. He then enrolled for a few months in the Faculty
of Divinity at St. Andrew's University, but finally gave up and took a position as a parish schoolmaster. His prospects in Scotland, without money and
without a patron, were dim. He heard of an opening in Upper Canada where
two leading merchants, Richard Cartwright of Kingston and Robert Hamilton
of Queenston, were looking for a tutor for their children. They offered him
free passage to Canada, and a stipend of £80 per annum for three years.
After considerable soul-searching, Strachan accepted the contract, and
reached Kingston on New Year's Eve, 1799, after a jolting sleigh-ride from
Montreal through the snow-piled forests along the shore of the St. Lawrence
River.

While conducting his classes in Kingston, he established a reputation for
himself as a hard-working academic, and more important, he won the patronage of Richard Cartwright. At the end of his contract, and with Cartwright's encouragement and support, the young immigrant was ordained by
the Anglican Bishop Jacob Mountain in Quebec in May 1803. He then proceeded to Cornwall to take over his first parish. With characteristic energy
and enthusiasm, he built what he called without hesitation or modesty "the
best church in the province," and a little later he had "the best school in
the colony."

John Strachan did not move to York until 1812. By that time he had
fashioned an élite corps of scholars imbued with loyalty, cohesion, and pride
in their traditions. It was inevitable that they would become the hard core of
the so-called Family Compact against which in later years the reformers of
Upper Canada, like the Baldwins, would batter their heads as if against a
block of Aberdeen granite. On the rolls of his Cornwall school, at one time
or another, were such men as John Beverley Robinson, Samuel P. Jarvis,
Robert Stanton, G. S. Boulton, W. B. Robinson, G. H. Markland, and P. Van
Koughnet. In their formative years Strachan was their teacher; in their ma-
turity, he was to be their political chief.

By 1802, the year in which Dr. Baldwin decided to settle in York, Major-
General Peter Hunter, the lieutenant-governor, had tightened up the administration of the province. While on state occasions he insisted upon being
carried about the streets in a sedan-chair, his relations with his officials
were forthright and soldierly. The citizens of York still recalled his reply
to their sonorous address of welcome upon his arrival three years before at

the King's Wharf in the harbour of York. His remarks were the epitome of military brevity: "Gentlemen,—Nothing that is within my power shall be wanting to contribute to the welfare of this colony."

That was all. In an early ordinance, he ruled that the heads of the various departments should stick strictly to business, and that their subordinates should be in regular attendance at their offices every day in the year excepting Sundays, Good Friday, and Christmas Day from ten o'clock in the morning till three o'clock in the afternoon, and from five o'clock in the afternoon till seven in the evening.

Once again, William Jarvis, who was still the secretary and registrar of the province, was the object of a governor's wrath when he dawdled too long over the issuance of land patents. It will be recalled that in the summer of 1797, The Honourable Peter Russell had had to launch an inquiry into the operations of Jarvis' department. The governor's threat of dismissal on this second occasion resulted in immediate action, and had a salutary effect upon the entire government service.

General Hunter's interventions in the administrative affairs of the province were more in the nature of sudden raids than prolonged campaigns. He attached greater importance to his military role as commander-in-chief of the two provinces of Upper and Lower Canada. Britain had been at war with France since 1793, and the disputatious government of the United States, whose sympathies lay with France, was a constant threat to the security of British North America throughout the period of Britain's preoccupation with Napoleon. For this reason, shortly after his arrival in 1799, Governor Hunter had carefully reviewed the military resources that were available to him. One unit that received his special attention was the Royal Canadian Volunteer Regiment. It had been raised some years earlier by Lord Dorchester as a permanent corps of Canadian troops. The men wore the uniform of the regular British infantry: scarlet with blue facings, a three-cornered hat with a cockade. They were armed with flintlock and bayonet. The force consisted of two battalions, one having been recruited in Quebec and consisting of French Canadians, the other in Montreal and consisting of English-speaking Canadians. Hunter's official assessment of the Regiment, in October 1799, was not encouraging:

> In both battalions there are a very considerable number of old men, and many others are too feeble to undergo the fatigues of military service. From what I have observed of their discipline, but little can be said in their favour.

With the conclusion of the Treaty of Amiens in 1802 with the French (the war broke out again the following year), the Royal Canadian Volunteer Regiment was disbanded, along with the Queen's Rangers. At the time of the demobilization of the volunteers, the English-speaking battalion had most of its companies scattered throughout Upper Canada: at Kingston, York, Fort George (Newark), Fort Erie, and Chippewa. Understandably, a number of the discharged volunteers chose to stay where they were. Many, like Lewis Bright, had fought with the British forces during the American Revolution, and it was natural that they would decide to establish themselves in the predominantly British province of Upper Canada. Bright chose to settle in York around 1802, and despite the charge of feebleness that Governor Hunter had levelled against the volunteers, he not only managed to father a brood of sixteen children, most of whom were born after he left the service, but by the time of his death in Toronto in 1842 he had attained the startling age of ninety-five.*

In Little York in 1802, as well as in the isolated settlements throughout the province, there were few opportunities for public merry-making and revelry. A wedding, therefore, was usually a popular excuse for the young bloods to indulge in a little hell-raising. Shortly after Dr. Baldwin moved in with the Willcocks' on Duke Street, Eugenia,[1] the youngest daughter of William and Phoebe Willcocks, was married to Captain Augustin Boiton de Fougères, one of the French Royalists who had taken up land in the Oak Ridges. He was, of course, well known to Quetton de St. George. The celebrations after the wedding were unplanned and unwanted. Ely Playter, a son of George Playter the Loyalist whose property was on the west side of the Don River above *Castle Frank,* carefully recorded in his diary the turbulent events surrounding the Willcocks wedding:

York 12th, Octr. 1802 —
Tuesday . . . Capt. Boiton and Miss Willcocks were married this afternoon and the young beaux of the Town remindfull of the happy occasion and the French Custom of Shivierieing the Parties a Number of them in disguise assembled and made a great noise about the old Esquires House, till, the Esquire, his Son [Charles] and Doctr. Baldwin came in a great Passion with their Guns and threatened to Shoot if the disguised Party did not disperse, some run of, one frenchman was taken, the guard that was in the Town, was sent for, the Constables call'd, and the noisey Party soon were all gone. About 10 OClock, all was quiet and we went to bed. . . .

Wednesday 13th . . . The weather was wet in the evening a small company of wild rakes gathered to keep up the Shivierie, but the night being rainy & dark they soon gave it up. . . .

Thursday 14th . . . after Tea all was prepared for continuing the Shivierie and such a noise with drums, Kettles, Cowbells and Horns was never before heard at York. They keep'd it up till Past Midnight, round the town but the old Esqr. nor none of his family made their appearance some of the parties in the appearance of Indians went to McDougalls, called for Liquor, and danced in the House. Then to A. Macdonnell's Pull'd him out of bed and made him treat, danced all over the House, and staid cutting capers till 2 OClock in the morning.
Friday 15th. See that the wild crew had thrown over Willcocks stack of Hay last night heard that the Esquire threatened vengeance on the perpetrators.

The origin of the custom of *Charivariing* in the early communities of the colony is explained by Thomas Canniff in *The Settlement of Upper Canada* which he published in 1872:

As Upper Canada was, in a limited sense, an off-shoot of Lower Canada, so but a few of the peculiarities of Lower Canada were introduced to the Upper. One was that of Charivariing, which means a great noise with petty music. It was introduced from France. The custom is now almost obsolete among us but time was when it was quite common. It

---

*Among Lewis Bright's children, with whom this narrative is later concerned, were Jane Bright who was to marry Charles Scadding, an older brother of the Reverend Henry Scadding, D.D., and Susan Bright, the wife of James Austin who bought the *Spadina* property from the Baldwins in 1866. Lewis Bright held the post of Messenger of the Legislative Council in York, from 1812 until 1840.

generally was indulged in at second marriages, or when an unequal match and marriage took place; when a young girl married an old man for instance, or if either party were unpopular. The night of the wedding, instead of being passed in joyous in-door pleasures by the wedded ones, was made hideous by a crowd of masked persons, who with guns, tin-pans, pails, horns, horse-fiddles, and everything else that could be made to produce a discordant noise, disturbed the night until silenced by a treat, or money. Sometimes those meetings resulted in serious consequences to one or more of the party, by the bridegroom resorting to loaded firearms.

In the case of William Willcocks or "the Old Esquire" as Playter called him, this was not the first time his house on Duke Street had been marked for special attention by a band of revellers. Three years earlier, when word had finally reached York of Admiral Nelson's victory over the French in the Battle of the Nile which was fought in 1798, Colonel Shank, the officer commanding the Queen's Rangers, had ordered a *feu de joie* to mark the occasion, and contributions of wood were solicited from the citizens. At sunset a great bonfire was lit on the shore of the frozen Toronto Bay, and the fun-making went on until late into the night. It was customary on such occasions for the inhabitants to show a light in their windows, or, as the Honourable Peter Russell did on that memorable evening, illuminate all their rooms. For some reason Willcocks declined to participate in the town's rejoicing, and his windows were "broke in consequence of his not illuminating."

At the beginning of 1803, with his school now meeting regularly in one of Mr. Willcocks' rooms, Dr. Baldwin became absorbed in another venture. The Legislature had concluded that there were not enough lawyers in the province to handle the volume of conveyancing and litigation that was attendant upon settlement of its vast territory. Accordingly, an Act was passed "to authorize the Governor, Lieutenant-Governor, or persons administering the government of the Province, to license practitioners in the law." It was not necessary that the candidates qualify themselves by a formal course of study, or that they submit to the tedium of clerk-ship. They simply had to satisfy Chief Justice Henry Allcock (a political friend of William Willcocks') that they grasped the essentials of English law. Baldwin was quick to seize his opportunity. He borrowed Blackstone's "Commentaries on the Laws of England" from Receiver General Peter Russell, and after browsing through it had no trouble in satisfying the learned chief justice that he had attained the required standard of knowledge. On April 3, 1803, the doctor was duly licensed to practice law and act as an advocate in the courts of the province. Three other men also benefited from this extraordinary short-cut to membership in the ancient profession: D'Arcy Boulton Jr., John Powell, and William Dickson of Niagara, who, in a duel a few years later, killed his fellow-lawyer William Weekes. The wags of the town liked to refer to the privileged group as "heaven-descended barristers."

The following month, on May 31, with his new professional qualification in hand, (he was also practising medicine and teaching school), Dr. Baldwin married Margaret Phoebe, the second daughter of William and Phoebe Willcocks. The marriage ceremony was performed quietly in York and the couple continued to live with the Old Esquire on Duke Street. There is no record of a "Shivierie" having occurred to celebrate the event.

William Willcocks had earlier acquired a piece of property at the northwest corner of Frederick Street and the present Front Street. To relieve the overcrowding of his house on Duke Street he decided to build a small, frame house there for his daughter Phoebe and William Warren Baldwin. They were comfortably settled in it by the following spring, and on May 12, 1804, Phoebe gave birth to their first son, Robert, who, as the Honourable Robert Baldwin, was to play a leading role in the struggle for responsible government in Canada. It has been said that Dr. Baldwin proudly marked the occasion by closing his school for the day, and granting the boys a holiday.[2]

The following year, in November 1805, a second son was born to Phoebe and William, and he was christened Augustus William Baldwin — "little Billy" as Elizabeth Russell called him. Shortly after, Dr. Baldwin became concerned over Phoebe's health, and Miss Russell's diary contains this entry for Sunday, February 9, 1806:

> Dr. Baldwin here in the forenoon, after which he took his wife and Maria Willcocks and little Billy up to Mrs. Adjutant McGill's to stay some days to try change of air for Phoebe.

This entry is of special interest because the house they visited was *Davenport,* which had been built by Ensign and Adjutant John McGill of the Queen's Rangers on the 200-acre farm lot (No. 25) he had been formally granted by the Crown in 1798. His house, which would have been built before his Patent was issued, stood on the Davenport Hill, to which it gave its name, and lay immediately west of William Willcocks' farm lot (No. 24), the later *Spadina* property.

It was natural that the meandering lane that led past his place from Yonge Street, following the ancient Indian trail at the foot of the hill, would come to be called the Davenport Road since the McGill house was the principal landmark along that route in the earliest days of settlement.

The name *Davenport*[3] has generally been accepted as the invention of Lt. Col. Joseph Wells, who bought the McGill property in 1821, and after whom the present Wells Hill district is named. But two years before the Wells purchase from the Widow McGill, we find Dr. Baldwin reporting in a letter to his friend St. George who was then in France: "Mr. Loring lives at *Davenport* — a very worthy small man and pleasant neighbour." Clearly, Loring was renting *Davenport* from the McGill family at that time, and the name was in general use before Lt. Col. Wells bought the property.

Miss Russell's diary note also illustrates the belief of the early settlers of York in the health-giving properties that were to be found in the air on the Davenport Hill, or the "mountain" as it was sometimes called.[4] They were often afflicted with fever and ague, and they blamed their unhappy condition on the yellow vapour that hung over the marshes at the mouth of the Don River, just to the east of the town. One sufferer in 1801 complained "there is a marsh about ½ mile from where I live from which a thick fog arises every morning." He said nobody who lived in York could escape the malaise caused by the swamplands. In the autumn of 1803, the colourful Lord Selkirk visited York and commented critically upon the location of the blockhouse and the Parliament Buildings at the eastern end of the town, close to the Don River. He also testified to the immunity to the ague that was enjoyed by the settlers farther up Yonge Street, in the district of the Davenport Hill:

> This situation is found to be unhealthy from the neighbourhood of a

marsh of 1000 acres formed by the mouth of the Don . . . this marsh is not found to affect the Garrison or more distant part of the Town at about a mile or mile and half distant — A party of Soldiers stationed in the Block house last summer were constantly affected by Fever and Ague, while the Garrison on a dry bank 2 miles off was quite healthy— the old town was also more unhealthy than the new part which is farther from the Marsh — and up Yonge Street a few miles from the Town no fever at all existed. — The prevalence of Easterly winds last summer blowing off the marsh rendered the Town more than usually unhealthy.[5]

And shortly after Dr. Strachan's arrival some years later in York, his daughter "a sweet infant, exceedingly interesting" died of the ague from the marshes at the mouth of the Don.

Chapter 4

A House of Modest Aspect

In 1806 Dr. Baldwin became convinced that his father-in-law's land specu-
lations were about to plunge the Old Esquire into the whirlpool of another
bankruptcy, with the consequent seizure of all his property including the
house occupied by Baldwin on Frederick Street. There was a solid basis of
fact for the doctor's anxiety. Willcocks was still burdened with the mortgage
he had made in John Gray's favour in 1800, and he had further encumbered
his property in 1804 with a mortgage to Robert Hamilton, the wealthy
Queenston merchant. Early in 1806, Elizabeth Russell had to intervene in a
bitter quarrel concerning his debts between Willcocks and St. George which
occurred in *Russell Abbey*. She faithfully recorded the event in her diary:

> Willcocks came at dinner time and ate roasted apple. After tea was over
> Mr. St. George came and sat the evening. Willcocks and him were talk-
> ing about the former's debt to Mr. Gray of Montreal. Willcocks thought
> that St. George took Mr. Gray's part and began to grow in a passion
> with St. George and had he been let go on he would have been in a
> violent rage and insulted St. George, but I put a check to his going on
> by speaking a little sharp and telling him that there was quite enough
> of it. He had got primed with his grog which he often is. — He drinks
> a great quantity of brandy wine & water mixed together. However they
> went away good friends together.[1]

As a lawyer, Dr. Baldwin was particularly sensitive to the stresses that
were building up in Willocks' affairs. The chilling prospect of being evicted
from his father-in-law's house by a mob of angry creditors roused him to
action. He turned to his friend and patron the Honourable Peter Russell
with whom he now considered himself to be on terms of easy familiarity.
Russell owned a small cottage with a pleasant garden at the northeast corner
of the present Bay and Front Streets. He had bought it in 1798 from John
Denison who had continued to occupy it until he moved to Russell's farm,
Petersfield, a few years later. Russell had tried to sell it in 1803 without
success notwithstanding that it was a choice waterfront property consisting of
almost an acre. Baldwin, knowing that it was available, now approached
Peter Russell with a view to buying it.

While Russell was still prepared to dispose of the property, he imposed
the curious condition that the ownership of it had to lie with the infant
Robert Baldwin, then just two years of age, and that his mother and father,
Phoebe and William Warren Baldwin, could only have the right to occupy
the property during their lifetime. Dr. Baldwin tried to assure him that the

simplest way to carry out his wishes would be for Russell to sell him the property, and he would pass it on to his son under the terms of his own will. This procedure was not acceptable to the receiver general. He well knew that a will made today could be changed tomorrow. Furthermore, regardless of his will, if Baldwin was the outright owner, he could sell or mortgage the property at any time. It could also be reached by his creditors. It is odd that Russell should have asked Baldwin to pay him for the property and yet deny him the fruits of absolute ownership. As might be expected, Dr. Baldwin's pride was deeply hurt. He wrote to Russell on July 27, 1806:

> Before I proceed further I cannot conceal how much it wounded me to perceive that you thought it necessary to secure to Phoebe and Robert the property independent of my will. I only lament that I am so little known after so long an interchange of reciprocal kindnesses in which, no doubt, I am still deeply the debtor.
>
> To them I feel myself so entirely devoted that I could not hesitate an instant to fall in with your suggestions. The present conveyance, which is submitted to your judgement, renders me only tenant for life without any power of alienating, while the bond makes me personally responsible for the debt; it is true it will descend as an obligation on my heirs, but then it cannot attach to this property in particular and in no way can it defeat the inheritance to Robert; which was your wish, if I am not mistaken. . . . I am only a quack in law, and may therefore be mistaken, but I think the form correct — it is taken *mutatis mutandis* from Blackstone.
>
> It appears to me that you do not perceive the necessity of my doing anything towards a domestic establishment. Be assured, sir, it is incumbent on me. Poor Mr. Willcock's houses are at the hourly mercy of his creditors, and his present plans with the best intention in the world [are] I fear little likely to extricate him . . . your house is comfortable of a modest aspect and likely to suit the extent of our ambition — you cannot think the principal unsafe as I owe no debt to speak of, and the payment of the interest is perfectly within my power.[2]

Dr. Baldwin went on to ask that the initial payment of interest be deferred until the first of January 1807, because it was impossible for him to move before that time. He also assured Russell that the principal owing under the proposed loan would be paid off in advance of its due date.

The papers were finally signed by the sceptical receiver general in August, 1806, and Dr. Baldwin moved into Russell's cottage the following year with his wife Phoebe and young Robert Baldwin, his second son having died in the spring of 1806. At last he had a place of his own that was beyond the reach of the Old Esquire's creditors — and yet in a narrow, legal sense the property was not his at all: it belonged to his son, Robert. Paradoxically, the first property Dr. Baldwin did own and occupy in York was the later *Spadina* tract that was left to him by his father-in-law "poor Mr. Willcocks" upon his death in 1813. Dr. Baldwin's fears of rapacious creditors running the old man to ground were never realized. Perhaps in later years he reflected upon the irony of his early misgivings as the Old Esquire's various farm properties, acquired as by a player in a desperate game, descended by inheritance upon the Baldwin family like the falling of a gentle, beneficent dew.

Many years after, in 1835, Dr. Baldwin was to build the imposing "Baldwin Family Residence" on the Front Street site he had bought from Peter Russell. And the same year his son Robert Baldwin, then age thirty-one, deeded the property to his father.[3] Technically, the condition of ownership imposed by the receiver general was finally frustrated.

In his *Toronto of Old,* which was published in 1873, the Reverend
Dr. Henry Scadding refers to the northeast corner of Bay and Front Streets as
having once been the site of Dr. Baldwin's "town residence" by which, of
course, he meant the substantial house raised by the doctor in 1835. He does
not seem to have been aware that the Baldwins' ownership of the property
extended as far back as 1806. "Advancing a little further," he says as his
imaginary pilgrim strolled along Front Street towards Bay Street, "we came
in front of one of the earliest examples, in these parts, of an English-looking
rustic cottage, with verandah and sloping lawn. This was occupied for a
time by Major Hillier, of the 74th Regiment, aide-de-camp and military
secretary to Sir Peregrine Maitland."

Maitland arrived in Upper Canada as lieutenant-governor in 1818.
By that time Dr. Baldwin had removed himself and his family to his new
Spadina after a brief sojourn at *Russell Abbey* where they lived with Elizabeth Russell after the War of 1812. He must have rented the rustic cottage
to a number of tenants, including Major Hillier, before he decided to demolish it and build his town house there in 1835. The actual period of his
early occupancy of the site was from 1807 to 1814, and it was in this house
that his sons Henry (1807), William Augustus (1808), and Quetton St.
George (1810) were born.

As the year 1806 drew to a close, York was saddened to hear of the
death in England of the popular John Graves Simcoe, the first lieutenant-
governor of the province, in his fifty-fifth year. The following year, as
Dr. Baldwin was establishing himself in his cottage on the present Front Street,
the shadow of illness and death also fell upon the family circle of *Russell
Abbey.* The Honourable Peter Russell suffered a stroke in April 1807, from
which he languished until his death a year later, and Phoebe Willcocks,
William Willcocks' wife and the mother of Phoebe Baldwin, died in May
1807. She had been something of a shadowy figure in the social life that
revolved around *Russell Abbey.* Elizabeth Russell, apparently, did not have
a high opinion of her. While her diary refers frequently to the visits of
William Willcocks, Phoebe Willcocks is rarely mentioned as a caller at the
Abbey. Miss Russell made this entry on January 8, 1806:

> In the evening, a little before tea came Mrs. Willcocks entirely by her-
> self. She said she was some time at the Courtyard gate before she could
> open it. She drank tea and sat great part of the evening. We sent Milly
> and John home with her. She seldom comes of herself except when she
> has something to communicate or a favour to ask. Tonight was to
> express her wish that Charles [Phoebe Willcocks' son] should succeed
> to James Clark's place in case of his not being able to do the duty of it
> from his ill state of health or death. In the former case it would allow
> him half the salary during his life — Peter told her that he had already
> applied to the President [Alexander Grant] for a friend, (It was Dr.
> Baldwin but he did not tell her so.) and told him that he had already
> allotted it to another. My brother did not tell her who, but it is the
> President's son-in-law; this he told Peter in confidence. — 4

This passage reveals the continuing role of the Honourable Peter Russell as
the patron and benefactor of the Willcocks family (Miss Maria Willcocks,
Phoebe Baldwin's older sister, that year obtained the appointment of housekeeper to the Executive Council, a position she held until 1815); it also
reveals that Dr. Baldwin, too, was dipping into the springs of the old man's
influence when he tried to obtain for himself the position of clerk of the

Provincial Parliament. The job, Elizabeth Russell tells us, had already been given to Alexander Grant's son-in-law. Grant occupied the office of governor temporarily, with the title of president and administrator, after Peter Hunter's death in 1805. Dr. Baldwin, however, was successful in another direction in 1806: he secured for himself the office of master in chancery, and also the position of acting clerk of the Crown and Court of King's Bench.

Later, in 1807, after the death of his wife, the Old Esquire again became involved in a political campaign. He had supported Judge Allcock, as we have seen, in York's first tumultuous election in 1800 only to have his candidate's victory nullified. In this second instance he threw his support behind Judge Robert Thorpe who was also successful at the polls but was forced to withdraw from the province shortly after taking his seat in the House of Assembly. Thorpe had at one time been chief justice of Prince Edward Island. In 1805 he was appointed puisne judge of the Court of King's Bench in Upper Canada. He was a troublemaker and a demagogue. He used his judicial position as a platform for slashing attacks on the government in general, and on the lieutenant-governor in particular. His utterances in court ran the gamut from the legal points at issue to withering indictments of the whole apparatus of government. Francis Gore, who had become lieutenant-governor in 1806, concluded that Thorpe's outbursts contained a larger element of sedition than honest dissent, and he was responsible for his discharge from judicial office in the province.

The whole affair was disappointing to William Willcocks. As soon as Judge Thorpe had taken his seat in the Assembly, the Old Esquire applied for a regular salary as judge of the Home District Court. The application was not supported by the candidate on whose behalf he had laboured. Indeed, his petition was dismissed ignominiously by the House without any discussion at all. As one observer has noted, Willcocks gave no sign of reform leanings after that bitter experience.[5] But his son-in-law, Dr. Baldwin, who had also supported Thorpe's candidature, from that time on identified himself increasingly with those in dissent. In fact, Francis Gore was quick to see this pattern developing. In a letter written at the time he referred to Baldwin as "an Irishman, ready to join any party to make confusion." And from distant Cornwall the Reverend John Strachan grumbled:

> The fame of your election extends to this remote part of the Province, it seems to have equalled Westminster. If this turbulent Judge proceeds in the manner he has been doing, the peace and harmony of the Province will be destroyed. . . . You see we enter a little into your Politics, in truth the discontents which this man may very easily raise will render the situation of every respectable man in the Province much less agreeable.

While brooding over this setback in his hopes of financial succour, and doubtless feeling the pangs of loneliness following his wife's death the year before, William Willcocks sought increasingly the solace of the congenial company of *Russell Abbey*. He began to toy with the idea of proposing marriage to Elizabeth Russell. Admittedly, his cousin Peter Russell's health was showing no sign of improvement, but Willcocks was now seventy-two and the object of his growing fancy was fifty-four. Neither, he argued quite rightly, was growing any younger. And so in March 1808, with the musky warmth of spring pervading the air of York, the Old Esquire penned a note to Miss Russell. Judging from his portrait, he must have reminded her of a frolicsome satyr, the inhabitant of some bosky dell, when he delivered his proposal to her in *Russell Abbey*. The note read:

> My dearest love
> Though I sit many hours in your company I have not an opportunity to converse with you on the subject next my heart — We having both agreed on our closer union — the sooner it can be accomplished the better. I am old and you are not growing young. Therefore as little time should be lost as convenience and propriety will admit of. — I do not wish our marriage to take place before the middle of May — but that as you may think best. I leave to your prudence the mentioning of it to your good brother. I wish for some conversation with you
> Ever your
Willcocks

Willcocks expressed his preference that the marriage not take place before the middle of May because of his wife's death the previous May. Propriety demanded a year of mourning. His reminder that the spinster was "not growing young" was perhaps wanting in tact, but on the whole, the letter was practical and direct, its message unobscured by any flight of romantic fancy. And Miss Russell's reaction was the same. She thought he had taken leave of his senses. She was astonished at his "impudence and folly." She noted in her diary a couple of days later: "the Old Fool came as usual to dinner." For a few weeks she treated Willcocks with studied disdain, but later relented, and the Old Esquire was finally restored to his place by the fireside of *Russell Abbey*.

Later in 1808, just a few months before Peter Russell's death, Willcocks' son Charles, for whom his mother had sought employment two years before, was again importuning the ailing Russell, this time with the object of interesting him in purchasing some property. The receiver general's response was clear and unequivocal. He wrote on June 11, 1808:

> Having a great deal of land in this Province which I am very desirous of selling, and not being able to procure a purchaser for any part of it, I am the last man who would be inclined to add to my stock. Circumstanced as I am at present I really am not able to part with the smallest sum without inconvenience.

Russell's letter testifies to the plethora of land in Upper Canada at that time, and the difficulty in selling it to advantage. The rewards in holding large tracts in the sparsely settled province were still a long way off — they awaited the opening up of the country to extensive immigration, better communications, and an industrial counterbalance to the simple agrarian economy of that day. While desirable property located within the little towns of the province slowly appreciated in value as their populations increased, the large landowners, like Russell, did not live to see their judgment confirmed in assembling great parcels of wild lands. And, as their holdings were diffused through successive generations of inheritors, the inevitable fragmentation and final exhaustion of their interests occurred.

Dr. Henry Scadding, whose father had owned extensive property on both sides of the Don River, reflected on this fact, somewhat enigmatically, sixty years later as he toiled over the manuscript of *Toronto of Old* in the parsonage of Holy Trinity Church:

> Survivors of the primitive era in Upper Canada have been heard sometimes to express, (like Lord Clive, after his dealings with the rajahs,)

their surprise that they did not provide for themselves more largely than they did, when the broad acres of their adopted country were to be had to any extent, almost for the asking. But this reflection should console them; in few instances are the descendants of the early very large land-holders much better off at the present hour than probably they would have been, had their fathers continued landless.

In accumulating thousands of acres of land in Upper Canada during his term of office, Russell was simply responding to the custom of his day. It was an age of great landed estates — the Simcoes at *Wolford* in Devonshire held thousands of acres, the Russell family at *Woburn Abbey* in Bedford-shire held thousands more. A broad land portfolio bespoke membership in an elevated tier of society. Landless at home, Russell's vast holdings in the new colony provided him at once with a feeling of security for himself and his sister, and an assured position in the narrow, self-conscious society of Upper Canada.

Posterity has not been generous in its assessment of Peter Russell. He has been depicted as a parsimonious land-grabber, and an exploiter of his position of public trust. Being a bachelor and his sister a spinster, the Russells left no descendants to argue their case on their behalf.

Shortly after his arrival in York, Governor Peter Hunter wrote caustic-ally to John King, the under-secretary at the Colonial Office in England, about Russell:

> The Executive Council are all good men, but I cannot help observing that your Friend Peter Russel is avaricious to the last degree, and would certainly as far as depended on him, have granted lands to the Devil and all his Family (as good loyalists) provided they could have paid the Fees.

This stricture has been widely quoted by historians, and has unduly prejudiced our assessment of Peter Russell's important contribution to the early development of York. And Dr. Henry Scadding, by gentle innuendo, leaves the Hunter view of Russell largely unimpaired. He has written:

> His position as Administrator, on the departure of the first Governor of the Province, gave him facilities for the selection and acquisition of wild lands. The duality necessarily assumed in the wording of the Pat-ents by which the Administrator made grants to himself, seems to have been regarded by some as having a touch of the comic in it. Hence among the early people of these parts the name of Peter Russell was occasionally to be heard quoted good-humouredly, not malignantly, as an example of "the man who would do well unto himself."

Scadding later fills nearly a page of *Toronto of Old* listing the properties that Russell offered for sale in the *Gazette and Oracle* in 1803, totalling thousands of acres, adding:

> Of the lands enumerated he styles himself, at the close of the advertise-ment, the proprietor. We have no desire, however, to perpetuate the popular impression, that all the said properties had been patented by himself to himself. This, of course, could not have been done. He simply chose, as he was at liberty to do, after acquiring what he and his family were entitled to legally, in the shape of grants, to invest his means in lands, which in every direction were to be had for a mere song.

It should be noted as well that the lands which Dr. Scadding carefully listed would hardly have been advertised for sale under the nose of the critical Governor Hunter had they not been acquired by the receiver general in a proper manner.

The irony of Russell's treatment at the hands of posterity deepens when we recall that in 1797 he took a strong stand against laxity in issuing grants of lots within the Town of York. Writing to D. W. Smith, the surveyor general, he said: "I shall do all in my power to prevent the lots of York to be taken up as objects of Speculation."

And later, in the same year, he stated his position to the surveyor general with greater force:

> Nothing but the utmost vigilance in the Council, in you, and in me can put a stop to these Impositions on the King's Bounty. — But with respect to the Town of York, I am determined to prevent as far as I can a Monopoly of the Lots in it. — I must therefore request that no assignments for a Town Lot issue from your Office without having first received my sanction — that I may have an opportunity of Examining the Parties, and by cross questions discover the probability of their becoming settled here —

It is likely that Governor Hunter's view of Russell was hastily formed and unfairly influenced by Chief Justice John Elmsley and William Jarvis with whom Russell had had serious differences of opinion in matters of policy affecting the province before Hunter arrived. It was not long, however, before Hunter lost confidence in Elmsley's advice, and as we have seen, he later threatened Jarvis with dismissal.

Because of their assured salaries and fees, the holders of senior government positions in early Upper Canada were in a position either to augment their personal landholdings, as Peter Russell chose to do, or remit substantial sums to their bankers in England. Lieutenant-General Peter Hunter chose the latter course as has been revealed by Brigadier-General E. A. Cruickshank in his *Memoir of Peter Hunter,* published in 1934:

> Besides the pay of his rank in the army and his salary of £2000 a year as lieutenant governor, he was entitled to a fee of a guinea for each patent issued for a grant of land and a similar fee for signing commissions for civil appointments. He remitted large sums from time to time to his brother in London.

Referring to Russell's position as a substantial landholder, Edith G. Firth has pointed out that there is no evidence that he ever received in free grants more than the 6000 acres to which he was entitled. He was entirely within his right to buy additional land, as Dr. Scadding conceded, and this he obviously did with vigour and enthusiasm. Whether he was wise in doing so is another question. Much of the land he acquired was unmarketable in his lifetime. It was largely for that reason, a few months before his death, that he could not "part with the smallest sum without inconvenience."

Chapter 5

The Death of
the Honourable Peter Russell

The hazy, humid summer of 1808, so typical of York, had now passed. The ripeness of autumn had settled upon the town, and the leaves of the sumac and maple were already touched with scarlet. In the rough fence-rows that enclosed the settlers' houses, clusters of goldenrod and Queen Anne's lace were stirring in the gusting wind. Soon the equinoctial gales would sweep the lake, warning the townsmen to hasten their preparations for the onslaught of the Canadian winter. The clouds of summer dust that had hung oppressively over the thoroughfares of York had finally been dispelled by the soft September rain. And in *Russell Abbey,* on the 30th day of September, the Honourable Peter Russell breathed his last.

The pace of life quickened noticeably around the Abbey for a few days as a throng of callers made their way along the lakefront to the famous residence of the receiver general to offer their sympathy to the sorrowing Elizabeth Russell. An impressive and solemn funeral befitting a senior government official had to be carefully worked out. A carpenter was hastily summoned to construct a coffin, and the Garrison was asked to muster a guard to accord full military honours to the lamented captain in recognition of his earlier service.

The funeral was held on October 4. Francis Gore, the lieutenant-governor, was chief mourner and the final sermon was preached by the Reverend Okill Stuart, who led the worshipping community of the Church of England in York, which was to become the Church of St. James. It is probable that the interment took place in the old Military Burying Ground close to Fort York, to the west of the present Spadina Avenue. In 1794, Governor Simcoe's infant daughter Katharine had been buried there. While St. James' Church was later to have its own cemetery on King Street, it was not until 1810 that the church plot was enclosed by a rail fence. At the same time the ground around the entrance, which then faced Church Street, was cleared of stumps. In later years, Dr. Baldwin arranged for the remains of Peter Russell to be re-interred, along with those of his sister Elizabeth, in St. Martin's Rood, as Baldwin named his private cemetery near his house *Spadina.*

As Governor Simcoe's successor as senior representative of the Crown, Russell's contribution to the day-to-day administration of the government of Upper Canada was of a high order. For three years as president and administrator he laboured in the difficult and perplexing days of early settlement, and had more to do than anyone else with the establishment of the operations of government on an orderly and efficient basis. He shares the distinction with Simcoe of having nurtured Toronto in its infancy, and having set it on a firm course towards its destiny as a great metropolitan city. One writer has put it this way:

> Simcoe dreamed of an ideal capital; Russell built York, and the roads to make York readily accessible. Simcoe looked far into the future; Russell contented himself with current practicalities. And Simcoe got his statue, while Russell is unlamented and almost forgotten.[1]

Peter Russell had made his will on August 22, 1808, just a few weeks before his death. Thomas Ridout, his son Samuel, and Stephen Heward[2] had filed awkwardly into his bedchamber to witness the signing of the document. As always in circumstances of the kind, the will must have been the object of speculation and conjecture on the part of those of the *Russell Abbey* circle who allowed themselves to hope that they would be recipients of the old man's bounty. After all, William Willcocks was Peter Russell's cousin, and a cash bequest or a farm property would be a flattering and tangible recognition of that relationship. And Dr. Baldwin, one of Peter Russell's physicians, could not help recalling Russell's insistence in the summer of 1806 that his Front Street property be transferred in such a way that its ownership would lie with the infant Robert Baldwin. Perhaps the receiver general had made further arrangements in his will along those lines which would benefit the doctor's family, if not himself.

After the funeral the will was read. The many thousands of acres of Upper Canada land that fell within its ambit, the whole estate in fact, was left solely to Russell's half-sister Elizabeth. No one else was mentioned.

"I give devise and bequeath," Russell had stated firmly, "all my lands, tenements, hereditaments and all and singular other my estates, real and personal and of what nature or kind soever in the said Province of Upper Canada or Elsewhere unto my dear Sister Elizabeth Russell of York in said Province Spinster. To have and to hold unto the said Elizabeth Russell her heirs and assigns forever."

During the months that followed, Dr. Baldwin found consolation in the fact that he was kept busy helping Miss Russell settle her brother's extensive estate. Francis Gore, perhaps noticing Baldwin's proficiency in this type of legal activity, approved his appointment in November, 1808 as registrar of the Court of Probate for the province.

In the same month, the doctor's father, Robert Baldwin the Emigrant as he has come to be called to distinguish him from his famous grandson, was visiting York from the family farm in Clarke Township. Now aged sixty-seven, he was faced with the prospect of all his children leaving the farm. In many ways he was deeply attached to his squire-like life in the backwoods of Durham County; he enjoyed the camaraderie of the pioneer settlement, and never lost his delight in contemplating nature as it revealed itself to him through the changing Canadian seasons. But the time was not far off when he could no longer sustain the operation of the farm by himself. He knew that soon he too would have to withdraw to York.

He pondered the seemingly inconsolable grief of Elizabeth Russell. When her brother was alive, the Russells had always been hospitable to him and his family on their visits to York. Perhaps now Miss Russell would recognize that her need of companionship was as great as his own. Like

William Willcocks, he decided to propose marriage to the heiress, and he did so in a letter written in York in November, 1808:

> Permit me to now declare these sentiments which have long lain dormant in my bosom and unknown to mortal but the Bearer who can vouch that it is no sudden thought but was kept secret. . . . The moment that announced your being your own mistress also announced your being left sole executrix. This, which to most others would have been a source of exaltation and joy, produced in me a contrary effect. Fearing that the acquisition of fortune may place you beyond my Hope. . . .
>
> Let what ever lawyer you please put your entire fortune beyond my reach by keeping it both now and the disposal hereafter totally in your OWNE power. . . .
>
> Grant me this request, that you will seriously consider this letter before you refuse me and also be convinced that no man on the whole continent of America as disinterestedly and sincerely loves you as the one who ardently wishes to have it in his power to subscribe himself by a still dearer name than that of
>
> Your friend,
R.B. York 3 Nov. 1808[3]

No record of Elizabeth Russell's reply exists, but she chose to remain unattached. Preoccupied with her sorrow, she evidently turned Robert Baldwin's proposal aside more lightly than that of William Willcocks when he had cast her in the role of *femme fatale* a few months earlier.

The process of winding up her brother's affairs dragged on, but Miss Russell was greatly comforted by Dr. Baldwin's solicitous attention to her needs, both legal and medical. John and Sophia Denison remained at the *Petersfield* farm and continued to manage it efficiently. She saw a good deal of the Willcocks and Baldwin families, and dined with them at the doctor's cottage on Front Street every Sunday.

But her brother's death had opened up a deep and dark abyss in her life. "I feel the loss of him more terribly every day—" she wrote to her friend Elizabeth Keirnan in Devon, "for in him I have not only lost a kind friend and affectionate brother but my adviser and protector. It was a great comfort to him to think that I still should find one in my cousin Edward Willey." Her letter was written from York on September 18, 1809, almost a year after Peter Russell's death. Her cousin, Colonel Edward Willey, was then living in Yorkshire where he died a short time later.[4]

The following year, in another letter to her friend written on October 12, 1810, she struck a despondent note concerning her health, and spoke nostalgically of the remoteness of England to which she was never to return:

> My own health is but indifferent and spirits extremely low — as being so is not to be wondered at when I reflect on my having lost all my nearest and dearest relations and left in a distant country from all my remaining friends — in an ill state of health and little hope of ever getting well of the *Disorder* I labour under and I much fear it will be a long time before I shall be able to return to England. The difficulty of parting with my property here added to the danger of the Seas and the great fatigue that travelling would now be to me. However, I will not give up the pleasing hope of some time or other having the happiness of seeing you. It would give me very great pleasure indeed to make one of your fireside. . . . If it was not for the goodness of Doctor Baldwin who is married to one of Mr. Wilcoxes Daughters I know not what I should have done . . . he had indeed been most kind and friendly to me.

Miss Russell's reference to the "danger of the Seas" reflects the ever-present fear of ocean travellers at that time of capture by Napoleon's ships. In 1810, D'Arcy Boulton, then the solicitor general of Upper Canada, obtained six months leave of absence to visit England. His ship was captured by a French privateer, and Boulton was imprisoned in Verdun until 1814. Elizabeth Russell was particularly disturbed by the incident because she had entrusted some letters to him for delivery in England.

In a further letter to Mrs. Keirnan, written on May 30, 1811, two and a half years after her brother's death, she confided that she felt his loss "more and more every day." And her *Disorder,* which she at last disclosed as being dropsy, was no better. In fact, later that summer her condition became critical. Dr. Baldwin, who was attending her, grew alarmed and sent to Niagara for the surgeon of the 100th Regiment who hurried to York to find her, as she later described it, "nearly on the Bed of Death." The surgeon recommended a minor operation, but she demurred at first and kept him hovering around *Russell Abbey* for several days. Finally, word was received in York that his regiment was leaving Niagara, and he was under orders to return immediately. In the circumstances Miss Russell grudgingly consented to the operation, and later reported to her friend in Devon that "18 pints of water was taken from me." The operation was successful and, as she was surprised to find, quite painless. Her health gradually improved. "I have been taking an extract of an Herb," she wrote, "which cured Sir James Craig [the late governor-general of the Canadas] of a dropsy with which he was afflicted for several years — the plant grows in great abundance in the woods." She added that she was able to make the concoction herself.

The herb or plant that Miss Russell used may have been purple foxglove. Though not indigenous to Canada, British settlers may have introduced it to the country at an early date, as was the case with other herbs and plants. They would have been aware of the digitalis contained in its leaves and of its value in treating such heart-induced disorders as dropsy.

Elizabeth Russell was confined to her house for most of the summer of 1811. Even the simple pleasures of her garden, which she had tended with stubborn devotion for over ten years, had been denied her. From her window in the Abbey, overlooking the garden and the Toronto Bay, she had seen the lilac and snowball blossoms bloom and fade — the trees she had planted long ago under her brother's approving eye. She sat listlessly in her room watching the sailing vessels glide across the glassy surface of the Bay and recalled the November day in 1797 when she and her brother arrived on that desolate shore from Niagara as a violent storm broke over the little settlement. As she reflected on these things, the crisis of her illness approached, and she conferred with Dr. Baldwin, in his capacity as her lawyer, about the will she knew she must make.

The document was quickly prepared, and on August 3, 1811, with Dr. Baldwin doubtless officiating, Thomas Ridout and his son Samuel, together with John Detlor,[5] visited *Russell Abbey* to witness Miss Russell's signature. The ailing spinster must have been comforted and reassured by Dr. Baldwin's reminder that the two Ridouts had witnessed her devoted brother's will three years before.

Elizabeth Russell continued to live at *Russell Abbey* until her death in 1822 at the age of sixty-eight. But the will she made in the summer of 1811, in a state of grief and despondency, was never changed. It lay for over ten years in Dr. Baldwin's strongbox. Finally, upon her death, Dr. Baldwin was to take over the administration of her vast estate as her sole executor and trustee.

The Reverend Dr. Henry Scadding, a tireless recorder of Toronto's early history, did not publish *Toronto of Old,* his major work, until 1873. Many years before, in 1841, he had been married by Bishop Strachan to Harriet, the daughter of John Spread Baldwin, Dr. Baldwin's younger brother. She died a little over two years after their marriage, and was buried at *Spadina,* in Dr. Baldwin's St. Martin's Rood Cemetery. Dr. Scadding had one daughter, Henrietta, who also married into the Baldwin Family, she becoming the wife of Robert Sullivan in 1866. Sullivan was a grand-nephew of Dr. William Warren Baldwin.

In the light of Dr. Scadding's close connection with the Baldwin family, and the ease of access he must have had to their papers and records, it is puzzling to find him so frequently in error in his factual references to Dr. Baldwin. As a result, generations of innocent writers have measured their length on the ice patches of fable and fancy that lie hidden beneath his Victorian prose. In no instance are his lapses in connection with Dr. Baldwin better illustrated than in his casual misstatement of the terms of Elizabeth Russell's famous will — a document of public record that was readily available to him for examination.

The venerable historian makes several references to the disposition of Miss Russell's property in his widely quoted *Toronto of Old.* "On the death of Mr. Russell," he wrote, "his property passed into the hands of his sister, who bequeathed the whole to Dr. William Warren Baldwin, into whose possession also came the valuable family plate, elaborately embossed with the armorial bearings of the Russells." A later reference modifies this statement: "Mr. Russell's estate passed to his unmarried sister, Miss Elizabeth Russell, who, at her decease, devised the whole of it to Dr. W. W. Baldwin *and his family."*

Not so. The basic provisions of Miss Russell's will are not in accord with these statements. While Baldwin received a generous cash bequest of £600, her estate, after payment of her debts and other legacies, was left to her cousins, Maria Willcocks and Phoebe Baldwin, the surviving daughters of the Old Esquire, William Willcocks. Phoebe, of course, was the wife of Dr. Baldwin. The language of the will is clear:

> . . . and further it is my will that after the payment of all the above mentioned legacies all the rest residue and remainder of my said real estate shall be divided equally between my Cousin Maria Willcocks and Phoebe Baldwin each to have and to hold her respective share to her respective heirs and assigns for ever to the use of the said Maria Willcocks and Phoebe Baldwin their heirs and assigns forever. And further it is my will that tho I expect the said William Warren Baldwin the Executor and trustee of this my will to make no unecessary delay in carrying the same into effect he shall not be harrassed by the several legatees above-mentioned but that he shall have a reasonable time allowed for the sale of the Lands and that he shall in no instance be sued or put to costs for the recovery of any of the aforesaid Legacies till three years from the time of my decease nor are the aforesaid legacies to bear any interest till after the sale of the aforesaid Lands and I do give and bequeath my personal Estate to my Executor towards the payment of my said debts and Legacies and I do hereby appoint the said William Warren Baldwin to be the Executor and Trustee of my last will and testament.

The distinction to be drawn between Dr. Baldwin's role as executor and trustee, and that of beneficiary, is especially important when we read these further lines of Dr. Scadding's which were inspired many years later as he contemplated Spadina Avenue:

> The Russell bequest augmented in no slight degree the previous possessions of Dr. Baldwin. In the magnificent dimensions assigned to the thoroughfare opened up by him in the neighbourhood of Petersfield, we have probably a visible expression of the large-handed generosity which a pleasant windfall is apt to inspire. Spadina Avenue is 160 feet wide throughout its mile-and-a-half length; and the part of Queen Street that bounds the front of the Petersfield parklot, is made suddenly to expand to the width of 90 feet. Maria Street also, a short Street here [now Soho Street], is of extra width. The portion of York, now Toronto, laid out by Dr. Baldwin on a fraction of the land opportunely inherited, will, when solidly built over, rival Washington or St. Petersburg in grandeur of groundplan and design.

Again, Dr. Scadding's stirring passage is pleasing but inaccurate. His reference to the "large-handed generosity" of Dr. Baldwin has been echoed by unwary writers for a century. The lands upon which the spacious Spadina Avenue was developed by the genial doctor were never his to give. As we have seen, after Elizabeth Russell's death, they were owned by Maria Willcocks and her sister Phoebe Baldwin. It was in his capacity simply as advisor to the two principal beneficiaries, his wife and Maria Willcocks, that Dr. Baldwin later laid out Spadina Avenue which, incidentally, had an original width of 132 feet, not 160 feet as stated by Dr. Scadding.

The legacies provided for in Elizabeth Russell's will are of interest because of the light they cast upon her circle of friends both in England and in Upper Canada.

The first bequest mentioned is "the money and Stock belonging to me in the British funds" which were left equally to the children of her cousin the late Colonel Edward Willey of Yorkshire, with twenty pounds to be paid "to their Mother for Mourning." And out of the sale of her real estate Dr. Baldwin was authorized to retain £600 for his own use, and £400 was left to his wife Phoebe for her separate use. Phoebe's sister, Maria Willcocks, received a legacy of £300, and the four sons of Dr. Baldwin then living, in 1811, namely Robert, Henry, William, and St. George, were each left £100. Dr. Baldwin's sisters, Alice and Mary, were remembered with bequests of £50 as was their father Robert Baldwin. But her "old friend and kindred William Willcocks Esquire" was granted only £20 for Mourning. Both Robert Baldwin the Emigrant, and William Willcocks, predeceased Elizabeth Russell, and their bequests therefore lapsed.

Remembering her "much beloved friend" in Devon, Mrs. Elizabeth Keirnan, Miss Russell left her £400. Mrs. Sophia Denison, the wife of John Denison the faithful manager of the *Petersfield* farm, was also left £400 "for her sole and separate use exclusive of her husband and for which her receipt alone shall be good this last bequest to be so secured and that the said Sophia Denison shall have and enjoy the interest thereof during her life the principal to be let out or vested in Lands for the Sole use of her daughter Elizabeth Denison." John Denison was left £50, and he was also excused payment of any debts which might be owing to Miss Russell. Finally, Mary Scarlet, formerly Mary Thomson, Miss Russell's companion, was given a legacy of £100, and her father Archibald Thomson and his wife were each left £10 for Mourning.

In providing the largest cash bequest for Baldwin, (as land values stood in those days, his £600 legacy was worth 600 acres of choice Township of York land), Miss Russell was doubtless recompensing him for his attention to her needs after her brother's death. She was probably also aware that the fees he would be entitled to as her executor and trustee, as well as her estate solicitor, would result in his receiving further benefits of a substantial nature.

The plan of Miss Russell's will was carefully worked out — at least in most of its details. She requested that her funeral expenses should be "such as propriety and decency would require without unnecessary show." She described herself as "being weak in Body but of sound and perfect memory and understanding." And the provision thoughtfully inserted by Dr. Baldwin relieving him as her Executor from possible harassment by her beneficiaries, and giving him three years to settle her legacies, testifies to his clear-headed understanding of the problems involved in winding up an estate holding large tracts of land. But all this leaves unanswered the conspicuous omission, if it was an omission, of any reference to the "valuable family plate, elaborately embossed with the armorial bearings of the Russells" which Dr. Scadding mentions in an earlier quoted passage. "Plate" at that time of course meant sterling silver, not the plated-ware in general use today. Scadding states that this early York treasure was bequeathed to Dr. Baldwin.

The disposition of all her personal property, which would have included the Russell silver, was dealt with briskly in a single sentence: "I do give and bequeath my personal Estate to my Executor towards the payment of my said debts and Legacies. . . ."

It is difficult to escape the conclusion that had any such valuable heirloom silver been part of her estate, Miss Russell would have roused herself to deal specifically with it. It is hard to believe that as a woman of means and sensibility she would have authorized its sale for the payment of her debts and legacies. If the Russell plate had existed in York (other than in Dr. Scadding's imagination), we may be certain Dr. Baldwin would never have sold it if it had fallen into his hands. Since the doctor attached great importance to the primacy of the senior male heir in a family, the silver would undoubtedly have been passed on to his oldest son, the Honourable Robert Baldwin. But no mention is made of the Russell silver in the later wills of either Dr. Baldwin or the Honourable Robert Baldwin. Having provoked our curiosity, Dr. Scadding has left us to speculate on the fate of the legendary silver of early York.[6]

Chapter 6

1812 Overture

During 1811, three important legal positions in the provincial government had become vacant: that of solicitor-general which had been filled by D'Arcy Boulton, now Napoleon's prisoner in France; the office of attorney-general which was left vacant by William Firth, a friend of Dr. Baldwin's, when he returned to England after a disagreement with Francis Gore over his fees; and finally, the vacancy in the Court of King's Bench caused by the dismissal of the intransigent Judge Thorpe.

Dr. Baldwin was now thirty-six years of age. He had been practising law for eight years. In addition to holding several minor judicial appointments, he was a bencher of the Law Society of Upper Canada, and in 1811 was elected its treasurer. On the face of it he had every reason to hope that he might be nominated to fill one of the lucrative legal positions now open in the province. All eluded his grasp. The position of solicitor-general was reserved for Boulton; William Campbell (later Chief Justice Sir William Campbell of Duke Street) was brought from Nova Scotia to succeed Thorpe as a judge of the Court of King's Bench; and John Macdonnell, a practising lawyer in York who had been called to the bar five years after Dr. Baldwin, and who sat in the Assembly for Glengarry, was appointed acting attorney-general in place of William Firth.

This setback in Dr. Baldwin's ambitions left a residue of frustration and bitterness. His family responsibilities had now become painfully onerous. His old father, Robert Baldwin the Emigrant, had finally made the break from the farm in Clarke Township and was living with the doctor's growing family in the cottage at Bay and Front Streets. And the Old Esquire, William Willcocks, was also making his home with them. Dr. Baldwin was probably glad to have him under his roof where he could keep an eye on him. In a letter to his friend Quetton de St. George he said: "If we can keep the old man from involving himself by useless schemes at mill building, he will leave something — we endeavour to make him as comfortable as we can. I fear his old habits of speculation will still haunt him—" and, perhaps conscious of his debt to his father-in-law in whose houses he had lived for the first four years of his married life, he added, "however, let him do as he will; while he lives and I have a house he shall have a home."[1]

In the close-knit society of Little York, rivalry between the various factions seeking preferment for themselves was intense. The position of these fluid groups tended to shift with the appointment of each successive governor, around whom life in the provincial capital largely revolved. It was the age of patronage, and in the jostling for position that went on amongst the officials and their wives, animosities often developed. They sometimes led to ill feeling between entire families. They even led to street brawls and duels.

It has been suggested that Dr. Baldwin's failure to obtain a senior position for himself in 1811 was due to the machinations of the so-called Family Compact, but that oligarchical group did not attain its privileged position in the affairs of Upper Canada until after 1818 when Strachan had been appointed to the Executive Council.[2] While the players were gathering in the wings, the principal actor, the Reverend John Strachan, under whose banner they were to form their ranks, was still in Cornwall—and his brilliant lieutenant, John Beverley Robinson, later attorney-general and then chief justice, was studying law in York. Dr. Baldwin's association with such men as Thorpe and Firth, with whose political views he was known to be in sympathy, undoubtedly harmed him when senior positions in the province were being filled upon the governor's recommendation to the British Colonial Office.

The following spring, brooding and sensitive, with no important position in sight, Dr. Baldwin took offence at some remarks made to him in court by the newly appointed attorney-general, John Macdonell. He demanded an apology through the intermediation of Lieutenant Thomas Taylor, a British officer stationed at Fort York. Macdonell refused. The formalities having been completed, Dr. Baldwin instructed Lieutenant Taylor to arrange the time and place for a duel. Duncan Cameron, whom Baldwin later described as "a bird of ill omen," was selected by Macdonell as his second, and a site on the Toronto Island, or Peninsula as it was then, was settled upon.* The antagonists were to face each other in the light of an April dawn.

Elizabeth Russell once said of Dr. Baldwin: "He is a poor dear hearted creature and always fears the worst." Quite naturally, he spent the night before his duel fretfully writing letters to his friends and his wife, and he also made a short will. He arose at daybreak and with Lieutenant Taylor slipped unnoticed from the house at Bay and Front Streets, and headed for the Peninsula along the track by the Bay. As they made their way they saw Macdonell and Cameron in the distance, crossing the ice in a sleigh. When they reached the blockhouse, which was located just west of the present Parliament Street, they paused long enough for Baldwin to sign his will in the presence of two witnesses. They resumed their march, and as they rounded the eastern end of the bay they noticed sheets of early-morning mist rising from the Don marshes. Only the melancholy cry of a gull broke the silence as they moved slowly towards their rendezvous.

Cameron and Taylor, the two seconds, made their arrangements quickly, and Macdonell and Baldwin, their pistols cocked, were placed back to back. As the duelling code required, upon the first command the adversaries walked apart, on the second they wheeled about, and on the third they were to fire. As Dr. Baldwin turned and raised his pistol, he was astonished to see Macdonell standing motionless, his arm unraised. Cameron called out urging Baldwin to fire, whereupon the doctor deliberately fired wide, whistling a shot through the trees and out over the lake. That ended the matter, and the duelists shook hands and withdrew.

---

*The Toronto Island resulted from the violent storms of 1858 which drove a navigable channel through the Peninsula at the eastern end of the Toronto Bay.

Dr. Baldwin later interpreted Macdonell's unwillingness to fire at him as an admission that he had been in the wrong. In any event, he was satisfied with the outcome, and felt that his honour had been redeemed. For Macdonell the incident was simply a fleeting reprieve from possible death. Six months later, as Lieutenant-Colonel Macdonell, provincial *aide de camp* to Major General Sir Isaac Brock, he lay dead in a field at Queenston, a bullet through his head. He fell shortly after Brock, and did not live to see the ignominious defeat and surrender of the American forces.

Baldwin and Taylor trudged back to town, and as they skirted the Don marshes, we are reminded of Dr. Baldwin's boating trips a few years before with the Honourable Peter Russell and his sister Elizabeth up the Don River to *Castle Frank,* the old Simcoe house which Russell had once tried to buy without success. John Denison, the manager of the receiver-general's *Petersfield* farm, had lived in it briefly before moving to the house then occupied by Baldwin on Front Street. *Castle Frank,* which had been named by Governor Simcoe for his son Francis, was now in ruins. Though not completed in their time, it was the focal point of the few pleasurable hours the Simcoe family had passed together while they were in York.

On the day of Dr. Baldwin's duel, April 3, 1812, Wellington's army was moving into its siege positions around the Spanish fortress town of Badajoz. After a week-long attack its walls were finally breached, and the delicate mechanism by which Napoleon ruled Spain was shattered. Two men identified with the early history of York were prominent in Wellington's famous victory at Badajoz: young Francis Simcoe, the owner of *Castle Frank,* aged twenty-one, died a hero's death and was buried near the town. And Lieutenant-Colonel Joseph Wells, Dr. Baldwin's distinguished neighbour ten years later at *Davenport,* won a gold medal for valour.

During the summer of 1811, at the time when Elizabeth Russell lay ill in *Russell Abbey,* the Old Esquire, William Willcocks, also made his will. As we have noted, he was living with the Baldwin ménage on Front Street, and at age seventy-six found it difficult to get around. In her correpondence at that time, Elizabeth Russell mentioned that he had been "troubled with a sore leg for several years." The state of his infirmity is confirmed by the fact that the witnesses to his will, which was signed on July 4, 1811, were Robert Baldwin the Emigrant, his daughter Alice Baldwin, and Hamilton Walker, a visitor in town from the District of Johnstown (Carleton County). Both Robert Baldwin and Alice Baldwin were part of Dr. Baldwin's crowded household, and since they were not receiving a benefit under the Old Esquire's will, it was a matter of practical convenience for them to witness the document.

Of special significance was the gift of his 200-acre farm lot in the Township of York to Dr. Baldwin: "I give and devise to my son-in-law William Warren Baldwin and to his heirs and assigns my 200 acres of land in the Second Concession of the Township of York." Willcocks referred, of course, to Farm Lot 24 in the Second Concession from the Bay, upon which Dr. Baldwin was to build his *Spadina* house a few years later.

The Old Esquire's will contained a number of other provisions of interest. He appointed D'Arcy Boulton, solicitor-general, and Dr. Baldwin co-executors, and his oldest daughter Maria Willcocks a co-executrix. As we have seen, Boulton at the time was imprisoned in France, but Willcocks was doubtless confident that he would return safely to Upper Canada before long and be able to assist with the administration of his estate. Boulton did, in fact, return to York in 1814 and was appointed attorney-general.

The Old Esquire's testamentary instructions were direct and practical. "I bequeath my soul to God who gave it and Body to the grave," he said, "to be interred with as little expense as decency will admit." His assessment of his son Charles Willcocks was expressed by a trifling bequest of twenty guineas "to be paid to him by my executors in one year after my decease." To his grandsons Robert and Henry Baldwin, the oldest of Phoebe and Dr. Baldwin's four sons then living, he left "my Mill or Mills together with my house and land in Markham and all the buildings I may have there at the time of my death." This provision referred to his well-appointed farm called *Millbrook,* close by the present village of Buttonville, near Markham, to which the Baldwin family, along with Elizabeth Russell and Maria Willcocks, withdrew in 1814 following the two American invasions of York. It has been stated by at least one authority that Dr. Baldwin inherited *Millbrook* from his father-in-law, but the above provision makes it clear that the extensive property was left to two of Dr. Baldwin's sons, not to him.[3]

The particular reference to a mill, house, and other buildings in this provision, and the omission of any reference to a house or out-buildings in connection with the *Spadina* tract left to Dr. Baldwin, clearly indicates that the 200-acre *Spadina* property had not been developed to any extent by Willcocks during his lifetime, other than by the construction of a simple cabin on the property in order to satisfy the early legal requirements of settlement and occupation.

Further confirming the view that *Spadina* was an undeveloped property is the specific mention of his house on the waterfront which he left to his daughter Maria Willcocks: "I give and devise to my daughter Susanna Maria Willcocks my house, lot of ground and water lot which I have in the Town of York." This was the house that stood at the northwest corner of Frederick and Front Streets, in which the Honourable Robert Baldwin had been born in 1804, and in which Joseph Cawthra later established the foundation of one of the early fortunes of Upper Canada. Later, the building became celebrated as the scene of the type riot in 1826 when it housed the crusading William Lyon Mackenzie's printing office. It was attacked by a band of youthful sympathizers with the Family Compact, and part of the equipment was rolled across Front Street into the Bay. However, Maria Willcocks had sold the property by then, realizing £500 for it in 1819.

Despite Dr. Baldwin's oft-expressed concern that his father-in-law would become involved in another bankruptcy, the stock of real estate he left at his death in 1813 was impressive. In addition to the *Spadina* tract, Dr. Baldwin was left "200 acres being Lot Number 16 in the Sixth Concession of the Township of Vaughan." And Willcocks' valuable 800-acre farm property, in the Township of Whitchurch, later known as *Larchmere,* on the shore of Lake Willcocks, was left to Maria Willcocks and her sister Phoebe Baldwin. Many years later William Willcocks Baldwin, the Honourable Robert Baldwin's oldest son, and the Old Esquire's great-grandson, lived for a time at *Larchmere.* The house was finally destroyed by fire, and the property sold.

Writing to a friend in England on June 12, 1812, her own illness safely behind her, Elizabeth Russell reported: "Poor Mr. Wilcox is very infirm and has been so a long time but lately so much worse and think he cannot hold out long. He and an unmarried daughter [Maria Willcocks] live with Doctor Baldwin."

William Willcocks probably shared her gloomy opinion of his condition because a few days later, on June 16, he added a codicil to his will. It clarified but did not substantially change the terms of the will he had made the year before. It did, however, specifically authorize Dr. Baldwin to make certain sales of land if necessary "for the payment of my debts to Mr. Hamilton" and any other debts outstanding at the time. This reference, of course, was to Robert Hamilton the Queenston merchant, after whose son the city of Hamilton later took its name. It will be recalled that in 1804 Willcocks had mortgaged the *Spadina* property to Hamilton. This debt was finally paid off in June 1814, by D'Arcy Boulton, Dr. Baldwin, and Maria Willcocks acting as executors of the Willcocks estate.

The codicil of 1812 is of additional interest because of the persons who were involved in witnessing it. They were John Large who had emigrated some years earlier from Cork, Ireland, and who was a friend of the Willcocks and Baldwin families. He lived for many years at *Millbrook* and farmed the property for the Baldwins after they inherited it from the Old Esquire. He died at an advanced age, and was buried in St. Martin's Rood Cemetery at *Spadina* in 1837. The second witness was John Mills Jackson for whom Jackson's Point, Lake Simcoe, is named. His daughter married Dr. Baldwin's brother, Captain Augustus Warren Baldwin of *Russell Hill* in 1827. Jackson had been sympathetic to Judge Thorpe in the 1806-07 anti-government movement with which Willcocks and Dr. Baldwin were also identified. The third witness, surprisingly, was John Beverley Robinson, Dr. Strachan's former pupil who was later to occupy a powerful position in the Family Compact.

The fine, legal hand of Robinson is discernible in the clear phraseology of the codicil which he must have prepared at the request of William Willcocks, otherwise he would hardly have been involved in signing the document as a witness. It corrected and clarified the original will which we may assume was drawn up hastily by Dr. Baldwin in 1811.

In the light of Dr. Baldwin's later fight against the Family Compact, it is one of the ironies of the early history of York that old Willcocks, no doubt unwittingly, named D'Arcy Boulton to be an executor of his estate along with Dr. Baldwin. And to deepen the irony, he called in John Beverley Robinson a few months before his death to elucidate his will by codicil, and amplify its sketchy provisions. Both Robinson and Boulton were to hold positions of influence in the later provincial oligarchy to which Dr. Baldwin was bitterly opposed.

William Willcocks died on January 7, 1813, in the Baldwin house which once stood at the northeast corner of today's Bay and Front Streets. The Town of York was preoccupied at the time with the war against the Americans and the Old Esquire's death passed virtually unnoticed. It is probable that Dr. John Strachan buried him in the cemetery of St. James' Church on King Street, but a later fire which destroyed the church also obliterated a number of the wooden grave-markers around it. For this reason, we may assume old Willcocks was not re-interred later in Dr. Baldwin's *Spadina* cemetery, St. Martin's Rood, as were Peter and Elizabeth Russell who had also died long before he established this private burial ground on the Davenport Hill in 1829.

Dr. Strachan had arrived in the provincial capital from Cornwall shortly after word had reached York of the declaration of war by the United States against Great Britain on June 17, 1812. The year before he had been disappointed in not obtaining the pastoral charge of Kingston and had thought of returning to Scotland. Lieutenant-Governor Francis Gore, on his way back to England, had stopped off in Cornwall to urge him to accept Bishop Mountain's proposal that he go to York to succeed the Reverend Okill Stuart, the first rector of St. James' Church, and the master in charge of the Home District Grammar School (the Blue School). Strachan had at first demurred. For one reason he had never been attracted to life in the provincial capital which he thought was dominated by petty groups bickering amongst themselves for advancement. He also regarded it as a precarious church mission in a remote part of the colony. But after a committee of citizens from York urged him to reconsider his decision, and General Sir Isaac Brock had enlarged his appointment to include the position of Chaplain to the Garrison, Strachan finally accepted. The fact that a number of his former pupils of the Cornwall Grammar School, men like John Beverley Robinson, J. B. Macaulay, Thomas G. Ridout, and Robert Stanton were then living in York, preparing themselves for important careers, must have also influenced his decision. Notwithstanding the disadvantages of Little York, here at least would be the nucleus of a congenial coterie.

While Strachan was settling himself and his family in York, General Brock won a brilliant victory at Detroit in August 1812, when the American General Hull was compelled to surrender his army. The stirring British victory at Queenston Heights followed in October, but Upper Canada was stunned by the death of its popular leader Sir Isaac Brock.

Shortly before the American invasion of York, in April 1813, Dr. Baldwin was seated one day at his writing desk in his parlour which overlooked Front Street and the Toronto Bay. Glancing out his window, he noted: "We have a large ship of 28 to 30 guns on the stock just by my door." He referred to the *Sir Isaac Brock,* a frigate which was in course of construction on the waterfront at the foot of Bay Street. At that time the shore of the Toronto Bay extended along the south side of the present Front Street. As the Americans were keenly aware, the frigate, when completed, would be the largest afloat on the lake. It would give the British the edge in the struggle for naval supremacy when it joined the rest of the fleet then at its winter anchorage at Kingston.[4] Over seventy men were employed in the work, and it was natural that even before the ship was launched it would be given the name of the province's lamented hero, Sir Isaac Brock. There was, of course, no practical security surrounding the building of the ship. The Americans were kept fully informed by sympathizers in York as to its size, armament, and progress of construction. They were planning a water-borne assault from Sackett's Harbour at the eastern end of Lake Ontario on Newark, but they did not wish to proceed with that stage of their offensive without first eliminating the danger that was posed by the *Sir Isaac Brock.* York, therefore, was singled out as the first target for attack, the main objective being to capture the *Brock* which was nearing completion on the stocks beside Baldwin's cottage.

On April 26, 1813, the American squadron, consisting of fourteen ships carrying 1700 men, was sighted off the Scarborough Bluffs, just to the east of York, and the alarm was sounded throughout the town. The following morning the American force sailed past York intending to effect a landing around the site of the old French Fort Rouille,* but a strong easterly wind

---

*The original location of Fort Rouille is today marked by a cairn on the Canadian National Exhibition grounds.

drove the squadron further west, and the Americans finally scrambled ashore, under covering fire from their ships, in the present Sunnyside area.

As the American force brushed aside the small British detachment that tried to prevent its landing, and swung easterly towards the town, Dr. Baldwin, John Large, Robert Baldwin the Emigrant, and Quetton de St. George met hurriedly at *Russell Abbey* to decide upon a course of action to ensure the safety of the ladies and Dr. Baldwin's children. It was decided to send them up Yonge Street to seek sanctuary at Baron de Hoen's two-room log cabin at the northwest corner of the present Eglinton Avenue and Yonge Street. The Baron owned a 200-acre farm lot there, known as Township Lot 1 in the First Concession west of Yonge Street.

Miss Russell stacked her phaeton so high with clothing and supplies from the Abbey that there was no room for anybody to ride in the carriage. The party straggled along behind it as it creaked and swayed over the corduroy roads. Included were Elizabeth Russell, Dr. Baldwin's wife Phoebe, and their four boys, the youngest of whom, St. George, was carried most of the way by Dr. Baldwin's sister, Mary Warren Baldwin; Robert Baldwin the Emigrant toiled along in the procession with the ailing Major Fuller, an old patient of Dr. Baldwin's. Maria Willcocks completed the family picture and assisted the dejected Elizabeth Russell. Mary Warren Baldwin had earlier witnessed the arrival of the American fleet and had noted with poetic detachment: "Nothing could equal the beauty of the fleet coming in, it preserved the form of a crescent, while the sails were as white as snow."

Before they had reached their destination, the *Russell Abbey* party heard an explosion far to the southwest. The ground seemed to quake, and the sombre forest suddenly became silent around them. They were later to learn that the sound they heard was caused by the explosion of the grand magazine at Fort York, in which scores of American soldiers were killed or wounded, including the American commander, General Zebulon Pike, who was mortally wounded by the flying debris and died later on a ship in the bay.

The American forces occupied York until May 1 when, with their wounded, they boarded their ships. The sails "white as snow" hung dejectedly from their yardarms for a week as they awaited a favourable wind to carry them out of the harbour and across the lake. They finally cleared Gibraltar Point on May 8, to the vast relief of the townsmen.

As Major-General Roger Sheaffe withdrew his small force of British regulars from the town to fall back on Kingston, he set fire to the *Sir Isaac Brock* to prevent it from falling into the hands of the enemy. He then instructed two militia officers, Lieutenant-Colonel William Chewett, the surveyor, and Major William Allan, a Scottish storekeeper, to make the best terms they could with the American commanders. Characteristically, Dr. Strachan offered his services and moved swiftly to the centre of the stage. He wrangled with the United States General Dearborn and cajoled the American Commodore Chauncey into accepting a reasonable settlement. He won for the militia a parole and immediate transfer of the sick and wounded from the Garrison to the town for treatment; the security of private property was guaranteed, but all public stores had to be surrendered. Dr. Baldwin, who by then had given up the practice of medicine, had been pressed into service to help the wounded and dying. When he finally returned exhausted to his Front Street house, he looked out sadly upon the smoldering ruins of York's proud ship. For days the air was heavy around his place with the pungent smell of burning tar and pine. His concern was mitigated by the knowledge that his family was safely concealed at Baron de Hoen's farm four miles from town.

York suffered the destruction of its parliament buildings, barracks, and the *Sir Isaac Brock*. The losses to the British regulars were 62 killed and 76 wounded, mainly in resisting the American landing; the Americans lost 55 killed and 257 wounded, chiefly as a result of the explosion of the grand magazine. By the following December York's sagging spirits were restored when word reached the town that British forces had crossed the Niagara River, captured Fort Niagara, and sacked Buffalo.

In the history of York, an event comparable in significance to the American attack was perhaps the emergence of the Reverend Dr. John Strachan as the natural leader of the provincial capital. Reluctant the year before to come to York, Dr. Strachan's star was soon to blaze in the heavens over the town with a fierce incandescence. York itself, after the inevitable purging of its American sympathizers, emerged finally from its ordeal on a surer footing, unified and strengthened by the force of a common danger overcome.

Chapter 7

Dr. Baldwin Builds Spadina

The American fleet returned to York on July 31, 1813. Dr. Strachan, in a state of godly wrath, seized a small boat and, with a white flag prominently displayed, rowed out to ascertain Commodore Chauncey's intentions. He took with him Dr. Grant Powell, a son of Judge William Dummer Powell. The only result of his visit to the American flagship, which was riding placidly at anchor in the Toronto Bay, was the promise he extracted from the commodore to return the town's library which had been carried off the previous May.[1]

Chauncey's stay was brief. His men removed a supply of flour from the establishments of William Allan and St. George; they released a few political prisoners from the jail; they sent an unsuccessful party up the Don River in search of government stores. And as they left they destroyed the lighthouse and storage buildings on Gibraltar Point at the entrance to the Harbour of York.

For a full year following the second invasion of York, the inhabitants lived in constant fear of further raids. Their anxiety mounted when the wind blew across the lake from the east because it favoured the American fleet on its run to York from Sackett's Harbour. In a letter to St. George, who was then in Montreal, written on July 20, 1814, Dr. Baldwin gave a vivid picture of the state of alarm prevailing in the capital, and of its effect in particular on Elizabeth Russell:

> The East wind now blowing puts us in great fear—I put up all my papers last night and kept my horse in to send them off—poor Miss Russell is so dejected that it appears like mental derangement—Mrs. Baldwin came in to town the other day and prevailed on her to go to Markham. Miss Willcocks remains for a day or two to put her house &c in order & pack up such things as Miss Russell may esteem most—She seems somewhat better since she went to the Country, but yet a strong tendency to derangement—it is impossible not to feel for her—[2]

We are left in the dark as to the outcome of Miss Russell's "strong tendency to derangement," but following the end of the war in December 1814, the Baldwin family moved into *Russell Abbey* to provide her with needed companionship and help restore her flagging spirits. She had stopped writing her diary during the war, and few insights are provided as to her later condition in Dr. Baldwin's infrequent and perfunctory references to her activities in his correspondence between the end of the war and her death in 1822.

Dr. Baldwin's father, Robert Baldwin the Emigrant, died in York, after an illness of only a few hours, in November 1816. The following year Dr. Baldwin himself was in poor health. "I am myself in very indifferent health indeed," he wrote to his friend St. George, now living in France, "my constitution seems to have undergone a change of a serious nature—to walk from home to your house fatigues me as if I had run a mile. It is the remains of the attack which had nearly carried me off last spring." In another letter written a month later, in August 1817, he told his friend that he still suffered from "the ill effects of much application."

Dr. Baldwin had succeeded his father to the legal position of surrogate of the Home District in December 1816, and he was also holding two other minor judicial positions at the time, that of judge of the Home District Court, which paid him only £10 to £12 per annum, and the more important post of master in chancery. The pressure of these offices, together with the steady growth in his law practice, was presumably the cause of his chronic state of fatigue, for he had abandoned his medical practice a number of years before.

In the summer of 1817, his younger brother, Captain Augustus Warren Baldwin, arrived in York. Recently retired from the Royal Navy on half-pay, he was looking around for a place to live in Upper Canada. A bachelor at the time, the captain had served with the Navy since 1794, and had taken part in a number of important naval engagements during the Napoleonic War, including the Battle of Trafalgar. In 1804, he had been a lieutenant on the British frigate that carried the Irish poet Thomas Moore, the close friend and biographer of Lord Byron, back to England from Halifax following his extensive American tour. After visiting Niagara Falls, Moore had sailed across Lake Ontario and may have put in briefly at the Harbour of York. The poet referred to York by its old Indian name in some verses he penned a few hours later while camping on the shore of the St. Lawrence River. The couplet ran:

> Where the blue hills of old Toronto shed
> Their evening shadows o'er Ontario's bed;

It was in the "blue hills of old Toronto" that Captain Baldwin decided in 1817 to make his home. Since Dr. Baldwin had earlier inherited the 200-acre property extending beyond the Davenport Hill, it made good sense for the two brothers to build adjoining houses on the hilltop. Dr. Baldwin persuaded Elizabeth Russell to sell his brother her 200-acre farm lot which lay immediately to the east of the *Spadina* tract. Like Dr. Baldwin's property, Miss Russell's Lot 23, Concession 2 from the bay, extended from the present Bloor Street to St. Clair Avenue. (See pages 24, 25.)

The deed to the "old sugar loaf lot," which Dr. Baldwin had first visited with Peter Russell in 1800, was signed by Miss Russell on August 29, 1817. It was witnessed by a John Bättyer, who was described as a labourer, and by Simon Washburn, one of Dr. Baldwin's law students. Captain Baldwin paid £200 for the property, or one pound per acre. It would appear that he got a bargain. Exactly five years before, on August 29, 1812, during the war with the United States, Miss Russell had sold the north half of Lot 22, Concession 3 from the bay, which lay immediately north of the present Upper Canada College, and extended to Eglinton Avenue, to a Stewart Grafton for £100, or again one pound per acre. That half-lot of 100 acres was more remote from York, and presumably of less value than the "old sugar loaf lot" with its frontage on the present Bloor Street which she sold to the captain on Dr. Baldwin's advice five years later at the same rate of one pound per acre.

Of course, immediately following the War of 1812, the economy of York suffered a recession. It had been stimulated by the continuous buying of supplies by the government commissary for the military and by projects like the building of the frigate the *Sir Isaac Brock,* but with the withdrawal of British troops from the province, business fell off sharply. By 1817, however, the pendulum of commercial activity had swung sharply the other way. One correspondent, writing in June 1817, noted that there had been a great influx of people that summer from the United States. He said: "The country is improving very fast—there are no fewer than 9 saw and 3 grist mills within 5 miles from where I live and more building. The Town of York increases in size very fast and they are now building 3 wharves which will extend a long way into the lake for the convenience of vessels loading and unloading."

From Elizabeth Russell's point of view, however, the amount of the purchase price was academic because she never received the money. A curious reference to the transaction is contained in the will of Captain Baldwin, made many years later, on August 14, 1850, long after Miss Russell's death in 1822. He stipulated that upon the death of his wife the property in question, known as *Russell Hill,* was to pass to his nephews, the Honourable Robert Baldwin and William Augustus Baldwin, the sons of his late brother, William Warren Baldwin. He went on to explain the reason:

> My intention being as this land together with other adjacent lands formed a part of the property owned by the late Miss Elizabeth Russell and was through the mediation of the said William Warren Baldwin separated from the said adjacent lands and sold by her to me for a sum of money which she never received through the defalcation of her Agent in London after a devise had been [made] by the said Miss Russell in favour of the said William Warren Baldwin of the same land together with the said adjacent lands that it should now fall to the family of the said William Warren Baldwin together with the said adjacent lands which were devised to the said William Warren Baldwin by the said Miss Russell and held by him 'till the time of his death as I have now no children left to inherit it.

At first glance it seems odd that Captain Baldwin felt it necessary to record the circumstances surrounding his purchase of Miss Russell's property over thirty years earlier, and particularly the defalcation of her London agent. The explanation must lie in the fact that he had a number of nieces and nephews living in Toronto when he made his will in 1850, the children of his late brother John Spread Baldwin,[3] for example, or his sister Barbara Sullivan, and he wished to make clear his reason for appearing to favour two beneficiaries of this larger class.

The reference to the embezzlement of Miss Russell's money can only be interpreted as a further argument on his part for leaving the *Russell Hill* property as his did, though its size was greatly diminished by the time of his death in 1866. Had the money reached Miss Russell, he argued, it would have formed part of her estate when she died. And since Dr. Baldwin's family were the ultimate beneficiaries of most of her assets, that money would have later found its way into his nephews' hands. The provision he made in his will respecting *Russell Hill,* he reasoned, simply restored the position of the 200-acre farm lot to its status before Dr. Baldwin persuaded Miss Russell to sell it to him.

It is to be noted that the clause in the captain's will is incorrect in stating that Dr. Baldwin held the lands adjoining *Russell Hill* " 'till the time of his death." As he was bound to do as Miss Russell's executor, he transferred the lots in question to his wife and Maria Willcocks in 1824, long before his death in 1844.

Following Captain Baldwin's arrival in York in 1817, Dr. Baldwin's nephew, young Daniel Sullivan, Jr., then aged seventeen, also emigrated to York from Ireland, in advance of his parents Daniel and Barbara Sullivan, Barbara being Dr. Baldwin's oldest sister. The boy's parents did not reach York until 1819. Young Daniel, a bright boy, was employed as a law clerk by Dr. Baldwin. He lived for a while with his uncle, John Spread Baldwin, in St. George's house not far from *Russell Abbey*. He wrote to his father in Bandon, County Cork, Ireland, on December 16, 1817:

> My uncle William still retains the name of Doctor though he has entirely renounced the medical profession. . . . He has two young gentlemen studying the law with him besides myself. The office is open from 10 til 4 and during that time we never want employment. He has lately built a handsome house three miles from town very pleasantly situated: the lot on which it is build he purchased from Miss Russel [sic]. . . . The Captain has purchased from Miss Russell the lot adjoining my Uncle William's; he is preparing to build next summer, and lives at present with my uncle William; their present residence is close by the new house into which they have not yet removed.

He also tells us that Dr. Baldwin has established his law office in *Russell Abbey:* "Miss Russell resides in town: it is at her house our office is kept."[4]

Young Daniel erred, of course, when he reported that Dr. Baldwin was building his house on a lot he had purchased from Miss Russell. However, his statement that the captain was living with his uncle William in a residence close by the new house is of interest. In a letter written the following year, in 1818, Dr. Baldwin referred to this temporary accommodation. He said: "The Captain is building also in our neighbourhood—he lives with us in our present rented tenement while his own is building."[5]

Dr. Baldwin also reported that he was very busy "hurrying on the plastering" of the house he had built almost three miles from town, and that "the journey in and out every day though troublesome in many respects conduces much to the health of myself and my boys."

The question naturally arises as to the location of the "rented tenement" in which the doctor and captain were living in 1817 and 1818 while their houses were under construction. It is quite certain that they had rented *Davenport* from the Widow McGill which would have provided them with a convenient location, being just a few minutes walk along the brow of the hill to the site of their new houses. Further weight is given this conclusion when we recall that Dr. Baldwin reported in a letter written in the summer of 1819 that Major Loring was then living at *Davenport*. As we have already had occasion to note, Major Loring was clearly occupying *Davenport* as a tenant, because Lt. Col. Joseph Wells did not buy the farm lot from the Widow McGill until 1821. Finally, Dr. Baldwin's family had been on friendly terms with the McGills for many years; he had taken his wife Phoebe to *Davenport* when she was ill in 1806, and when he thought she would benefit from "a change of air" on the Davenport Hill.

Alice Baldwin, writing to her cousin John Baldwin in Cork, Ireland, on August 27, 1818, commented: "Augustus is so busy with his farm, Masons

The original *Spadina* house (1818-1835). A mix-up in the cataloguing of the three views of *Spadina* in the J. Ross Robertson Historical Collection resulted in this sketch being recorded as the "Second Spadina House" whereas it is in fact the first, although painted long after the house was destroyed by fire in 1835. The word *Spadina* is an Indian term signifying a sudden rise in land. Dr. W. W. Baldwin borrowed it from the local, native dialect to describe the magnificent site of his house on the Davenport Hill overlooking the Town of York. The word is correctly pronounced Spad-eena.

—Metropolitan Toronto Library Board

and Carpenters that it seems a hard task for him to keep up a correspondence."[6]

This progress report on her brother's house, which Captain Baldwin was to call *Russell Hill,* shows that its construction was lagging behind the building of *Spadina.* Since Dr. Baldwin was "hurrying on the plastering" in September 1818, we may assume that his new house was completed in time for the Baldwin family to move in by Christmas. In the case of Captain Baldwin's *Russell Hill,* the evidence points to a completion date in 1819.

Dr. Baldwin provided a picture of his new house in a letter he wrote to his friend St. George on July 29, 1819:

I have a very commodious house in the Country—I have called the place Spadina, the Indian word for Hill—or Mont—the house consists of two large Parlours Hall & stair case on the first floor—four bed rooms and a small library on the 2nd. floor—and three Excellent bed rooms in attic storey or garrett—with several closets on every storey—a Kitchen, dairy, root-cellar wine cellar & mans bedroom underground—I have cut an avenue through the woods all the way so that we can see the vessels

Russell Hill (1819-1871) was the home of Captain Augustus Warren Baldwin, R.N., a younger brother of Dr. W. W. Baldwin. He retired to York in 1817 and immediately purchased a 200-acre farm lot from Elizabeth Russell for £200 upon which he built this house in 1819. On the brow of the Davenport Hill, it lay just to the east of his brother's *Spadina.* Samuel Nordheimer acquired 25½ acres of the *Russell Hill* property after the captain's death in 1866, and built *Glenedyth* on the site of the old Baldwin house in 1872.

—Metropolitan Toronto Library Board

passing up and down the bay—the house is completely finished with stable &c and a tolerable good garden, the whole has cost about 1500£ the Land you know was the gift of poor Mr. Willcocks.[7]

Two other notable houses were also in course of construction in the Town of York in 1818 while Dr. Baldwin and his brother were building their houses on the Davenport Hill in York Township. Dr. Strachan was raising what Dr. Baldwin described as a "magnificent house,"* of brick construction, at the northwest corner of the present Front Street and University Avenue. Baldwin estimated its cost to be between £5000 and £6000. And D'Arcy Boulton, Jr., was completing his gracious brick residence, *The Grange,* which still exists as part of the Art Gallery of Ontario.

The *Spadina* house, proudly described by Dr. Baldwin, was of frame construction. A brick residence at that time was something of a novelty in York, and we may be certain had it been built of brick he would have so described it. Moreover, a brick residence of the ample proportions he

*Dr. Strachan's house was so described by Dr. Baldwin in a letter to St. George of July 29, 1819 (see Note 7). The house was demolished in 1896.

mentions could not have been built for as little as £1500. Though Dr. Strachan's house on Front Street was more elaborate, its brick construction was the main factor in skyrocketing its cost to over £5000.

The *Spadina* dwelling was placed 300 feet back from the crest of the Davenport Hill overlooking York. In order to provide himself with a clear view of the lake, and create a spacious lawn in front of his house, Dr. Baldwin removed the trees immediately between the house and the brow of the hill. It could only have been in that limited sense that he "cut an avenue through the woods all the way" so that he could observe the vessels on the bay. Since the elevation of the Davenport Hill at that point is 248 feet above lake level, it is difficult to imagine that the doctor found it necessary to remove very many trees on his own property below the hill, or on Elizabeth Russell's 300-acre farm that extended further south to the present Queen Street. Certainly, his development of the broad Spadina Avenue after her death in 1822 had little or nothing to do with enhancing the view of Lake Ontario that he already enjoyed from his hilltop house.

The site of the doctor's *Spadina* was located a little to the east of the north-south centre line of his Farm Lot 24. As a result, when in the late 1820's he began laying out Spadina Avenue on Maria Willcocks' Park Lot 15, the Bloor Street frontage of his *Spadina* property was located at the head of the avenue and his house commanded an impressive view of the new thoroughfare with its ornamental Circle above College Street. It was an imaginative piece of planning in those days and lent attraction to the district for purposes of subdivision and sale. There is no evidence that Dr. Baldwin ever sought to extend Spadina Avenue north of Bloor Street and therefore across his own property. There was no need for him to do so. From the earliest days of his occupancy, he reached it from Yonge Street, thence along Davenport Road.

Spadina Avenue, which took its name from Dr. Baldwin's house, was originally laid out with a width of two chains, or 132 feet, double the size of the conventional road allowance of one chain, or 66 feet. In the plan or subdivision of the three old Russell Park Lots, 14, 15 and 16 in the Township of York, which was not registered by the Baldwin Estate until 1860, the width of Dr. Baldwin's visionary avenue was still shown as being 132 feet. The widening of the road to 160 feet, a dimension which Dr. Scadding ascribed to Dr. Baldwin in an earlier quoted passage, did not occur until long after the doctor's death.

The extension of Spadina Avenue south of Queen Street, almost to the Toronto Bay, arose from Lieutenant-Governor Francis Bond Head's decision in 1837 to open up part of the old Toronto Military or Garrison Reserve for subdivision and settlement. Deputy Surveyor General Hawkins accordingly prepared a plan, which was approved by Captain Richard H. Bonnycastle of the Royal Engineers on February 18, 1837. Clarence Square and Victoria Square formed part of the subdivision, and a new road, called Brock Street, was laid out through the Garrison Reserve as an extension of Spadina Avenue.

In order to conform with the unusual dimensions of Dr. Baldwin's avenue to the north, the surveyor was forced to provide a 132-feet-wide road allowance for the new Brock Street. Its name was finally changed to Spadina Avenue in 1884.[8] The jog that occurs today at Bloor Street, where Spadina Avenue swings to the west and then proceeds north on what is known as Spadina Road, results from a plan of subdivision registered in

1873 by Dr. Baldwin's grandson, Robert Baldwin, who at the time was the owner of that part of the original *Spadina* tract. When he drew up his plan of subdivision, which included the area around Walmer Road where it leads north from Bloor Street, he anchored the east limit of his plan on the new Spadina Road.

The origin of the name *Spadina* is explained by Dr. Baldwin in his letter to St. George. It was derived from an Indian term "Ishapadenah" meaning a hill or a sudden rise in the land. It was always pronounced "Spa-*dee*na" by the Baldwin family. Indeed, many years later, Dr. Percy J. Robinson, the author of *Toronto During the French Régime,* who had a broad knowledge of the Indian dialects spoken in the region around York, stated emphatically that the only possible pronunciation was "Spa-*dee*na" because there was no hard "i" in the Indian language.[9]

Dr. Baldwin entered upon the tenure of his new *Spadina* with a feeling of exhilaration and relief. His 200-acre domain provided him and his young sons with a freedom they had not known when they were living with the fastidious spinster of *Russell Abbey.* They held joyous picnics in the darkly shaded glen just a short walk from the house, through which the Castle Frank stream meandered on its way to the Don River. And on summer evenings, with his troop of boys at his heels, the doctor rambled along the brow of Davenport Hill, pausing every now and then to view the distant town beneath its plumes of smoke and, beyond it, the ships with their glinting sails far out on the lake.

In the serenity of his new home, Dr. Baldwin reflected upon his improving fortunes. His law practice was growing steadily, and he had joined forces with a partner in acquiring land for development in Cavan Township which adjoined Clarke Township where the original Baldwin farm was located.[10] And, perhaps most important, the spinster of *Russell Abbey* was showing no signs of wanting to return to England, if indeed she was capable of doing so, nor of changing the will she had made during her illness in 1811. In the natural course of things, Dr. Baldwin would soon be required to withdraw her will from his strongbox, and as her executor launch into the administration of her extensive estate. With these practical considerations in mind he was encouraged to expand his idea of founding a Baldwin dynasty in Upper Canada which would endure forever. The building of *Spadina* was simply the first step. Like the Russell family's *Woburn Abbey* in Bedfordshire, *Spadina* was to be the Baldwins' principal seat.

In his *Toronto of Old,* Dr. Henry Scadding explained Dr. Baldwin's dynastic dream:

> A liberal in his political views, he nevertheless was strongly influenced by the feudal feeling which was a second nature with most persons in the British Islands some years ago. His purpose was to establish in Canada a family, whose head was to be maintained in opulence by the proceeds of an entailed estate. There was to be forever a Baldwin of Spadina.

Chapter 8

The End of an Era

In 1829, Dr. Baldwin turned his attention to establishing a suitable family burial ground on his *Spadina* property. He chose a site behind his house on the crest of the south bank of the ravine, close to the boundary line that divided his farm lot from that of his brother, Captain Baldwin of *Russell Hill*. The half-acre cemetery, which was only a few minutes' walk from their houses, contained a burial vault set into the side of the hill just below its summit.[1] Beneath it, the Castle Frank stream flowed unhurriedly towards the Don River. Dr. Baldwin named the cemetery St. Martin's Rood after the fourth-century saint of that name whose monastery in France had been the training ground for the earliest Celtic missionaries who had roamed as far as Ireland. The doctor may have been influenced in his choice of name by the fact that his son, Quetton St. George, died at *Spadina* in November 1829, at the age of nineteen. His remains were the first to be committed to the new burial ground.[2] The boy's father would have recalled that in the Old Country the counterpart of Canada's Indian Summer was called St. Martin's Summer. His youngest son had died just as that short reprieve from winter had settled upon the *Spadina* farmlands.

Elsewhere on his *Spadina* estate, which extended from the present Bloor Street to St. Clair Avenue, Dr. Baldwin had taken steps earlier to develop the section surrounding his house into a gracious country seat. After Elizabeth Russell's death at *Russell Abbey* in 1822, Maria Willcocks, Phoebe Baldwin's sister, had taken up her residence at *Spadina* with the Baldwin family. In her honour, the narrow drive that led southeast from the doctor's house to the foot of the hill was called Aunt Maria's Road. It was the principal approach to *Spadina* from Yonge Street, and a "great Gate," as it was referred to in a number of legal documents of the time, framed its entrance on Davenport Road.[3] The gate served both *Spadina* and *Russell Hill* since the drive passed through it and then diverged, one lane leading east across the boundary line where it gradually ascended to Captain Baldwin's house, the other swinging west and climbing the hill to *Spadina*. A further carriage drive across the hilltop provided a direct link between the two Baldwin houses, a section of which led north to St. Martin's Rood.

With Aunt Maria's Road in place, Dr. Baldwin next honoured his wife's sister by cutting a walk for her from the farmyard at the rear of *Spadina* to the stream at the foot of the ravine. "Miss Willcocks was very fond of poultry," J. Ross Robertson wrote in his *Landmarks of Toronto*, and to gratify her Dr. Baldwin had this path cut through the woods and enclosed it with a fence of split rails, and every day in pleasant weather Miss Willcocks would drive her ducks and geese down the walk to the stream. . . . Shortly after the building of *Spadina* house, Dr. Baldwin built a little cottage of logs, heavily thatched, along the path about half way down the hill. This was a tiny affair, not more than ten feet long and six feet wide. It was fitted with seats and a table, and was a favourite resting place for those wandering along the goose walk, which by this time had been dignified by the name of the Glen walk. In this cottage was kept a book, still in possession of the Baldwin family, and visitors of poetic inclination were invited to write verses in it. The cottage was burned down about the year 1850, but the poetry inspired in it remains.

The writer added that the verses in the book dated from 1820 to 1827.

Three months before young Quetton St. George Baldwin's death at *Spadina,* his father had purchased the southwest corner of King and Yonge streets. The parcel had a frontage on King Street of 130 feet, with 57 feet on Yonge Street, and the doctor paid £750 for it. It was part of the one-acre Town Lot 2 which had been granted by the Crown to a Theophilus Sampson in 1801. Instead of having himself recorded as the owner, Dr. Baldwin had the title to the property registered in the names of two of his sons, William Augustus and Quetton St. George.[4] In doing so, and thereby excluding his oldest son Robert from the transaction, we may assume that the doctor had it in mind that as a result of the condition imposed by the Honourable Peter Russell in 1806, Robert Baldwin was already the legal owner of the corner property at Front and Bay streets.

After Elizabeth Russell's death, Dr. Baldwin continued to maintain his law offices at *Russell Abbey.* A letter written there by his son Robert, at 4 a.m. on June 27, 1825, clearly suggests that the Baldwins were also using the place for their living quarters whenever it was necessary for them to remain in town overnight.[5] Young Robert Baldwin was called to the bar of Upper Canada that year, and joined his father as a partner in the Baldwin firm. By 1829, it made good sense for the doctor to follow the expansion of the city westward, and after he had purchased the King and Yonge Street property, he built a two-storey, frame structure on the site with law offices on King Street and second-floor living quarters overlooking Yonge Street.

In the spring of 1834, two months after the Town of York had been incorporated as the City of Toronto, Maria Willcocks fell ill at *Spadina.* She made her last will and testament on May 29, and it was witnessed by Dr. Christopher Widmer, a leading Toronto physician, and by two law students, Edward Hitchings and Henry Latham, who presumably were under articles to Dr. Baldwin and his son in their new offices on King Street.[6] Since she and her sister, Phoebe Baldwin, had been the principal beneficiaries of Elizabeth Russell's estate, as well as that of their father, William Willcocks, Maria Willcocks' assets were substantial. In disposing of them, we may be sure she had the benefit of Dr. Baldwin's advice. In any event, she named him and his son Robert as her executors and trustees, and the affectionate regard in which she held the doctor was confirmed in her first reference to him in her will where he is described as her "dearly beloved Brother in law"; Miss Willcocks referred to his wife in the same sentence simply as "my dear Sister Margaret Phoebe Baldwin." Under the general plan of her will, Dr. Baldwin and his wife were given a life interest in the bulk of her estate, with their children and their families receiving the residue; the doctor was additionally given authority to dispose of any part of her property with the exception of a few lots on King Street and Newgate Street (Adelaide Street) in Toronto. Maria Willcocks died at *Spadina* the following August 8, 1834, at the age of sixty-six.[7] She was buried in St. Martin's Rood Cemetery. With her death, most of the pioneer land holdings of the Honourable Peter Russell and William Willcocks were united at last in a single family mosaic in which Dr. Baldwin's *Spadina* lay prominently at the centre.

The doctor and his son applied for probate of Maria Willcocks' will a few weeks after her death, and it was granted by the Court of Probate of Upper Canada on September 6, 1834. The following year, as the Baldwin law firm was in the midst of settling Miss Willcocks' affairs, *Spadina* was razed to the ground by a fire of unknown origin. Of frame construction, the two-storey house that had been a conspicuous landmark on the Davenport Hill since 1818 was reduced to a smoking ruin. Faced with the choice of rebuilding *Spadina* on a grander scale, or relocating his house elsewhere, Dr. Baldwin elected to build a new residence for himself on the site of the "house of modest aspect" that he had moved into in 1807 at the corner of Front and Bay Streets. Not only was the location convenient to his new law offices, but it also provided him with the opportunity of constructing an imposing house of solid brick in the centre of the most desirable residential district in the city. His neighbours along Front Street facing the Bay were Judge L. P. Sherwood, Judge James B. Macaulay, Judge W. Dummer Powell, H. J. Boulton, and Dr. Strachan — and further west, between John and Simcoe Streets, the impressive red-brick Parliament Buildings of Upper Canada completed the shoreline vista. At the same time, Dr. Baldwin also decided to rebuild *Spadina* on a smaller scale than before, for use simply as a country house.

This sequence of events is confirmed by a number of references in the Baldwin Papers to Dr. Baldwin's building activities at that time. In a letter written in September, 1835, to John Large at *Millbrook,* for example, the doctor informed his correspondent that "The big house is almost finished and the carpenter gone—they promise to leave us this Wednesday. I am just setting off to see what is doing at *Spadina."*[8] And when the Front Street house had been completed shortly after, it must have occurred to Dr. Baldwin that the ownership of the property still remained with his son Robert. To correct the situation, Robert Baldwin and his wife Augusta Elizabeth transferred the property to Dr. Baldwin by deed on November 26, 1835.[9] In January 1836, Robert Baldwin's young wife died in the new "Baldwin Family Residence" as it was called, an event recorded with intense sorrow by her husband.

Insofar as the *Spadina* ruins were concerned, it is evident that Dr. Baldwin did not begin rebuilding that house until the spring of 1836, because it was not until the following July that he was in a position to report to Robert, who was then in England, that the single-storey dwelling was "rough cast all over" and that it looked "extremely pretty." In the same letter, Dr. Baldwin informed his son that he had just finished some work on the "West Crescent Road," a reference to the thoroughfare that curves round the west side of the Circle on Spadina Avenue just north of the present College Street.[10] By that date the 132-foot-wide avenue had been extended as a rough, dirt road to the base of the doctor's 200-acre *Spadina* farm lot on the present Bloor Street where, as today, it ended.

In *Toronto, No Mean City,* Professor Eric Arthur has described

The second *Spadina* house (1836-1866). This single-storey house, like the original *Spadina*, was of frame construction. Dr. Baldwin built it in 1836 on the ruins of the old. When James Austin bought 80 acres of the *Spadina* property from Dr. Baldwin's grandson in 1866, he demolished this dwelling and built the third *Spadina*, now extant, on the foundations of the two earlier Baldwin houses. This scene was painted in water colours for the J. Ross Robertson Historical Collection by a British artist, F. V. Poole, who first exhibited in England in the 1890's. The subject of this sketch had disappeared long before he painted it.

—Metropolitan Toronto Library Board

Dr. Baldwin's Front Street house, concluding that the doctor designed it himself:

> Rather extravagantly, one would think, the first-floor plan provides for three parlours, a library, and a large closet. All rooms are trimmed or panelled in walnut. The basement plan indicates a kitchen 25' x 19', a wine cellar 25' x 10' and a meat room 10' x 10'. The only clue to dining arrangements is a dumbwaiter in the kitchen that served one of the parlours. On the outside, the balustrade beneath the cornice would be an unforgivable solecism to the purist. The sketches would indicate Dr. Baldwin was himself the designer.

Notwithstanding the elaborate style of his new house on the Bay, Dr. Baldwin continued to regard his *Spadina* estate as his principal seat. He still liked to be known as "William Warren Baldwin of *Spadina*," and was so described in a number of later legal documents.

The long, slow fuse of William Lyon Mackenzie's planned uprising against the oligarchy of Upper Canada flickered ominously throughout the autumn of 1837. Finally, in the first week of December, it burst into flame. With

Mackenzie at their head, his supporters gathered at Montgomery's Tavern on the outskirts of Toronto determined to march down Yonge Street, seize the capital, and set their grievances right. In order to gain time to organize their defences, the agitated government leaders hit upon the idea of sending a representative to talk to the insurgents. Sir Francis Bond Head, the lieutenant-governor, was prepared to grant them amnesty on condition that they disperse to their farms and villages, and he wanted his offer communicated to them as quickly as possible. The search for a suitable envoy led to Robert Baldwin who, like his father, held a prominent place in the ranks of the moderate Reformers. While no favourite of the radical Mackenzie, he was at least not linked with the Family Compact, which was the special object of Mackenzie's hatred. Baldwin agreed to intercede with the rebels, but stipulated that someone join him on his mission. Dr. John Rolph, also a Reformer and, like Dr. Baldwin, a doctor turned lawyer, agreed to accompany him. Shortly after noon on December 5, the two men, along with a carpenter displaying a flag of truce, rode out to Gallows Hill to talk things over with Mackenzie. The skeptical rebel leaders demanded that Sir Francis' offer of amnesty be confirmed in writing, and Baldwin and Rolph turned back to the city to get it. By then, having regained his confidence, the governor had decided to break off negotiations with the insurgents. Baldwin and Rolph felt it their duty to canter back up Yonge Street to inform Mackenzie of his change of heart. Robert Baldwin then returned to his father's house on Front Street where he maintained an anxious vigil throughout the night.*

The same evening the lights burned late in Dr. Strachan's study farther along Front Street. For some reason, Sir Francis Head summoned his advisors to meet with him at Strachan's house in order to draw up a plan to deal with the threat to his authority.[11] As at the time of the two American invasions of York in 1813, when Dr. Strachan had taken charge during the town's hour of crisis, the archdeacon led the meeting in preparing the strategy for the following day. The impulsive Allan Napier MacNab of *Dundurn* in Hamilton advocated a pre-dawn attack against the rebels with himself leading the charge. Strachan wisely vetoed the plan, preferring to see Colonel Fitzgibbon, the hero of Beaver Dam, in command of the operation. It was finally decided that the hastily mobilized militia would advance up Yonge Street at noon the next day, with Fitzgibbon and MacNab at their head, and that the column would include a few artillery pieces as well as two military bands. It wasn't much, but it was enough. After a brief skirmish, the rebels broke and fled.

While the flame of Mackenzie's rebellion was reduced, it had not been extinguished. The British government could no longer ignore the grievances that his treason had exposed in Upper Canada. And their new awareness of the defects in their system of colonial administration was further intensified by Louis-Joseph Papineau's ill-fated rebellion in Lower Canada the same year.

And so it was in 1838 that the Earl of Durham was commissioned by Lord Melbourne's Whig government to visit British North America and enquire into the causes of unrest, take such steps as were necessary to stabilize

---

*Baldwin was incensed to learn later that Dr. Rolph was deeply implicated with the rebels. In a whispered conversation after Baldwin had turned away, Rolph had urged Mackenzie to attack the city without delay.

The original *Davenport* house was built around 1797 by Lieutenant John McGill, Adjutant of Simcoe's Queen's Rangers. His 200-acre farm lot lay to the west of the *Spadina* property, and extended to the present Bathurst Street. Lt.-Colonel Joseph Wells, a retired British army officer, bought the farm in 1821 for £750. He demolished the McGill dwelling, but retained the name *Davenport* for his new house which he occupied until his death in 1853. Davenport Road, once an Indian trail, is called after the McGill home, an early landmark on the hill. The *Davenport* of Colonel Wells' day, illustrated here, was noted for its spacious and well-kept lawns which extended from the house to the crest of the Davenport Hill at the head of Howland Avenue.
—Metropolitan Toronto Library Board

the political situation, and bring in recommendations "respecting the form and future government" of the Canadas. A wealthy and influential British peer, Lord Durham and his party reached Quebec City on May 27. They remained on board the *Hastings* for two days while their vast stock of baggage, including His Lordship's family plate and furniture, was being unloaded. When they finally disembarked, the crowds in the ancient town were fully recompensed for their patience. They watched in astonishment as Lord Durham passed through the narrow streets on his way to the Castle of St. Louis. He rode his own white charger and was dressed in a brilliant uniform embroidered with silver; he wore the collar of the Bath, and was attended by a large retinue which included eight aides-de-camp, two more than the Duke of Wellington had required when he had commanded the allied forces on the Continent.[12]

It was not until the following July, 1838, that the Durham mission reached Upper Canada. The party left Montreal on July 10, stopped briefly at Cornwall and Kingston, and then sailed by steamer directly to Niagara where it arrived on July 13. The Durhams put up at the Clifton House Hotel, and Lady Durham wrote to a friend in England that the Falls that lay before them were "the most sublime and beautiful spectacle in creation," and her elated husband reported to Lord Melbourne, "They infinitely surpass the most extravagant notion I ever entertained of their sublimity. No man ever lived, but Milton," he added, "who could adequately have described them."

After spending five days at Niagara, where Lord Durham was also impressed with the city of Buffalo, and enthusiastic over the possibilities of the Welland Canal, he and his party steamed into the Toronto Bay on the *Cobourg* at five o'clock on the afternoon of July 18. Lady Durham noted in her journal that her husband was so ill after his exertions at Niagara that the boat had to delay its arrival for half an hour to enable him to prepare for his reception.

Toronto was *en fête* for His Lordship's one-day visit: a public holiday was declared, the fire, hook and ladder companies turned out in his honour, and numerous delegations, including a band of Indians from the Credit, were there to greet him. *The British Colonist* estimated that the crowd that surged around the Queen's Wharf, the Parliament Buildings, and the City Hall that hot, July day exceeded 12,000. "We were rather struck with the appearance of the streets," Lady Durham recorded later, "which seemed to be better built and to consist of better houses than in any place we had seen. There also seemed to be some pleasant houses and gardens looking toward the lake." Undoubtedly, Dr. Baldwin's new family residence facing the Bay would have caught her eye as the procession passed along Front Street.

The following day, July 19, a levee was held at Government House. The vice-regal residence occupied the southwest corner of King and Simcoe streets, and lay just to the north of the Parliament Buildings. The reception began at twelve noon, and Sir George Arthur, who had succeeded Sir Francis Head as lieutenant-governor the previous spring, introduced a number of officials and leading citizens to the distinguished visitor. Among them were Dr. Baldwin and his son, Robert. At some point in the proceedings that day, the two Baldwins spent twenty minutes chatting with Lord Durham about their ideas concerning constitutional reform. Their historic discussion, which is said to have been arranged by appointment, must have occurred either before the levee began, or following it later in the afternoon. In any event, none of the three men involved could have foreseen the far-reaching consequences of their brief meeting. Lord Durham expressed an interest in their views and asked them to write to him fully about them. He then ended the conversation and turned to receive some other visitors.

As the Baldwins returned to their house on the lakefront, it is easy to imagine the thoughts that rose in their minds: the points they had omitted in their discussion doubtless concerned them, as well as those they might have made with greater force and clarity; Dr. Baldwin might have been too effusive, perhaps garrulous; his son, characteristically, solemn and reserved; they must have speculated about Durham's responses to the things they did manage to say; whatever their conclusions, they would have been encouraged by his request that they write to him. And this they did. Dr. Baldwin mailed off a discursive letter shortly after, and it was followed by a clearer exposition of the subject of colonial responsible government by his son three weeks later. As a result of the Baldwin correspondence, their concept of responsible government was substantially adopted as a basic principle of Lord Durham's later recommendations. Regarded as the most significant document ever produced on the subject of British colonial administration, Durham's famous *Report* was to become not only the blueprint for political reform in the Canadas, but for other British colonies as well.

Lord Durham's mission left Toronto later that afternoon to return to Kingston. He boarded a steamer at Brown's Wharf on the Bay, and again an immense crowd was on hand to watch his departure. When the boat finally cast off at 6 P.M., a violent storm was breaking overhead. As His Excellency's craft steamed past Gibraltar Point and turned into the lake, the guns at the garrison fired a farewell salute. They were barely audible against the sound of the thunder that was rolling across the city.[13]

Lord Durham returned to England in December 1838, and his *Report on the Affairs of British North America* was completed and delivered to the Colonial Office by the following February. Included in its recommendations was the proposal that the old provinces of Upper and Lower Canada be united under a single parliament. Though it was cool to the recommendation that a system of responsible government also be granted, the British government accepted the principle of legislative union, and Charles Poulett Thomson, a member of Lord Melbourne's cabinet, was appointed governor-general and despatched to the Canadas to bring it about. Having obtained approval of the measure in Lower Canada, Thomson arrived in Toronto at the end of 1839 with the object of gaining the support of the assembly of Upper Canada for the proposed union. The Tory Family Compact had set its face unalterably against the idea, and the Reform Party, which had the decisive voice, was only slowly brought round. Throughout the negotiations, Poulett Thomson, who was shortly to become Lord Sydenham, relied heavily upon the influence and support of Robert Baldwin, the chief spokesman for the Reform Party in Upper Canada. When the critically important approval of the provincial assembly was finally won, the governor-general named Baldwin to be solicitor general west in the new administration.[14]

In the spring of 1841, after the Act of Union had been promulgated, the town of Kingston, Toronto's ancient rival, was pushing forward with its preparations for the opening in June of the first union parliament. The seat of government was to rotate between Kingston, Montreal, and Toronto, and Kingston's new General Hospital was being converted into a sumptuous legislative chamber, while *Alwington House* on the outskirts of the town was being refurbished as Lord Sydenham's official residence. In the light of the arduous negotiations that he had faced in bringing the union to fruition, to say nothing of the gout with which he was habitually afflicted, it was perhaps excusable for Lord Sydenham to write deprecatingly of the lavish quarters that were being prepared for the new assembly members. He reported that they "would be thought magnificent by us Members of the English House of Commons. But the fellows in these Colonies have been spoiled by all sorts of luxuries, large armchairs, desks with stationery before each man, and heaven knows what, so I suppose they will complain."

As the country awaited with mixed feelings the first meeting of the United Parliament, Dr. Baldwin, now the elder statesman of reform, still sought to influence events in pursuit of his goal of responsible government. Lord Sydenham, whose hands were tied in the matter by Lord John Russell, the powerful new colonial secretary, expressed his impatience over Dr. Baldwin's continued meddling in political affairs in a letter he wrote to Lieutenant-Governor Sir George Arthur on March 15, 1841. He confided irreverently to Arthur that he thought he could handle Robert Baldwin if he could keep him away from "that mischievous old ass, his father."[15]

It was in 1828, when *Spadina* was his year-round house, that Dr. Baldwin had first enunciated the idea of a form of colonial government which, modelled on the Imperial Parliament, would consist of "a provincial ministry responsible to the provincial parliament and removable from office by His Majesty's representative at his pleasure and especially when they lost the confidence of the people as expressed by their representatives in the assembly." Having sat as a member of the provincial assembly during the 1820's, the doctor's earlier frustrations in not being able to obtain an important government appointment for himself were revived. The indifference of the Executive (the lieutenant-governor and his Executive Council) to the wishes of the popularly elected assembly roused him to increasingly outspoken criticism of the deeply entrenched provincial oligarchy. Before Elizabeth Russell's death in 1822, Dr. Baldwin stood to lose a good deal if she changed her will, and the minor offices he already held, such as his post as master in chancery, would have been jeopardized.[16] After Miss Russell's death, however, when the foundation of his family fortune was laid, the doctor felt himself on firmer ground. No longer under the constraint of cautious dissent, he exchanged his umbrella for a shillelagh and strode confidently into the lists of reform. By 1829 we find him writing to the illustrious Duke of Wellington, the British prime minister, to inform him of the grievances of the gathering forces of reform in the province;[17] among the suggested remedies that were outlined was his famous concept of a "provincial ministry responsible to the provincial parliament." Since no action was taken by the British government on the doctor's proposals, it was natural when Lord Durham appeared in Toronto ten years later that Dr. Baldwin had seized the opportunity of again making his views on the subject known.

Late in 1843, when his health was failing, Dr. Baldwin was named by the new governor-general, Sir Charles Metcalfe, to the Legislative Council of the United Canadas. His appointment gave Dr. Baldwin the right to use the title "Honourable," but he was destined to enjoy the distinction for only a few weeks. Before he could take his seat, he died. He glimpsed but did not touch the fabric of his dream of responsible government. Four years had still to pass before the "great Ministry" of his son, Robert Baldwin, and Louis LaFontaine was to secure full acceptance of his lofty and enduring principle.

Dr. Baldwin's end came at his house on Front Street after an illness of only a few months. He died on Monday, January 8, 1844. He was in his sixty-ninth year. "When I first arrived from Kingston," Robert Baldwin wrote to Louis LaFontaine a few days later, "I found him looking much better than I had expected and he continued to do so for a week or ten days after my return. On Christmas Eve I observed his appetite seemed to fail him and though he appeared cheerful on Christmas morning he ate little and seemed to linger with us in the evening, remaining a full hour beyond his usual time of retiring, as if he had a presentiment of its being the last he was to spend with us here. He had to be carried upstairs to his room that night and never left it after."[18]

The funeral took place at St. James' Cathedral at 11 A.M. the following Friday. "All the shops in King Street, through which the remains passed," the *Toronto Banner* reported, "were closed in respect to the memory of the deceased." In his lifetime, the doctor had been connected with innumerable societies and associations: they included the Law Society of Upper Canada and the Society for Converting and Civilizing the Indians, and Propagating the Gospel Among Destitute Settlers in Upper Canada; he was a director of the Home District Mutual Fire Insurance Company, and acted as a volunteer cashier of the Home District Savings Bank, an institution that was formed to encourage labourers and tradesmen to be "industrious and frugal;" he was interested in the formation of the York Mechanics' Institute (the forerunner of the Toronto Public Library), and served as a member of the Committee for the relief of the Poor and Destitute of the City of Toronto; during the cholera epidemic of 1832, he was named president of the York Board of Health, and he also lent his support to the Bible Society of Upper Canada.

It was scarcely surprising that his funeral attracted a large crowd. "As the deceased gentleman was one of the oldest members of the bar of Upper Canada," the *British Colonist* noted, "the profession attended in their robes; the members of St. Patrick's Benevolent Society, of which Dr. Baldwin when living was President, were also present in a body with crape round their arms." The report added that Bishop Strachan "was also at the funeral" and that the burial service was read by the Reverend H. J. Grasett, the assistant minister of St. James'.

Many of the "immense concourse of people" that attended the funeral walked through a drenching rain from the cathedral on King Street to St. Martin's Rood on the Davenport Hill to witness the final entombment rites.

Dr. Baldwin had made his last will on August 25, 1842.[19] In it he gave his wife Phoebe the use of the 200-acre *Spadina* estate for her lifetime, as well as the family residence on Front Street. Upon his wife's death, both properties were to pass to his oldest son, the Honourable Robert Baldwin, subject to the condition that William Augustus Baldwin, the doctor's younger son, be allowed to occupy *Spadina* for a period of three years after his mother's death.

The provision affecting William Augustus Baldwin is of interest. The later squire of *Mashquoteh* had married Isabella Clark Buchanan in 1834 when he was twenty-six. His aunt, the ailing Maria Willcocks, recognized the event by presenting him with the deed to her Farm Lot 23 in the Third Concession from the Bay.[20] It consisted of 200 acres and extended from the Third Concession Road Allowance (St. Clair Avenue) to the present Eglinton Avenue. Lying just to the west of today's Upper Canada College, it forms the core of Forest Hill Village. Maria Willcocks had obtained the property in 1824 as part of her entitlement to Elizabeth Russell's extensive land holdings which she shared with her sister Phoebe Baldwin.[21] (See map—pages 24, 25.)

When Dr. Baldwin made his will, William was still living with his wife and family at *Spadina*. His wife died in 1850, and the same year Phoebe Baldwin transferred to her bereaved son her interest in the south half of Farm Lot 22 in the Third Concession from the Bay. That parcel consisted of 100 acres. It lay just to the east of the full farm lot young Baldwin had been given earlier by his aunt, and like her property, it was based on and extended north from the present St. Clair Avenue. The parcel, which today is largely occupied by Upper Canada College, was also received by Phoebe Baldwin in 1824 as part of her share in the estate of Elizabeth Russell.[22]

Phoebe Baldwin died in her Front Street residence in 1851, the same year

William Augustus Baldwin built himself a house which he called *Mashquoteh* on the property his mother had just given him. Its name was derived from an Indian term signifying a meadow or a clearing in the woods. Described as being "of hewn timber, from the Baldwin estate, filled in with brick and roughcast," the two-and-a-half-storey dwelling stood on what is now Avenue Road, just south of Heath Street. It was demolished in 1890 to make way for the extension of Avenue Road to the gates of the new Upper Canada College. William married again in 1852, his second wife being Margaret Fry MacLeod. They were to occupy *Mashquoteh* together, with its domain of 300 acres, for over thirty years;[23] later, two successive *Mashquotehs* were to be built, just to the west of the original house, and these also were to be occupied in a smaller setting by William's descendants until comparatively recent times. It is ironic, in the light of Dr. Baldwin's dynastic dream respecting *Spadina* and the weight he attached to the primacy of the eldest son, that the tenure of *Mashquoteh* by the descendants of his youngest son should have surpassed by many decades the Baldwin occupation of *Spadina*, which was conceived by Dr. Baldwin as the perpetual seat of the head of the family.

The day after he had signed his will, Dr. Baldwin penned a rambling letter to his wife which was to be read after his death. It set out in considerable detail his ideas as to how she should dispose of the furnishings and effects of his two houses. In guiding her, he took the opportunity to reaffirm his belief in the primacy of the eldest son, and the honour to which he felt he was entitled as the head of a family. "This head," he wrote, "is always by the appointment of Providence — one child only can be born first — and this in all human societies barbarian as well as polished has been received as the appointment of Providence." It must be assumed after a marriage of forty years that Phoebe Baldwin was fully aware of her husband's views on the subject. Perhaps she never agreed with him. Perhaps the doctor felt that a final colloquy on the matter would carry greater force when it was heard as a voice speaking from the tomb. Perhaps it was simply a case of having the last word. In any event, at the end of his long life, Dr. Baldwin still clung to his belief that society was uplifted and the human family ennobled when it recognized that the eldest son was named by Providence to be the revered head of a family.[24] Ironically, it later fell to the Honourable Robert Baldwin to introduce the legislation that repealed in Canada the ancient British law of primogeniture that favoured the eldest son in the case of those dying intestate.

Also, in 1851, *Spadina* was again to become the year-round home of the head of the Baldwin family. In that year, the Honourable Robert Baldwin retired from political life. Worn out by long years of fighting for his "one idea" of responsible government, a battle he and LaFontaine had finally won, and disillusioned over the diminishing support of his Reform Party colleagues in Canada West, he resigned abruptly on June 30 from his post as attorney general west. A lonely widower aged forty-seven, he had grown old before his time. His health had been undermined by the demands of public office, and now he sought only the peaceful oblivion of domestic life. "It is time to separate from society when we can no longer be of any use to it," Montaigne had written nearly three centuries before. Robert Baldwin embraced his precept. Though he retained the Baldwin family residence on Front Street, by the end of 1851 he had withdrawn completely to the rural solitude of *Spadina* where he was to remain until his death in 1858.

In addition to having played the chief role in attaining acceptance of the principle of colonial responsible government, Baldwin could reflect with deep satisfaction upon the legislation that he and LaFontaine had fashioned during their "great ministry" of 1848-51. Outstanding among their accomplishments were the Municipal Corporations Act, which was commonly called the Baldwin Act and which reformed the basis of local government in Canada West (the later province of Ontario); an act to revise the judicial system; and an act to transform Toronto's King's College into the nonsectarian University of Toronto (over the bitter opposition of Bishop Strachan, Baldwin's former schoolmaster). But in broad political terms, perhaps Robert Baldwin's greatest achievement was in the *entente* that he effected with the French in Canada East (the later province of Quebec): it was only because of the close working arrangement that he enjoyed with LaFontaine's reform forces that he was able to achieve the great goal of responsible government — a fact that seems to have been forgotten in Canada's political life today.

The single-storey *Spadina* house to which Baldwin retired was considerably smaller than the one he had moved into as a boy in 1818. And judging from a letter written to him when the United Parliament was sitting in Montreal, the second *Spadina* was not well built. During Baldwin's absence from the city, Lawrence Heyden, his brother-in-law, was looking after his affairs. He wrote on August 14, 1848: "The foundation of Spadina House is repaired — it was in a bad state & sunk originally only two feet in the ground." Heyden's letter also revealed the kind of leasehold arrangements the large landowners of the district, like the Baldwins and Colonel Wells of neighbouring *Davenport,* were making with the local farmers:

> Mr. Brough has been again speaking of the fences on Spadina farm; the line fence between the Capt [*Russell Hill*] and you was the last complaint. I went out to the Capt & found that he had just commenced repairing it. Brough says that he will lose severely by trying to work the place in its present state except he gets an additional term. He wants 7 years from the expiration of his present lease.—1 Apl 1851—for the additional term he offers a pound an acre which seems a fair rent; it is what Col Wells gets now & his farm I understand was in first rate order when given to the tenant; still he is going to leave next spring. I would be thoroughly inclined to accept Brough's offer—it is in my opinion the full value, & he appears to be a good tenant. I told him that you would build a Barn next winter or spring if convenient to you.

In the same letter, Heyden complained of the difficulty he was having with the York County Registry Office in obtaining registration at an acceptable cost of the massive Deed of Partition that had been worked out the previous June under which Robert Baldwin and his brother, William Augustus of *Mashquoteh,* apportioned between themselves the unallotted lands of their forbears. The partition encompassed a broad inheritance: it divided up such locally historic properties as "The Russell Abbey Block" and "The Spadina Avenue Block," as well as a number of farm tracts that were scattered throughout the townships of Whitchurch, Whitby, and King. Heyden wrote:

> The Registration of the Deeds of Partition come to over £13—in the County of York. I objected to the charges & the deeds remain in the Registrar's office yet. I will take them out this week protesting against the charge. The Registrar charges full fees for every township in the District mentioned in the Deed; he says that the act requires him to register in a separate book for each township & that he must enter the

Memorial in full in each Book—Ridout is I think wrong. I wanted him to take the opinion of the Court but he refused. He says that he has taken opinions enough, & told me good humoredly that you might sue him.[25]

After he had established himself at *Spadina,* desiring more space for privacy and reflection, Robert Baldwin built a one-and-a-half-storey clap-board cottage about fifty feet north of his *Spadina* house. It contained a deep cellar of fieldstone which provided a needed storage area for the harvest of his orchard and garden. More important, having retired from his King Street law practice in 1848, a large, downstairs room provided him with ample space for his voluminous legal files, family papers, and estate accounts. The cottage faced the east, and its main entrance was shaded by a covered ver-andah. Two windows in the library overlooked the *Spadina* kitchen garden and, significantly, they also afforded a clear view of the family cemetery that lay at the crest of the glen a few hundred feet to the northeast. The trim, little cottage was finished off with a cupola in which was suspended a heavy, iron bell, a precaution that was probably inspired by the memory of the dis-astrous fire of 1835 that had gutted the first *Spadina* house.[26]

Though retired, Baldwin was by no means forgotten. In a flattering letter in 1855, the Honourable John A. Macdonald urged him to accept the posi-tion of chief justice of the Court of Common Pleas. Baldwin declined on grounds of ill-health. Earlier, the Convocation of the University of Toronto, which Baldwin had largely created, had elected him chancellor only to have him refuse the office for political reasons. In 1854, the governor-general, the Earl of Elgin, informed him that Queen Victoria had conferred upon him the distinction of Companion of the Order of the Bath. Baldwin accepted that honour gratefully.

In February 1851, Augusta Elizabeth, Robert Baldwin's daughter, had married the Honourable John Ross, just before her father's retirement from public life. Ross was a well-known Toronto lawyer, Reform politician, and was to serve as speaker of the Legislative Council from 1854-56, and after that, as president of the Grand Trunk Railway. Starting in 1854, he accumu-lated over fifty acres of land on the Davenport Hill at the northwest corner of Davenport Road and Dufferin Street.[27] He built a pleasant house for him-self on the edge of the hill, and after the United Parliament had moved to Toronto in 1855, his place became a favourite retreat of John A. Macdon-ald. Though a considerable distance west of his father-in-law's *Spadina,* Ross' carriage would have passed his place each day as it jogged towards York-ville and Yonge Street along the Davenport Road. We may be sure a close relationship existed between the two households, and that the master of *Spadina*'s advice was often sought by Ross in political matters. Despite his withdrawal to his country seat, Baldwin continued to exercise considerable influence over his political contemporaries. An illustration of this fact is found in a letter that was written to John A. Macdonald by the Honourable

---

The Honourable Robert Baldwin (1804-1858), the son of Dr. William Warren and Phoebe Willcocks Baldwin. He played a leading role in the struggle for Responsible Government in Canada, and retired to *Spadina* in 1851. Upon his death in 1858, he was buried in St. Martin's Rood Cemetery, the Baldwins' burial ground on the *Spadina* property.

—Metropolitan Toronto Library Board

John Ross who was in England at the time. Writing from the Reform Club in London on September 18, 1855, he commented: "I have thought a great deal of the Upper Canada judgeship when Macaulay retires, and trust you have made up your mind to give it to Hagarty. . . . If you like to talk the matter of the judgeship over privately with Baldwin I think he would give you some advice you would be glad to get."[28] Ross referred to the well-known Toronto lawyer John H. Hagarty, Q.C., who had succeeded Dr. Baldwin in 1846 as president of the St. Patrick's Society. It is probable that John A. Macdonald visited Robert Baldwin at *Spadina,* and discussed the appointment with him. In any event, Hagarty was raised to the Bench as a puisne judge of the Court of Common Pleas the following February. Later, he was to attain the office of chief justice of Ontario, and in 1897 he received a knighthood.

Also in 1855, Robert Baldwin responded to an appeal to donate some of the land he owned in "The Spadina Avenue Block" for the building of an orphanage. When Jenny Lind, the famous Swedish singer, had appeared at the St. Lawrence Hall in 1853, she had given the receipts of one of her concerts to the mayor of the city for a deserving charity. Part of her donation was directed towards the building of a home for the destitute children of Toronto, and a site was found on the north side of Sullivan Street, between Spadina Avenue and Beverley Street. It was located on the Honourable Peter Russell's old 100-acre Park Lot 14, and lay a little to the north of the point where he had placed his *Petersfield* farmhouse half a century before. The Sullivan Street parcel was 140 feet deep. Robert Baldwin contributed a frontage of 155 feet, and the Honourable William Cayley, 19½ feet.[29] The Orphans Home & Female Aid Society occupied the property until 1882 when it moved to new quarters on Dovercourt Road.

Robert Baldwin's last days at *Spadina* were marred by melancholy notwithstanding that many of his family were still around him. His daughter, Phoebe Maria, kept his house, and his youngest son and namesake had returned to *Spadina* after service with the mercantile marine. His eldest son, William Willcocks, resided at *Larchmere,* the Old Esquire's farm at Lake Willcocks; his uncle, Captain Augustus Warren Baldwin, still lived next door at *Russell Hill;* his brother William Augustus, who was to father sixteen children, was comfortably settled at *Mashquoteh;* and his youngest daughter, Eliza Ross, was attending to the needs of her growing family on Dufferin Street.

And yet, Robert Baldwin was a lonely man. He had never fully recovered from the blow that had fallen upon him when his young wife, Augusta Elizabeth, had died in 1836, over twenty years before. As he sat by the window of his cottage library late at night, his eye must often have wandered across the somber fields to the monuments of St. Martin's Rood where she was buried. Doubtless on such an occasion, he painfully wrote his burial instructions to his daughter, Maria. One writer has described them:

> He kept the letters which had passed between him and his wife, both before and after their marriage, with the most religious care. Often when all the rest of the family were in bed he spent hours in re-reading them. He never left home without taking one or more with him as he wished to die with one of them near him. On his death he left these letters, together with copies of them, to his daughter Maria, accompanied by a list of last requests. He asked that the originals might be placed on his breast in his coffin covered with a handkerchief that had belonged to

William Willcocks Baldwin (1830-1893) inherited the 80-acre *Spadina* property in 1858 from his father, the Honourable Robert Baldwin. He sold it at public auction in 1866 to James Austin.

—Public Archives of Ontario

his wife. He had kept the handkerchief that had covered the face of his dead wife. Might the same handkerchief be used to cover his! The chairs on which the coffin of his wife had rested would be found marked. Might his coffin rest on the same chairs! He asked that his coffin might be placed to the right of his wife's and that a "small iron chain be passed round the two coffins and locked, so as to chain them together." Should he die under circumstances that should render it impossible to find his body, "Let an empty coffin be in like manner placed in the tomb by the side of my E."[30]

Robert Baldwin suffered a heart attack early in December 1858. He died at *Spadina* on the ninth day of the month. In the knowledge that his life was ebbing away, he had a short will quickly prepared, "As it has pleased Almighty God to visit me heavily and suddenly at this time." He signed it on the day he died in the presence of his two physicians, James H. Richardson and William R. Beaumont.

The funeral was held at *Spadina* on Monday, December 13, and despite the bad weather, hundreds of people climbed the Davenport Hill to attend the service. Bishop Strachan, reflecting gravely upon the man who had been his head boy at the Home District Grammar School in 1819, drove out to *Spadina* in his carriage to observe the entombment rites which were conducted by the Reverend Mr. Grasett. And honouring Robert Baldwin's long association with the Law Society of Upper Canada, as founder of The Advocates' Society, and as a distinguished bencher and treasurer, the legal profession, including the judges of the Superior Courts, attended in their gowns. The *Globe,* in its issue of December 14, reported that "During the afternoon business was suspended in most of the stores on the principal streets of the city, and a similar mark of respect was paid to Mr. Baldwin's memory in the city of Hamilton, by recommendation of the Council."

William Willcocks Baldwin was only twenty-eight when his father died and left him the hilltop portion of his *Spadina* property as part of his substantial patrimony. It comprised, of course, the main house and out-buildings. "I devise to my son William," Robert Baldwin had said in the first provision of his deathbed will, "that part of my Spadina property lying to the north of the Davenport Road."

Young Baldwin, who was now the head of the family, had married Eliza MacDougall in 1854, and after her death the following year, he was married again in 1856 to Susanna Mary Yarwood. It would appear that he never occupied *Spadina* on any permanent basis, choosing to remain at *Larchmere* after his father's death. In 1866, however, he is listed in the Toronto Street Directory for the first time, and is shown as living in the Town of Yorkville.

In an earlier will (1840) that was incorporated into his deathbed testament, Robert Baldwin had moralized over the responsibilities of the head of a family; his remarks at that time were directed to his son William, who was then only ten, and to whom he was leaving many important properties:

> I look upon it as the duty of the head of a Family like ours, not merely to use without impairing the property which he inherits from his Ancestors, but by diligence industry and economy to increase the same, so as to be able besides providing properly for the rest of his Children to transmit the family estates to his heir enlarged as well as improved according as God has prospered him That as the family increases in each succeeding generation, if such should be God's Blessed will the means of good in the hands of their head may be increased likewise and that the exertion to fulfil such obligation may ever preserve in activity that mental energy which can alone preserve any family from falling to decay.

The lean years at the close of the U.S. Civil War weighed heavily upon young William Baldwin. The rents from his inherited lands were insufficient for his needs, and he had already mortgaged his *Spadina* property twice.[31] Knowing that a vigorous group of new capitalists was emerging in mid-Victorian Toronto, eager to create landed estates of their own, he decided at the end of 1865 to sell his family seat. A few weeks later, in an auction room on King Street East, Dr. Baldwin's dynastic dream was finished.

NOTES TO PART I

Chapter 1

1. John Scadding (1754-1824) was Simcoe's farm manager at *Wolford* in Devonshire and accompanied the governor to Upper Canada. He was granted a substantial property on the east bank of the Don River in 1793. In a letter written that year Mrs. Simcoe reported, "Mr. Scadding seems very well satisfied with his sixty pounds a year as clerk." He returned to England with Simcoe in 1796 where his three sons were born, John (1807-1845), Charles (1809-1892), and the later Toronto historian and rector of Holy Trinity Church, Henry (1813-1901). The Scadding family finally settled in York in 1821 in "a good large log dwelling" on their Crown grant lands. The father, John Scadding, was killed by a falling tree in what is now St. James' Cemetery. See T. A. Reed, *The Scaddings, A Pioneer Family in York,* Papers and Records of the Ontario Historical Society, Vol. XXXVI, (Toronto, 1944).

    Christopher Robinson (1763-1798) was born in Virginia and served with Simcoe's Queen's Rangers in 1781. He was demobilized in New Brunswick and came to Upper Canada in 1792. He settled in Kingston where he practised law, moving to York in 1798 where he died a few months later. See *Three Centuries of Robinsons, The Story of a Family,* Julia Jarvis, (Toronto, 1967).

2. Edith G. Firth, *The Town of York, 1793-1815,* (Toronto: University of Toronto Press, 1962), p. 11.

3. Russell Papers, Public Archives of Ontario, quoted in Firth *ibid.,* p. 17.

4. *The Lieutenant-Governors of Upper Canada and Ontario, 1792-1899,* D. B. Read, Q.C., Toronto, 1900.

5. Elizabeth Russell Papers, Central Library, Metropolitan Toronto.

6. Shepherd-White Papers, Public Archives of Canada, quoted by Mary Quale Innes, *Mrs. Simcoe's Diary,* (Toronto: Macmillan of Canada, 1965), p. 15.

7. The details of Berczy's troubled life and tragic end are recounted in John Andre's *William Berczy, Co-Founder of Toronto* (A Canada Centennial Project of the Borough of York, 1967).

8. Russell Papers, Central Library, Metropolitan Toronto, quoted in Firth, *op. cit.,* p. 46.

9. See p. 160, *et seq.*

Chapter 2

1. Russell to Osgoode, Quebec, Sept. 13, 1798 (T.P.L., Peter Russell Papers), quoted in Edith G. Firth, *Town of York, 1793-1815,* p. 226.

2. Russell to the Comte de Puisaye, Jan. 1, 1799; (T.P.L., Peter Russell Papers), quoted in Firth, *ibid,* p. 145.

3. Chewett's letter to D. W. Smith, from which these notes were taken, was shown to the writer by the late Verschoyle Blake of the Ontario Archives Office.

4. For a discussion of the Duke of Portland's proposal to Simcoe, and Peter Russell's ambitions, see Marcus Van Steen, *Governor Simcoe and His Lady,* (Toronto: Hodder & Stoughton Ltd., 1968), p. 145. The Duke of Portland was the British home secretary at the time.

5. Robert Baldwin was the second son of Alderman John Baldwin of Cork. With his brother, John, he produced a twice-weekly newspaper in Cork, the *Volunteer Journal,* but when the political cause faded that it was designed to support, he left the paper in 1785 and returned to farming. He died in York in 1816.

6. *Niagara Herald,* March 14, 1801. See Firth, *op cit.* p. 163.

7. See R.M. & J. Baldwin, *The Baldwins and The Great Experiment* (Toronto: Longman Canada Ltd., 1969), pp. 51-52. In naming that part of the escarp-

ment on his property "Sugar Loaf Hill," the receiver general perhaps recalled the famous Sugarloaf Mountain in County Wicklow, Ireland, which dominated the view from a number of county seats, like Charleville and Powerscourt.

Chapter 3

1. Eugenia Willcocks died two years later, in 1804. Her husband shortly after took charge of Laurent Quetton de St. George's store in Kingston. He left it in 1810 and returned to Europe.
2. Although Dr. Baldwin's school has become a commonplace of local history, the historical evidence surrounding its existence is sketchy. In addition to the doctor's announcement in the Upper Canada Gazette, a further reference to the school is contained in Nicholas Flood Davin's *The Irishman in Canada* (1877) p. 239. Speaking of Baldwin's project, the author says: "One of his pupils was the late Chief Justice McLean, who used to tell how the pupils got a holiday on the birth of the future statesman in 1804."
3. The origin of the name *Davenport* is unknown. It has been suggested that McGill's house was called after a Major Davenport who was once stationed in York. The British Army List does not disclose such a posting at the material time. Perhaps the word is a corruption of "Devenport," as it sometimes appears in early directories, and was chosen by McGill to commemorate his possible connection with the town of that name in England. His commanding officer, Lt. Col. Simcoe, who granted McGill his farm lot, was of course connected with Devonshire through his *Wolford* estate.
4. Metropolitan Toronto Central Library, Alexander Wood Letter Books — Wood to Mrs. Elmsley 23rd May, 1806 — quoted in *The Town of York* (1793-1815) p. 102, "On Sunday, or rather between Saturday and Sunday last, the fire (which had & still continues to rage furiously in the Woods) got to the Fence at Cloverhill. . . . Mr. McGill at the Mountain suffered but little tho' at one time he was threatened with total destruction."
5. See Edith G. Firth, *The Town of York 1793-1812*, p. 252, Lord Selkirk's Opinion of York.

Chapter 4

1. Extracts from Elizabeth Russell's Diary (M.T.C.L.: Elizabeth Russell Papers). This diary note was made on January 24, 1806, and is reproduced in Edith Firth, *The Town of York, 1793-1815*, p. 260.
2. Dr. Baldwin's letter to the Honourable Peter Russell, dated July 27, 1806, is lodged with certain Russell Papers in the Ontario Provincial Archives.
3. See Note 9, Chapter 8.
4. Extracts from Elizabeth Russell's Diary, *op cit.* This note appears in Firth, *op cit*, p. 259.
5. Henry E. Guest, *The Life of William Warren Baldwin,* a thesis written for the Faculty of Graduate Studies, University of Manitoba (Thesis G 9379, April, 1961).

Chapter 5

1. See Edith G. Firth, *Administration of Peter Russell,* Ontario Historical Society Papers & Records (1956) Vol. XLVIII No. 4, pp. 163-181.
2. Thomas Ridout (1754-1829) was appointed surveyor general of Upper Canada in 1810. Samuel Smith Ridout (1778-1855) was the eldest son of Thomas Ridout. He was sheriff of the Home District from 1815 to 1827 when he became registrar.
   Stephen Heward (177?-1828) held a number of minor government offices in York, and from 1819 until his death was auditor general of Land Patents. He was a brother-in-law of Sir John Beverley Robinson, a chief justice of Upper Canada.

3. Robert Baldwin's letter to Elizabeth Russell is quoted in R. M. and J. Baldwin, *The Baldwins and The Great Experiment,* (Toronto: Longmans Canada Limited, 1969), pp. 68-69.
4. The extracts from Elizabeth Russell's correspondence quoted in this chapter are taken from her original letters which are on file in the Baldwin Room of the Metropolitan Toronto Public Library.
5. John Detlor lost his life during the first American invasion of York in 1813.
6. Inquiries by the writer among descendants of Dr. Baldwin, and of the Royal Ontario Museum, yielded no knowledge of the Russell family plate.

Chapter 6

1. Dr. Baldwin's letter to his friend St. George was dated July 11, 1810. It is quoted in Henry H. Guest's thesis (G9379), Faculty of Graduate Studies, University of Manitoba (1961).
2. R. M. & J. Baldwin, *The Baldwins and The Great Experiment* (Toronto: Longmans Canada Limited, 1969), pp. 88-92 for an interpretation of Dr. Baldwin's position vis à vis the Family Compact, and the details of his duel with Macdonell as set out in the doctor's letter, which is quoted, to his absent friend William Firth.
3. See *ibid.*, p. 132, where the Conservation Report of the Department of Planning and Development (1956) is quoted as the authority for the inaccurate statement that the *Millbrook* property was inherited by Dr. Baldwin.
4. See Colonel C. P. Stacey, *Battle of Little York* (The Toronto Historical Board, 1971), and George F. G. Stanley, *Canada's Soldiers* (Toronto: The Macmillan Company of Canada Limited, 1960). Commodore Chauncey's newly built flagship, the *President Madison,* was a corvette of only twenty-four guns.

Chapter 7

1. John Strachan, *J. L. H. Henderson,* (Toronto: University of Toronto Press, 1969), pp. 18-20.
2. W. W. Baldwin to Quetton St. George, Montreal (T.P.L. W. W. Baldwin Papers), quoted in Edith G. Firth, *The Town of York, 1793-1815,* p. 332.
3. John Spread Baldwin had died in 1843 leaving surviving him his widow Anne Scott Shaw Baldwin (1798-1870), and seven children, among them Maurice Scollard (1836-1944) a later Bishop of Huron, Arthur Henry (1840-1908) a later rector of All Saints Anglican Church, Toronto, and Morgan (1834-1898) a later harbor master of Toronto.
4. The letter from Daniel Sullivan, Jr. dated December 16, 1817, is filed with certain Baldwin Papers in the Ontario Provincial Archives; the letter containing the reference to Dr. Baldwin's office in *Russell Abbey* is amongst the Baldwin Papers at the Metropolitan Toronto Central Library—both letters are quoted in Henry H. Guest's thesis.
5. R. M. and J. Baldwin, *The Baldwins and The Great Experiment,* p. 107 (Dr. Baldwin's letters are quoted).
6. Quoted in Henry H. Guest's thesis.
7. W. W. Baldwin to St. George (M.T.C.L. W. W. Baldwin Papers, 1) quoted in Edith G. Firth, *The Town of York, 1815-1834,* pp. 305-6. For a different, and more romantic interpretation of the origin of Dr. Baldwin's *Spadina* see Stephen Leacock *Baldwin LaFontaine Hincks,* The Makers of Canada Series (1910), p. 26. Leacock says of Dr. Baldwin, "He had the good fortune to fall heir to the property of a Miss Elizabeth Russell. . . . Desirous to use his new found wealth for the foundation of a family estate, Dr. Baldwin purchased a considerable tract of land to the north of the little Town on the summit of the hill overlooking the present city of Toronto. . . . To this property the name *Spadina* was given."

8. The information concerning Brock Street was provided by the Toronto City Archives.
9. The writer was a pupil of the late Dr. Percy J. Robinson at St. Andrew's College, Aurora, Ontario. He explained the correct pronunciation of the name "Spadina" as he autographed a copy of *Toronto During the French Régime* in 1936. See also Captain W. F. Moore, *Indian Place Names in the Province of Ontario* (Toronto: Macmillan Company, 1930).
10. Dr. Baldwin's partner was Charles Fothergill (1782-1840) who settled in Port Hope in 1817. From 1824 to 1830 he represented Durham in the Assembly. The first book of poetry published in York (*Wonders of the West, or, A Day at Niagara Falls in 1825*) was printed by Fothergill in 1825 while he held the post of King's Printer and editor of the *Upper Canada Gazette and Weekly Register*. For a discussion of Dr. Baldwin's land activities with Fothergill, see Henry H. Guest's thesis.

Chapter 8

1. A legal description of St. Martin's Rood Burial Ground is contained in a deed dated August 31, 1842, Connell J. Baldwin to William W. Baldwin, registered as No. 20336 Township of York.
2. The records of St. James' Cemetery list the removals from "Mr. Baldwin's Private Burial Ground—Spadina Vault" in September, 1874.
3. See Deed No. 20336, Township of York (Supra).
4. The Patent from the Crown of Lot 2 (1 acre) to Theophilus Sampson was dated June 30, 1801. The deed in favour of the Baldwin sons was dated August 21, 1829, registered Town of York as No. 6924 on August 29, 1829.
5. The letter is quoted in R. M. and J. Baldwin, *The Baldwins and The Great Experiment,* page 121.
6. See Memorial of the Will of Susanna Maria Willcocks registered as No. 25067 in the Registry Division of the County of Ontario and City of Oshawa (Whitby, Ontario). The Memorial is dated April 1, 1865, and was registered by William Augustus Baldwin of *Mashquoteh.*
7. St. James' Cemetery records—2 (Supra).
8. See R. M. and J. Baldwin, *op cit.,* p. 133 where Dr. Baldwin's letter is quoted in part.
9. Town of York, Instrument No. 12390, dated November 26, 1835, registered December 22, 1835. The property comprised Lot 4, Town of York Plan—see page 261, Book T.L. 20, Toronto Registry Office.
10. See R. M. and J. Baldwin, *op. cit.,* p. 148.
11. See J. L. H. Henderson, *John Strachan* (Toronto: University of Toronto Press, 1969), p. 60.
12. See Chester New, *Lord Durham's Mission to Canada,* (Toronto: McClelland and Stewart Limited 1963), p. 63 et seq.
13. *The British Colonist,* Thursday, July 26, 1838.
14. See J. M. S. Careless, *The Union of the Canadas, 1841-1857* (Toronto: McClelland and Stewart Limited, 1967).
15. *The Arthur Papers, III,* C. R. Sanderson, Editor, (Toronto: 1959), p. 387.
16. Henry H. Guest, *The Life of William Warren Baldwin,* (A Thesis, The Faculty of Graduate Studies, University of Manitoba, 1961), p. 225.
17. The Duke of Wellington was the prime minister of Britain at the time. E. G. Stanley (afterwards Earl of Derby) was asked to present the petition in the British Parliament. See George E. Wilson, *The Life of Robert Baldwin* (Toronto: The Ryerson Press, 1933), p. 21.
18. The letter appears in R. M. and J. Baldwin, *op. cit.,* p. 192.
19. A Memorial of the Probate of Dr. Baldwin's will is registered as Instrument Number 26653, Township of York.

20. Susanna Maria Willcocks conveyed the whole of Lot 23, Concession 3 to William A. Baldwin by Deed Number 10674, Township of York, registered April 18, 1834.
21. Dr. W. W. Baldwin, as executor of Elizabeth Russell's estate, conveyed the whole of Lot 23, Concession 3 to Maria Willcocks by Deed 4744 registered March 6, 1824. As part of her distribution, Dr. Baldwin also conveyed the whole of Park Lot 14 to Miss Willcocks (*Petersfield Farm*) by deed dated August 20, 1823, registered on August 5, 1824 as 4928, Township of York.
22. As Elizabeth Russell's executor, Dr. Baldwin conveyed to his wife Phoebe the 100-acre south half of Lot 22, Concession 3 by deed dated August 20, 1823, registered as Number 4928 on August 5, 1824. Phoebe Baldwin conveyed the 100 acres to her son William A. Baldwin by deed dated November 12, 1850, registered as Number 38490 on November 13, 1850.
23. In *Toronto of Old* (p. 426), Dr. Henry Scadding wrongly describes the owner of *Mashquoteh* as being "Mr. W. Warren Baldwin, son of Dr. W. W. Baldwin, the builder of *Spadina*."
24. Dr. Baldwin's letter to his wife Phoebe is dated August 26, 1842. Baldwin Papers, Metropolitan Toronto Central Library.
25. Baldwin Papers, Metropolitan Toronto Central Library. The Deed of Partition was registered as No. 32251W on July 28, 1848.
26. The bell was removed to *Mashquoteh* when the cottage was demolished around 1912. It is now the property of Mr. Archer Baldwin of Coboconk, Ontario.
27. Ross purchased Lots 16 and 17, Registered Plan 61, being a subdivision of part of Lot 31 Con. 2. The lots consisted of 25.2 acres each, and were acquired in 1854 and 1855. Ross died in 1871, and his wife Augusta Elizabeth sold the property the following year to Edward H. Foster. Also, in 1873 she sold The Circle on Spadina Avenue, just north of College Street, to the Hon. John McMurrich who turned it over to Knox College in 1874. Mrs. Ross inherited The Circle from her father, the Hon. Robert Baldwin.
28. Sir Joseph Pope, *Memoirs of The Rt. Hon. Sir John Alexander Macdonald,* (Toronto: Oxford University Press, 1930), p. 159.
29. The Baldwin deed was dated December 27, 1855 and was registered July 15, 1856 as No. 63232. The Cayley deed was dated December 29, 1855 and was registered July 15, 1856 as No. 63233. See also Frank N. Walker, *Sketches of Old Toronto* (Toronto: Longmans Canada Limited, 1965), p. 338.
30. George E. Wilson, *op. cit.,* p. 300.
31. William Willcocks Baldwin mortgaged the 80-acre *Spadina* property to William Gordon for £1216.13.4 on May 10, 1859. The mortgage was registered May 30, 1859, as No. 77131. He next mortgaged the property to Stephen Richards for £748.5.0 on September 14, 1863. That mortgage was registered the next day as No. 86233.

Part II

The Golden Key (1866-1936)

Chapter 9

King Street Auction

On a February morning in 1866, as a biting wind was gusting in from the Toronto Bay, James Austin left his private office in the Wellington Street Chambers of the new Bank of Toronto Building and turned briskly up Church Street. Glancing to his right, he saw that the St. Lawrence Hall clock, high in its weathered, green cupola, was within a few minutes of striking the hour of twelve. He quickened his pace along the creaking plank sidewalk that would lead him to King Street and the auction rooms of Wakefield, Coate & Company. Their land sales always began punctually at noon. A retired wholesale merchant living comfortably on Jarvis Street, Austin had a special interest in the land sales that were being conducted that day. Among the properties being auctioned was the historic *Spadina* estate of the Baldwin family which overlooked Toronto from its vantage point on the distant Davenport Hill. He had made up his mind to buy it.

As he approached King Street, the squat, Norman tower of St. James' Cathedral came into view. Still awaiting its lofty spire, the tower at that time was adorned with only a mantle of snow. Turning the corner, he joined the animated throng on King Street. The keen winter air seemed to add urgency to the motion of the gleaming cutters as they drove up to the town's leading shops. In contrast, the crowded horsecars of the five-year-old Toronto Street Railway, their sleigh runners in place, plodded slowly towards the St. Lawrence Market.

As Austin made his way along King Street, his mind was carried back to that distant day in October 1829, when he had arrived in the town of York, a lad of sixteen, from County Armagh, Northern Ireland.

His father, John Marks Austin, had been a farmer in Tandragee where James was born in a thatched, white-washed cottage on March 6, 1813. Like thousands of Irish emigrants at the time, dissatisfied with conditions at home and impressed with the glowing reports that were reaching Ulster of the attractiveness of Upper Canada for settlement, John Austin had gathered his modest means together and set sail for America with his wife and five children. After a passage of seventy days, ten of which were spent on the St. Lawrence River between Montreal and Prescott, the Austin family, weary and dispirited, had at last disembarked at Little York. James Austin later described the final stages of their journey:

> At that period the only mode of conveyance was by small flat bottomed boats propelled by French Canadians with poles along the shores of the St. Lawrence, except when a rapid was reached several yoke of oxen

107

were called into requisition and by means of a strong hawser, the boat was dragged through until still water was again reached. Having arrived at Prescott, the family embarked on board a small high pressure steamer called the "Queenston", and arrived after two days steaming in Muddy Little York, a very appropriate name as there were no side paths, sewers, or any mode of lighting the streets by night—it may easily be imagined what my father's disappointment must have been, as he was led to believe it was a flourishing town with all the appliances necessary to make it a place attractive to settlers—had it not been that the season was far advanced the family would have returned to their native home again as many others had done.

John Marks Austin spent two months in Little York fretfully assessing the situation. His two concerns were to find a farm for himself and his family, and employment for young James in York. "Very soon after our arrival," James Austin wrote laconically, "my father apprenticed me to Wm. Lyon Mackenzie for 4½ years to learn the printing business, and purchased a farm in the Township of Trafalgar and moved the remainder of the family to it in the month of December."[1]

Young Austin stuck doggedly to the fiery Mackenzie beyond the term of his apprenticeship. He witnessed at first hand the most turbulent period of his chief's prolonged agitation for political reform which culminated in the disastrous Upper Canada Rebellion of 1837. Fearing reprisals because of his association with Mackenzie, who fled the country with a price on his head, the young printer withdrew to the United States. He returned finally to Toronto and, with his fellow Irishman, Patrick Foy, established a wholesale grocery business in 1843. It became one of the most prosperous and influential firms of its kind in the province. During their long association they saw the city's population climb from fewer than 18,000 to nearly 45,000. The face of Toronto was transformed as new churches thrust their proud spires into the heavens over the town, handsome shops were opened up on King Street, St. Lawrence Hall and University College were built, and St. James' Cathedral was rebuilt by Bishop Strachan after the Great King Street Fire of 1849. Following the end of the Crimean War, or "Russian War" as it was then called, the two Irishmen decided to close out their partnership and invest their capital elsewhere. They had won for themselves what the Victorians liked to call "a comfortable competency," and James Austin had also learned that a golden key lay in the hand of a man whose capital was uncommitted in times of depression. Looking back many years later, he recalled the event:

> At the close of the Russian War a very severe crisis came upon the country, and want of confidence sprang up to such a degree that we in common with the business community generally were afraid to let goods out of our hands on credit. Of course under the circumstances business fell off to such an extent we considered it most conducive to our interests to dissolve a partnership which had been conducted on the most harmonious principles for the long period of sixteen years, it being evident to both of us that by collecting our means, and applying them in other channels more money was to be made, and that on a much more secure basis.[2]

One direction in which Austin had chosen to apply his means at that time was in purchasing shares of The Consumers' Gas Company of Toronto which had been established eleven years earlier.[3] His financial interest was promptly recognized by his election in 1859 to the company's board of directors.

As James Austin neared the auction rooms of Wakefield, Coate & Company, which were opposite Toronto Street, he also reflected for a moment upon the yeasty prosperity that the recent American Civil War had brought to Toronto. It had ended ten months before, and now commercial activity throughout Canada West had contracted sharply. The familiar cycle of war-inflated demand followed by depression was again asserting itself across the province. To many in the city's financial and commercial community, real estate was no longer a good investment. Indeed, the venerable William Gooderham, president of the Bank of Toronto, had just told his shareholders that the year 1865 had been "one of the most trying that the country had ever experienced." The seventy-five-year-old banker, who was also the senior partner of Gooderham & Worts, Millers and Distillers, had added that the bank's holdings of real estate, other than its own premises, were then worth less than $5,000. Moreover, by the end of 1866, with the collapse of the Bank of Upper Canada still reverberating across the land, even that small item was to be written off the Bank of Toronto's balance sheet. Gooderham was left to explain gloomily that "your directors have come to the conclusion that it is vain to base any estimate for the future on the probable rise in the value of real estate, and have dealt with the assets in their books accordingly."[4] James Austin had concluded otherwise. Deeply aware of the feeling of despondency that prevailed throughout the country during the harsh winter of 1865-66, he believed that the time for property investment was now at hand.

A sparsely built man, his black beard touched with grey, Austin had now reached the auction rooms. The place was always a popular rendezvous for curiosity seekers, idlers, and land speculators. In that day many land sales were transacted by public auction, and if an important property was on the market, a large and attentive crowd could be counted upon to squeeze itself into the rooms. The proceedings were invariably enlivened by the frock-coated Mr. Wakefield in whom the qualities of a gifted raconteur, tragedian, and comic character found their natural union—that is to say, he was a salesman *par excellence.*

Entering the establishment, Austin moved forward quickly to the front row of chairs which were arranged close to the auctioneer's platform. As he made his way through the crowd he noticed the Honourable John Ross, the late Robert Baldwin's son-in-law, warming his hands at a massive stove, intent in his conversation with the Toronto merchant John Macdonald. He nodded amiably to the two men as he passed. Ross, a striking figure in a black cloth coat with a rich mink collar and matching fur cap, had recently served a ten-year term as president of the Grand Trunk Railway, and was the head of an influential law firm in Toronto. He lived on the Davenport Hill at Dufferin Street. John Macdonald, Toronto's leading drygoods wholesaler, owned a great warehouse which occupied part of the block between Wellington and Front streets. He was also the owner of an extensive property on the Davenport Hill, at the top of the present Avenue Road, where a few years earlier he had built his rambling mansion *Oaklands.*[5]

James Austin knew that men like Ross and Macdonald were not attracted to the auction rooms out of curiosity. Their presence gave warning that their interest was of a practical nature. As men of means they were always interested in adding to their land holdings, particularly if an important property could be bought to advantage. The weight of their interest would be felt in the competitive bidding that lay ahead.

It was now noon, and Mr. Wakefield mounted the platform with impressive dignity. He paused and slowly turned up the gasolier above his head. The dimly lit room was further brightened by several sputtering gas lights on the walls which were simultaneously adjusted by his clerks. His partner, Mr. Coate, took his seat at a small table to the right of the platform, and with the solemnity of a parson searching for his text, leafed through he pages of the firm's great ledger. After urging some of the spectators, who were still standing at the back of the room, to seat themselves in the few remaining chairs, Mr. Wakefield began the proceedings by reading aloud from a paper in his hand.

"Acting upon the instructions of William Willcocks Baldwin, Esquire, a resident of this place," he intoned, "I offer for sale today the residence known as *Spadina,* together with its outbuildings, situated on eighty acres of land, extending north from the Davenport Road to the Third Concession Road [now St. Clair Avenue], being the northerly part of Farm Lot 24 in the Second Concession from the Bay."

Removing his steel-rimmed spectacles, his glance sweeping the room, Wakefield asked for the indulgence of his audience so that he might remind them of the importance of the occasion, and the historical significance of the property that was now being offered for sale.

He started by saying that the names Baldwin and *Spadina* had been linked together in the public mind for half a century. His client's great-grandfather, William Willcocks, an early settler in York, had obtained the property by grant from Governor Simcoe. He left the 200-acre farm lot to his son-in-law Dr. William Warren Baldwin who built his *Spadina* house on the crest of the hill overlooking York in 1818. The property then descended to the doctor's son, the Honourable Robert Baldwin, who in turn left the hilltop portion to his son Mr. William Willcocks Baldwin when he died at *Spadina* in 1858.

Mr. Wakefield went on to point out that Mr. William Willcocks Baldwin now felt that the Baldwin residence at the corner of Front and Bay streets was sufficient for his purpose. With the death the previous month of his esteemed uncle, Augustus Warren Baldwin at *Russell Hill,* next door to *Spadina,* he had concluded that it was no longer incumbent upon him to continue in his ownership of the *Spadina* farmlands. (There was, of course, another more compelling reason for the sale which Mr. Wakefield understandably declined to mention: the property was mortgaged to the hilt. Notwithstanding the depressed state of the real estate market, the sale of his ancestral seat was now required to help Baldwin extinguish his debts.)

Sensing that the crowd was becoming restless under a recounting of events with which most of them were familiar, Mr. Wakefield started the bidding. By agreement, the opening price was set at £2000, sterling, the equivalent of $8,000 in Canadian currency. The prospect of a bargain added zest to the proceedings, and the price rose quickly to £3000. It was then apparent that the contest had narrowed down to the Honourable John Ross, John Macdonald of *Oaklands,* and James Austin.

Choosing that moment to heighten the suspense, Wakefield broke in to extol the virtues of the property. The eighty acres of land, he explained, were served by the Castle Frank stream which flowed through the northerly part of the property on its way to the Don River. He dwelt at length on the idyllic beauty of the glen and, in a carrying whisper, reminded his audience that old Dr. Baldwin had placed his family's burial ground at the top of a leafy bank overlooking the picturesque ravine.

The bidding was resumed, this time with reverential dignity, and the price advanced slowly to £3500. Pausing and leaning forward as if to catch the faintest whisper, Mr. Wakefield asked, "Am I offered £3550?" The silence of the room was broken only by the hissing of a gaslight. "Do I hear £3550?" Mr. Wakefield called again sharply.

Raising his arm, James Austin finally answered, "£3550."

Mr. Wakefield continued, "I am offered £3550 for this choice property." He repeated the figure several times. And then nodding his head vigorously in Austin's direction, he crashed his gavel down like a thunderclap.

The crowd broke up in a hubbub of talk and, perhaps in relief, sporadic applause rippled across the back of the room. As Austin was leaving a well-wisher caught his arm and questioned the price he had paid for the property in the light of the depressed times. Austin replied tersely, "Things are worth what they'll bring on the market," and turning away he stepped out onto King Street. He had arranged for his sleigh to meet him at the door and climbing in and settling himself under a fur robe, he instructed his coachman to drive to his house on Jarvis Street. As they turned the corner at the St. Lawrence Hall, the clock high above them in its weathered green cupola struck the half hour after twelve.

A year later, from the grounds of the imposing new *Spadina* he had built on the site of the old, James Austin and his family were to listen to the rising sound of the church bells, and watch the fireworks blazing over the city, as Toronto celebrated the birth of the new Dominion.

Chapter 10

James Austin Builds a New Spadina

The cheerless winter of 1865-66 had finally yielded to an early spring, but the citizens of Toronto had few grounds for rejoicing. The depression, which had gripped the country since the end of the American Civil War, was showing no signs of letting up. Earlier hopes of a union between the two Canadas and the Atlantic provinces had collapsed. To cap it all, bands of armed Fenians were training openly along the American border, from Detroit to New Brunswick, and were expected to invade Canada at any time.

The Fenian Brotherhood was convinced that a blow struck successfully at Canada could force England to submit to the Fenian dream of a free and independent Irish Republic. Toronto, in fear of attack, hurriedly set up a Defence Committee for the protection of the city, and the dejected townsmen were urged by pulpit and press to contribute to the patriotic cause. William Cawthra, one of the town's wealthiest men, responded with a gift of $1,000 and soared to the top of the subscription list.

In the stone barracks west of Fort York, later known as the Stanley Barracks, the officers of the British 47th Regiment, who had done their best all winter to enliven an indifferent season with sleighing parties on the Toronto Bay and hearty regimental balls, were now confined to their dreary compound on the lakeshore to await the call to arms.

Old Bishop Strachan, in his eighty-eighth year, his hearing and sight failing rapidly, was still occupying the "Palace" he had built on Front Street in 1818, nearly a half-century before. His constant companion, "a tabby cat as big as a dog," passed the daylight hours blissfully asleep in his lap.[1] The venerable prelate had spent the winter fussing over his plans for an early meeting of the Anglican Synod which was intended to elect a coadjutor bishop to relieve him of his diocesan burdens. However, the Fenian threat had compelled him grudgingly to postpone his meeting until the fall. Now he could do nothing more than maintain a fretful vigil by his fireside.

Following the auction sale of his *Spadina* farmlands in February, William Willcocks Baldwin had launched into the task of removing his family's furnishings and effects from *Spadina*. By March 16, 1866, James Austin had registered his deed and taken possession of the eighty-acre property.[2]

While Baldwin was busy clearing out the old dwelling, Austin was developing his plans for his new *Spadina*. In making his decision to demolish Dr. Baldwin's second house and build a third *Spadina* on the site, James Austin was influenced by a number of considerations. In the first place, the location could not be improved upon. It afforded him a matchless view of

112

James Austin's *Spadina*, built in 1866 on the site of the two earlier Baldwin houses. Though the house was later enlarged by his son, Albert William Austin, the mid-Victorian character of the principal rooms is unchanged. The figures standing on the lawn are Miss Jane Watson, a governess, and James Austin. Seated, Mrs. James Austin and her daughter Mrs. George Allan Arthurs of neighbouring *Ravenswood*. The girls on the lawn are Mrs. Arthurs' daughters, Elma and Margaret (Mrs. Sydney Greene). Her oldest daughter, Ada, (Mrs. Victor Cawthra) is seen in the victoria with her uncle Albert W. Austin. Miss Catherine Bright, a sister of Mrs. James Austin, holds shyly to the verandah steps.

—Metropolitan Toronto Library Board

the distant city and the lake beyond it as a result of the 300 feet of open ground that Dr. Baldwin had cleared a half-century before between the house and the brow of the Davenport Hill.

In addition, the rear of the site was already served by driving sheds and stables, and Dr. Baldwin's old house was the hub of a network of private drives and lanes. A deep well, famous in the district because it drew its water from a clear spring beneath the Davenport Hill, was also convenient to the location. And the Honourable Robert Baldwin's cottage library, a comparatively new and solid structure with a cavernous cellar which the statesman had used for storing the produce of his orchard and garden, could be put to good use as a coachman's quarters close to the new *Spadina*.

There is no record of the architect employed by James Austin to prepare

the plans for his house. Indeed, the design probably came from the drawing board of a master-builder working from a pattern book as did many of the plans for the ample farm houses which are illustrated in the county atlases of that day. Mid-Victorian in style, Austin's *Spadina* was planned simply as a commodious and comfortable country house. The informality of its matching side verandahs, one providing a sheltered approach to the main door on the west, the other a cool retreat from the blazing afternoon sun, bespoke an overriding concern with practical comfort rather than architectural pretension. (See page 113.)

Austin retained the main entrance on the west side of his house because it was already served by two private carriage drives: one, the present Austin Terrace, led west across his property to the lot limit of the Wells estate (*Davenport*) where it turned and descended to the Davenport Road along the present Walmer Road Hill; the other, Aunt Maria's Road of the Baldwins' day, provided a more direct route to Yonge Street to the east. It descended the hill to the Davenport Road in the form of an "S" from the present Ardwold Gate subdivision. Part of this historic road, which was cut through the pine woods on the hillside by Dr. Baldwin around 1820, is still extant as a gravelled drive which curves across the *Spadina* lawn to the main entrance of the present house.

The early arrival of spring in 1866 enabled the builders to make a start on the construction of the house immediately after Austin had registered his deed. Labour was plentiful because of the general depression, and by mid-April masons and carpenters were swarming over the site. The dense woods in the present *Casa Loma* area rang with the shouts and curses of the draymen as they urged their horses up the steep carriage drive from the Davenport Road, sweating under loads of stone, lumber, and brick.

Before the work of demolition had begun, James Austin had taken pains to preserve Dr. Baldwin's massive, eight-panelled front door for use at the rear entrance of the house. Through this ancient portal, during the Baldwin regime, had passed many of the country's leading political figures, including the Earl and Countess of Elgin, Louis LaFontaine, John A. MacDonald, Francis Hincks, John Ross, and even Bishop Strachan who, it will be recalled, drove out to *Spadina* in his carriage on a bleak December day in 1858 to attend the funeral rites of his former pupil, the Honourable Robert Baldwin. The ancient door, over ten feet in height, with a heavy iron lock and crudely bolted knocker, is still in use today with its original, elliptical fan transom and sidelights.

The other known links with Dr. Baldwin's two *Spadinas* lie embedded in the basement of the present house. When his shallow cellar was re-excavated to a depth of five feet, in order to provide a more substantial foundation for Austin's brick dwelling, much of the doctor's foundation material — boulders and stones gathered laboriously from the surrounding fields — was used in the construction of the lower walls of the 1866 house. In recent times, a party of workmen tunnelling through the thick walls to install a modern heating system was astonished to encounter several large boulders,

---

When James Austin demolished Dr. Baldwin's *Spadina* in 1866, he preserved the doctor's old front door and incorporated it into the rear entrance of his new *Spadina*. With its original sidelights and elliptical fan transom, the historic door is still in use today.

—Photography by William Robertson

The reception room, at the end of the main entrance hall, is still hung in crimson damask, with gilt mirrors and valances. The room gives access to the drawing room on the right, and through the door on the left, to the present library, originally James Austin's dining room. In Edwardian times visitors were received in this room on Friday, the day designated for calling at *Spadina*.

—Photography by William Robertson

one over three feet in circumference, which had been part of Dr. Baldwin's original foundation.

The pace of building quickened during the lengthening days of May, and by the end of the month the buff brick walls, similar in colour to the brickwork of the St. Lawrence Hall and St. James' Cathedral, were rising proudly over the green *Spadina* farmlands.

At the end of May, a large force of Fenians, their numbers swollen by disgruntled members of the former Union Army, finally struck across the Niagara River and invaded Canada. Troops were rushed from Toronto to the Fort Erie area, and a confused battle was fought at Ridgeway, in which the recently formed Queen's Own Rifles of Canada received its baptism of fire. After a few days of inconclusive manoeuvring, the Fenians finally eluded their pursuers and slipped back into the United States.

Tension ran high in Toronto during the incident, and the masters and boys of the Upper Canada College Rifles had to be called out to mount pickets throughout the defenceless city. Early in June, with the stirring regimental band of the British 47th in attendance, a public funeral was held in Toronto for the five soldiers of the Queen's Own Rifles who had fallen at

The drawing room, *Spadina*, with its original Jacques and Hay furniture still in place. The decorative doorway with Ionic columns which leads to the main hall was substituted in 1910 for the earlier French doors. The 1866 board flooring with carpeting was also replaced at that time with a highly polished hardwood floor.

—Photography by William Robertson

Ridgeway. A vast multitude attended the ceremonies. The town then withdrew into a period of deep and bitter mourning.

The Fenian scare led at once to a revival of talk of the need for Confederation. The principles of union had been rejected by the Atlantic provinces the year before, but they were re-examined with a new urgency when New Brunswick as well was singled out for attack by the Fenians. As a result, in the closing weeks of 1866, the Honourable John A. Macdonald and his colleagues, including representatives from Nova Scotia and New Brunswick, gathered in London, England, to settle the terms of the British North America Act with the British government — the first step in the eventual union of all the Canadian provinces.

As the Confederation delegates were meeting in London, James Austin and his family were settling into their new *Spadina*. Susan, his wife, had some reservations about leaving her comfortable house in the heart of the city, and Austin had found it necessary to assure her that if she found it lonely they would return to Jarvis Street where they had lived since 1852. Their solid, brick house was on the east side of that thoroughfare, just below Gerrard Street. Having offered such an assurance, Austin wisely arranged

One of the fourteen cast-iron grille radiators scattered throughout *Spadina*.
—Photography by William Robertson

for his daughter Anne Jane Arthurs, who had married George Allan Arthurs of Toronto three years before, to occupy the Jarvis Street house while her wary mother acclimatized herself in the outer marches of the city.

James Austin, himself a Methodist, had been married by the Reverend H. J. Grasett (later Dean Grasett) to Susan Bright, the daughter of Lewis and Margaret Bright in St. James' Cathedral on November 28th, 1844. Lewis Bright was an old campaigner of the American Revolutionary War. He had settled in York around 1802, and was an original pewholder of St. James'. The father of sixteen children (three sons served with Brock at Queenston Heights), he lived to an advanced age, and died at Toronto in 1842. Before her marriage, Susan had lived with her widowed mother and two unmarried sisters in the old Bright house on Lot Street, at the northeast corner of the present Queen and James streets. The site is now occupied by part of the T. Eaton Company's downtown store. Of James and Susan Austin's marriage there were five children: Anne Jane (1845), Margaret Louisa (1848), Charles George (1851), James Henry (1853), and Albert William (1857). Charles died in 1864 in his fourteenth year — and as we have noted, Anne was married to George Arthurs in 1863 when she was just seventeen years of age.

Detail of one of the cast-iron grille radiators in *Spadina*. The owl and the squirrel represented the proven Victorian virtues of wisdom and industry. It will be noticed that the industrious squirrel is threatened with attack by a serpent.

As things turned out, James and Susan Austin and their three children made the adjustment quickly and happily to their new domain on the Davenport Hill. True, it was remote from the city. During the winter a strange stillness seemed to possess the land, and at night, from an upstairs window, only a few pale, flickering lights could be seen in the direction of Yorkville. South of Davenport Road, desolate fields and dark stands of pine stretched all the way to Bloor Street. (See page 123.) Their only neighbours were the Wells family at *Davenport,* near Bathurst Street, (See page 122) and to the east, Admiral Augustus Warren Baldwin's widow who held bravely to her lonely *Russell Hill* until the following year when she withdrew to Bond Street.

The new *Spadina* was found at once to be in satisfying harmony with its surroundings. Its lofty ceilings and spacious rooms seemed like a natural extension of the adjacent lawns and open fields. And no detail escaped the eye of the designer in his effort to relate the dwelling to its rural setting. In the rounded arches over the windows, for example, each of the carved keystones depicts a jack-in-the-pulpit or trillium from the *Spadina* glen, a lily-of-the-valley or rose from the garden, a thistle or clover leaf from the field. And the great oaks and maples, the hoary sentinels of the hilltop lands, are represented by a single leaf carved in stone.

Ravenswood, the mid-Victorian house of Anne Austin Arthurs and her husband George Allan Arthurs, was built on the *Spadina* hill in 1868. Mr. John Craig Eaton bought the *Ravenswood* property from Mrs. Arthurs in 1908, demolished this house and built his imposing *Ardwold* on the site.

—Mrs. E. Llewellyn G. Smith

Nor were the woodland creatures of *Spadina* overlooked by the meticulous designer. Throughout the house there are fourteen radiators with ornate cast-iron grilles and white marble tops. Among the scrolls, garlands, and geometric designs of the grilles can be detected, in single and solemn pose, the figures of a squirrel, an owl, and a sparrow. The creatures appear in alternating sections, the squirrel clutching a nut in its paws, the owl glaring balefully from an iron branch, the sparrow trailing a garland from its beak. (See page 119.)

A number of these nature-theme grilles found their way into incongruous settings: one is installed in the reception room at the end of the main hall where the walls today are still hung with crimson damask, where a gilt mirror stands on a white marble mantelpiece almost touching the fine plaster moulding of the ceiling twelve feet above, where a century-old crystal chandelier sparkles and dances in the glow of gilt valances, and where a porcelain urn

A view of the promonotory on the Davenport Hill, later called the "Battery," from which point James Austin and his family observed the skyrockets blazing over Toronto on the night of the Confederation celebrations, July 1, 1867. The brick and stone observation platform is still in use today.

—Private Collection

of classic proportions, supported by a marble-topped radiator, soars above the iron-enmeshed sparrows (See page 116).

In the formal drawing room, as well, to which the reception room gives access, the squirrels and owls, symbolic of industry and wisdom, are permanently enmeshed in two fanciful radiator grilles. This room, which the well-known portrait painter Kenneth Forbes once declared to be the finest example of a Victorian drawing room he had seen in Canada, is over forty-two feet in length. Two bay windows provide a vista of the sweeping lawn to the south, the city and lake beyond it. At each end of the room white marble mantelpieces, complementing the one in the adjoining reception room, support great gilt mirrors. The original furniture, selected by James and Susan Austin from the Toronto showrooms of Jacques and Hay in 1866, is still in place. And two crystal chandeliers, each with its gas fittings, add a final accent of Victorian elegance. (See page 117.)

A view of Toronto from the Bathurst Street Hill, oil on canvas, signed and dated Arthur Cox, A.R.C.A., 1875. The old toll-gate in the foreground bars the entrance to Davenport Road from Bathurst Street which had not then been extended north of Davenport. The Wells property (*Davenport*) is seen to the left with its private carriage drive descending easterly on to the Davenport Road, and to the south the Howland Plains stretching to Bloor Street. The scene was painted from a promontory in the present Wychwood Park.

—Private Collection

For the Austin boys, James and Albert, aged thirteen and nine, the *Spadina* farmlands were a source of unending excitement and adventure. They both attended Upper Canada College on King Street West, driving down in the morning with their father in his carriage, and returning in the afternoon in the creaking, horse-drawn cars of the Toronto Street Railway which plodded up Yonge Street to their terminal near the Red Lion Hotel, just north of Bloor Street. When free from school, the boys helped with the chores around the place, and delighted in exploring the dark and mysterious glen through which the clear waters of the Castle Frank stream sparkled and leapt on their way to the Don River. They also liked to wander along the crest of the Davenport Hill. From a vantage point on the Wells property close to Bathurst Street, they were able to look out upon the manoeuvres of the British troops from the Garrison on what were then known as the Howland Plains. The plains stretched from Bloor Street to the Davenport Road, along the east side of the present Bathurst Street. In that day Bathurst Street had not been extended north of the old tollgate at its entrance to Davenport Road.

But above all, the curiosity and interest of the Austin boys was most keenly aroused by the migratory flights of wild pigeons and hawks across the *Spadina* lands. Many years later, Albert W. Austin recalled shooting the

A view of Toronto from the *Spadina* farmlands on the Davenport Hill painted around 1875. Davenport Road lies at the foot of the hill as well as to the extreme left where it curves southward towards Yorkville and Yonge Street. The figure under the oak tree is young Jim Austin with his black retriever. The site from which the view was taken now lies in today's Ardwold Gate subdivision. Oil on canvas, unsigned.

—Mrs. E. Llewellyn G. Smith

wild pigeons, or passenger pigeons as they were sometimes called, in the woods as a boy:

> The wild pigeons (now extinct) made this wood their resting place after their long flight across the lake in the spring time. The wild pigeons caused great trouble at times by devouring the seed as fast as sown, and many were caught in nets, and afterwards sold for trap shooting. Unlike the tame pigeon, which, when released from the trap, will go in all directions, the wild pigeon would go straight away from the trap. If ever a bad shot was made, the bird was sure to be brought down by some one of the numerous outfielders who always seemed to know by instinct when a wild pigeon shoot was about to take place.
>
> While the wild pigeon predominated in the spring time, the fall brought millions of hawks from the north. These birds seemed to dread the cold more than others, and were the first to go southward. They would fly south until they saw the big Lake Ontario, when they would rest in the great trees of *Spadina* and prey on the young chickens. The hawks would then feel their way south around the Lake via Hamilton, rather than cross. On a clear day it was a beautiful sight to see these graceful birds in flight—against the blue sky. The woods also contained many woodcock and partridge.[3]

At midnight on June 30, 1867, the bells of St. James' Cathedral rang out joyously across the city to announce the birth of the new Dominion. Confederation was at last a fact, and Toronto the capital of the new province of Ontario. Thousands of visitors swarmed into the city to join in the July 1st celebrations. There were military displays, musical entertainments,

parades, bonfires, and banquets. James Austin's family watched the evening spectacle from a small promontory at the top of the Davenport Hill — a location they were later to call the "Battery." Rustic benches and chairs were set round, and the party remained until a late hour observing the rockets soaring over the city like comets, and in the nearby town of Yorkville, the blaze of bonfires and fireworks.

Anne and George Arthurs had journeyed up from Jarvis Street with their two young daughters to spend the holiday at *Spadina.* To mark the occasion, James Austin offered them a site on the *Spadina* property to build a house for themselves if they wished to do so. The Arthurs accepted his proposal with enthusiasm, and since Susan Austin was now happily reconciled to her life in the country, plans were set in motion for the selection of a location, commencement of construction, and the sale of James Austin's Jarvis Street house.

The Arthurs decided to place their dwelling, which was to be named *Ravenswood,* about 150 yards east of *Spadina,* close to the lot limit which divided the Austin property from Mrs. Baldwin's *Russell Hill.* (See page 120.) The old Aunt Maria's Road, which descended the Davenport Hill just in front of the new Arthurs house, served as their main carriage drive, although one branch of it continued to lead across the *Spadina* lawn, as it does today, to James Austin's main entrance. In 1868, as *Ravenswood* was being completed, Austin took steps to improve the other carriage drive which led to his house from the west. At the foot of the present Walmer Road Hill, where it enters the Davenport Road, he built an English-style gate-keeper's lodge, and on both sides of the long driveway from that point to his house at the easterly end of the present Austin Terrace, he planted rows of chestnut trees. In later years the densely shaded driveway became renowned for the dazzling beauty of its blossoms in the spring.[4] A few of the ancient chestnut trees of that time, blasted by a century of winter winds, still survive on the grounds of *Spadina* today.

During the final stages of the building of *Ravenswood,* the Arthurs lived briefly at *Spadina,* with James and Susan Austin, so that they could better supervise the construction of their new house. The Austin dwelling at 233 Jarvis Street was sold on March 25, 1868. The times again being buoyant, James Austin was gratified to receive $7,500 for it—and to have his judgment confirmed in having paid William Willcocks Baldwin £3,550, the equivalent of $14,200, two years earlier for the 80-acre *Spadina* property when real estate prices were severely depressed.

Baldwin also entered the real estate market again in 1868. This time he sold off the easterly 138 feet of the "Baldwin Family Residence" property at the northeast corner of Bay and Front Streets — part of the town lot which his grandfather, Dr. W. W. Baldwin, had bought from the Honourable Peter Russell in 1806. Baldwin received $8,000 for the parcel, but wisely retained the old corner house with its frontage of 77 feet on Front Street which he leased to advantage for many years. In 1866, he had moved to a place in Yorkville, and the city directory of that year records that he filled

---

Susan Bright Austin (1817-1907), the daughter of Lewis and Margaret Bright who settled in the Town of York around 1802. She married James Austin in 1844, and died at *Spadina* in her 90th year. Jane, one of her numerous sisters, married Charles Scadding, the older brother of the Toronto historian, the Reverend Dr. Henry Scadding.

—Private Collection

the post of "distributor of Law Stamps" at Osgoode Hall. While not en-
dowed with a strong constitution, William Willcocks Baldwin nonetheless
managed to discharge the duties of his office with unaffected dignity for a
long period, adding colour and continuity to the lengthy Baldwin association
with the Law Society of Upper Canada. (See page 97.)

Early in the morning of January 12, 1869, an air of suppressed excitement filled *Spadina*. The entire household had risen with the sun in preparation for Margaret Austin's marriage that day to Captain William Hamilton
Joice of the 13th Hussars, a British regular regiment stationed at the Toronto
Garrison. Maggie, as the Victorians called her, was the youngest daughter
of James and Susan Austin. She was now in her twenty-first year. The wedding was to take place at 11 o'clock at St. James' Cathedral on King Street,
to be followed by a wedding breakfast at *Spadina*.

Old Matthew, James Austin's coloured coachman, a runaway slave who
had turned up in Toronto during the Civil War, had spent the previous day
polishing to gleaming perfection the black panels and silver lamps of Austin's carriage—the same carriage he had lent in 1860 for the use of the
Prince of Wales (later King Edward VII) at the time of his sojourn in
Toronto. And *Spadina,* too, had been scrubbed and polished for the gala
event.

The wedding breakfast after the service was pronounced a memorable
success. Lieut. Colonel Jenyns, the commanding officer of the 13th Hussars,
gave his permission for the regimental band to play at the gathering, and his
scarlet-coated musicians arranged themselves in the bay window of Susan
Austin's parlour. Their arias, noteworthy for the vigour and determination
with which they were rendered, greeted the guests as they arrived at *Spadina*
half-frozen from the ordeal of the long drive from King Street.

After paying their respects to the bridal party in the reception room,* the
guests passed into the drawing-room where they clung stubbornly for a
while to the blazing fireplaces at each end of the spacious room. They were
revived and dislodged at last by generous glasses of steaming, hot punch.
Methodism hid its face that day at *Spadina*.

The reporter of the *Daily Telegraph* recognized a number of familiar
faces in the crowd: Colonel Anderson, Lieutenant-Colonel and Mrs. Jenyns,
Mr. and Mrs. C. W. Buntin, Mr. James E. Ellis, Captain Fryer, A.D.C.,
Mr. Gooderham, Mr. and Mrs. Frank Smith, Mr. and Mrs. Worts,
Miss Worts, Mr. and Mrs. Rice Lewis, Mr. and Mrs. Michie, Miss Fulton,
Mrs. William Arthurs, Mr. and Mrs. Robert Gooderham, Mr. Fred Cumber-
land, Jr., Mr. T. Allan, Mr. John Shedden, Captain Ford, Mrs. Bright,
Dr. Bardy, Mr. and Mrs. Scadding, "and a number of others, among whom
were many military gentlemen."

Finally, after several spirited toasts, the bride and groom fled down the
front stairs to a waiting carriage and the band played its last stirring number.
The remaining carriages were summoned, and the guests withdrew one by
one into the fading light of a January afternoon.

---

*The *Daily Telegraph* reported: "The bridesmaids, Misses Worts, Bright, Scadding
and Harrington, were all dressed alike, in white, low-necked, corded silk dresses,
with appropriate wreaths and trimmings. The groomsmen, Captain Clay and
Messrs. Wells, Ellis and Bieber, all of the 13th Hussars, were attired in the
ordinary black, with white gloves."

Later in the summer of 1869, the captain's regiment was recalled to England where it was stationed in the old cathedral town of York. Margaret's letters were awaited eagerly by her family who were relieved to detect in them no trace of homesickness, nor dissatisfaction with her life in an English barracks. In the void created by her departure from *Spadina,* and with her two boys absent at school all day, Susan Austin soon found an absorbing interest in Anne and George Arthurs' growing family at neighbouring *Ravenswood.*[5]

Chapter 11

The Men of Montreal

James Austin had reason to be pleased with the results of his efforts to further improve his hilltop property during the summer of 1869. In the glen behind the two houses, *Spadina* and *Ravenswood,* new footpaths had been cleared through the dense undergrowth, and rustic bridges built over the Castle Frank stream. And he had entirely rebuilt the low plank bridge (now the site of the Spadina Road bridge) that had carried vehicles across the creek in the Baldwins' day. In the rolling hills north of the glen, stretching on both sides of today's Spadina Road to the present St. Clair Avenue, the summer crops were well advanced. The new gardens, shrubs, and trees around the Austin and Arthurs houses were firmly established, and the lawns and carriage drives had taken on something of the character of the quiet parklands surrounding the Irish country houses Austin remembered as a boy in County Armagh.

Insofar as his financial interests were concerned, Austin found much to occupy his time. He kept an office in the new Bank of Toronto chambers at the corner of Wellington and Church streets, and drove into town in his carriage each day. Aside from attending to his own investments, which were then chiefly in land and mortgages, he devoted considerable time to the affairs of the Consumers' Gas Company of Toronto. He had been elected a director of that company, it will be recalled, in 1859, and in 1867 was appointed its vice-president. He was also a director of the Canadian Bank of Commerce, having been elected to that office as the bank opened its doors for business in May 1867.[1] In the summer of 1869, however, he was viewing that connection with growing uneasiness.

The Bank of Commerce, based in Toronto, had prospered from the start. Branches had been opened in London, St. Catharines, and Barrie. Now, just two years later, its ambitious president, the Honourable William McMaster, was talking about increasing the bank's capital from one million to four million dollars. Some of his shareholders disagreed with him. Men like James Austin, Frank Smith (later the Honourable Sir Frank Smith), and Joseph H. Mead, a rich Toronto fur merchant, felt there was simply not enough business in sight to justify so large an expansion of the bank's resources. They argued that even if the additional funds could be raised, the bank would be tempted to reach out too aggressively for new business, and thus expose itself to the fate that had just overwhelmed the Royal Canadian Bank. Established in Canada West in 1865, the Royal Canadian had quickly opened fifteen branches, and by 1867, as the Commerce was being launched, it had added five more. By 1869, though technically solvent, its affairs had become so involved it had to suspend operations. The frantic pace of expansion had left its management confused and winded. On the face of it, McMaster's dissident group of shareholders could hardly be blamed for their anxiety over what was felt to be a visionary scheme.[2]

Nor was that all. Just three years earlier, the financial condition of the province had been in a state of chaos. In 1866, the ailing Bank of Upper Canada, long identified with the Family Compact in Toronto, had finally collapsed. And the following year, the influential Commercial Bank of Canada, another Upper Canada institution, sank from sight under the weight of an unmarketable portfolio of American railroad bonds. Public confidence in the new province of Ontario's financial institutions was at low ebb.

McMaster, however, was not inclined to concern himself with the mistakes of the past. They were not of his making. The drummer he heard, and was to march to, at that moment was sounding the beat of a fast-moving business recovery. The country's spirits were rising. The depression at the end of the American Civil War had been forgotten. The talk was of expansion, and the opening up of the Canadian Northwest. The great age of the railroad was knitting together the old commercial centres of the East and would soon lead to the exploitation of the limitless, unsettled regions of the West.

But prosperity in those days did not mean a burgeoning demand on the banks for large capital sums: the economy of the country was still young and immature. In 1870, for example, only 181,679 Canadians were employed in manufacturing, and that figure probably included hundreds of blacksmiths and harness makers toiling throughout the new Dominion.[3] To the banks, prosperity generally meant a quickening in demand for a multitude of small credits—loans to the country's wholesalers and retailers, to importers of dry goods and groceries, to exporters of basic commodities like grain and timber. Because high volume implied a multiplicity of small transactions, it imposed a correspondingly heavy burden of vigilance on the management of a bank in granting and supervising its loans. Those in dissent with McMaster felt that the new Canadian Bank of Commerce had neither consolidated its position sufficiently, nor developed an adequate staff to cope with the huge increase in business that was now desired by its president. The Royal Canadian Bank fiasco was clearly a case in point—vaulting ambition that had overlept itself.

William McMaster, a fervent Baptist and a later benefactor of McMaster University, had arrived in York, a young Irish immigrant, in 1833. After amassing a fortune as a Toronto dry goods merchant, he turned his flourishing business over to his nephews and sought other channels for the release of his powerful energies. With a massive head sunk on a heavy neck he invited comparison with a bulldog, with which he shared in equal measure the qualities of stubbornness and tenacity. "A phrenologist," Nicholas Flood Davin wrote, "could not have a better text than the head of William McMaster."[4] An uncompromising teetotaler, McMaster built the Baptist Church at the corner of Toronto's Gerrard and Jarvis streets. He was also instrumental in raising McMaster Hall on Bloor Street, which still stands today adjacent to the present Varsity Stadium. His extensive property *Rathnelly* lay on the west side of Avenue Road, just below the Davenport Hill. He held interests in a number of financial institutions, and for a time was the Toronto director of the Bank of Montreal. It was inevitable, how-

A hundred years ago rustic bridges like the one shown here spanned the Castle Frank stream in the densely wooded *Spadina* glen. Today the creek has been swallowed by a trunk sewer, and the floor of the ravine, once profuse with trilliums, jack-in-the-pulpit, and wild violets, is now stripped of its natural growth.

—Private Collection

ever, that sooner or later his ruggedly individualistic personality would clash with that of E. H. King, the "Napoleonic" general manager of the Bank of Montreal. That bank had been pursuing increasingly restrictive policies throughout Canada West, and McMaster, his Christian patience exhausted, resigned abruptly in protest, and turned his wealth and influence to the creation of the Canadian Bank of Commerce.

"We do not oppose anyone," McMaster declared bluntly when, as its first president, he announced the objectives of the new bank, "all we seek is the good of the country. We believe that all the floating capital which some banks get hold of is loaned out of the country. Our policy is to benefit our respective localities by employing our own and the floating capital coming under our control, in the support of the trade and industry of the place."

His manifesto was a thinly veiled criticism of the Bank of Montreal. During the U.S. Civil War that bank had withdrawn gold from the province for highly profitable speculation in New York. Later, after writing off a million dollars in bad and doubtful debts in Canada West between 1863 and 1866, the despotic E. H. King had decreed that his bank would grant no further accommodation to the province's farmers, merchants, and produce dealers. Inevitably, such action by the largest bank in the land had severely restricted the credit resources of the new province of Ontario. It was interpreted by the mercantile and financial interests of Toronto as further evidence of the monopolistic designs of the financiers of Montreal who were known to have their eye on the rich, rural hinterland of southern Ontario, and beyond it, the Canadian Northwest. The glittering prize, the financial domination of Ontario, now seemed within E. H. King's grasp. The bank that William McMaster headed, then, was mainly conceived as a bastion of defence against the men of Montreal.[5]

A new class of capitalist, now emerging in Ontario, marked the final stage in the natural evolution of a group of men who a quarter of a century before had been carefully building their fortunes as millers, wholesalers, and shopkeepers. They were the embodiment of the Victorian ethic: they were doers not dreamers. Their wealth was the fruit of hard, unremitting toil, not the accident of inheritance. In their youth they had worn the habit of frugality unashamedly, like devout monks sworn to eternal poverty. Now as men of property they were proud and confident in their strength. Their word was their bond. They attended their churches and meeting houses each sabbath dressed in sombre frock coats scented with lavender water, and offered fervent thanks to their God, who they were certain had a good deal to do with their temporal success. But he was not a benevolent God. He was a God to be feared. "Watch out," they would say darkly, "for the man who hasn't the fear of God in his heart." And on the Lord's day their gas-lit houses would be shuttered and muted as if a corpse lay in the parlour. Loud laughter and jollity were taboo. Card-playing was forbidden. Only religious music was tolerated. The books that were read pensively on Sunday dealt with biblical subjects and pointed wholesome morals.

The wives of the Toronto Victorians, resigned to the black attire made popular by Queen Victoria's perpetual mourning, were serenely content to preside over their domestic establishments. During the week they drove out occasionally in their carriages to the best shops on King Street, or visited their favourite charities, but the management of their houses, the rearing of their children, and the coddling of their husbands were the focal point of their life and interest. They generally recruited their female servants from the local Orphans' Home, and lodged them in cellar bedrooms. They treated them with firmness and kindness, and their charges responded with a matching degree of respect and loyalty. The highest praise those Victorians could bestow was reserved for a man or woman who possessed the virtues of diligence and thrift. The only aristocracy they knew and believed in was one of human worth. The glitter of a ball at Government House was dismissed as a piece of tedious frippery, and they justified their own reluctant attendance on the grounds that the lieutenant-governor had to be upheld because of the stability and continuity he contributed to their congenial system of government. Young men who approached their heavily chaperoned daughters, unless they had means or a useful career in sight, were viewed with unmasked suspicion and hostility. Our Victorians were never misty-eyed about the subject of love. That was a condition, they believed, that was as ephemeral as a shadow playing on the pathway of life, unless, of course, worthwhile financial resources were present to give it substance.

And so, as William McMaster moved unrelentingly to expand his bank's assets, the grumblings of concern among some of his directors and shareholders became more audible. Throughout the winter months of 1869-70, James Austin pondered his course of action. He reflected upon the circum-

One of the shaded carriage drives on the *Spadina* property, this part led north from *Ravenswood* to the coachman's cottage overlooking the glen. The drive now forms part of the present Ardwold Gate road.

—Private Collection

stances that had led to his election as a director of the Commerce in May 1867: he had been appointed to fill the vacancy caused by the dramatic resignation of John Macdonald, M.P.P., his neighbour at *Oaklands* on the Davenport Hill. Macdonald, who was known as Toronto's "Merchant Prince," served as a founding director of the Commerce for the brief span of three weeks. Just as the bank was preparing to open its first Toronto office at the southeast corner of Yonge and Colborne streets, he had a sharp clash of opinion with McMaster, and stalked from the boardroom. His resignation caused a flurry of comment in Toronto's financial circles. James Austin was anxious to avoid a repetition of that painful occurrence. Veering off a collision course with McMaster, he decided to withhold his hand until the annual meeting in June 1870. He then quietly informed the president that he would not stand for re-election as a director of the bank.

During the summer of 1870, the burden of his association with McMaster laid aside, James Austin, now in his fifty-eighth year, settled back at *Spadina* to enjoy the life of a country gentleman. Word had earlier reached the Austin family from York, England, that Margaret Austin Joice had given birth to a boy in May: the child was to be named Charles Albert for two of Margaret's brothers. However, the gratifying news of the arrival of James and Susan Austin's first grandson was clouded by a later, disquieting, report from Margaret's husband, Captain William Hamilton Joice. He informed them that her recovery from her confinement was proceeding with painful slowness, and that it was her wish to return to Canada as soon as she and her infant son were able to travel. The dank and dismal English barracks at York were clearly no place for the period of convalescence that now seemed necessary for the ailing Margaret. Captain Joice assured James Austin that he would apply for leave of absence from his regiment at the earliest possible moment in order to bring Margaret and their son safely home to Toronto. Otherwise, the summer days at *Spadina* flowed on in unhurried monotony.

But elsewhere in Toronto, in the law offices of Ross, Lauder, and Mulock, a group of men was meeting fretfully throughout the humid, summer months as they struggled with the perplexities of launching a new bank. In June 1869, responding to the confident and prosperous mood of the country, they had obtained a charter for a bank to be located in Toronto. It was to be called The Dominion Bank. The preamble to its act of incorporation, which loosely described the purpose of the fledgeling institution, ran as follows:

> Whereas John Worthington, James Crowther, John Crawford, M.P., the Honorable J. C. Aikens, Walter Sutherland Lee, Joseph Gould, the Honorable John Ross, James Holden and Aaron Ross, and others, have by their Petition prayed that they and their legal representatives might be incorporated for the purpose of establishing a Bank in the City of Toronto; and whereas it would be conducive to the general prosperity of that section of the country and greatly facilitate and promote the agricultural and commercial growth of the said locality; and whereas it is but just that the said persons and others who see fit to associate themselves should be incorporated for the said purpose: Therefore, Her Majesty, by and with the advice and consent of the Senate and House of Commons of Canada, enacts as follows: . . .

The provisional directors who were named in the preamble were all prominent in the commercial and professional life of the Toronto district of that day: John Worthington, the first of the petitioners named, was a

well-known Toronto building contractor who owned one of the largest
quarries in the state of New York; James Crowther was a barrister of the
firm of Bell and Crowther; and John Crawford, also a barrister, had played
an important part in the promotion of the narrow-gauge Toronto and
Nipissing Railway. He was shortly to become Ontario's third lieutenant-
governor. The Honourable J. C. Aikens had been called to the Senate at
Confederation, and had become secretary of state in Sir John Macdonald's
first Dominion Ministry. The Honourable John Ross, the son-in-law of the
late Honourable Robert Baldwin, was the head of the firm of Ross, Lauder,
and Mulock. He had played an active role in public and business life, as
solicitor-general and speaker of the Legislative Council in the old province
of Canada, as senator and speaker of the Upper House in the new Dominion,
and for ten years as president of the Grand Trunk Railway. Walter Sutherland Lee, a Toronto financier, served for many years as the manager of the
Western Canada Loan and Savings Company.

The other three petitioners were all influential residents of Ontario
County: Joseph Gould was the leading business figure in the Uxbridge
district where his woollen mills, saw mills, and flour mills had contributed
to the general prosperity of the area. He had turned out at Montgomery's
Tavern with Mackenzie's ill-fated supporters, and later represented North
Ontario in the Legislature. James Holden, of Whitby, a former newspaper
man, was the chief builder and later the managing director of the Whitby
and Port Perry Railway, then under construction between the Scugog chain
of inland lakes and Lake Ontario. As Dr. O. D. Skelton put it: "In
Mr. Holden's eyes, the first link in a railway to Georgian Bay, a railway which
in its turn was to be only the first link in a road to the Pacific." Aaron
Ross, a director of the same railway, was a wealthy merchant of Port Perry.[6]

Though not named in the petition for incorporation, William Mulock,
a young partner in the Ross firm, played a dogged part in the long series
of meetings that were to ensue before The Dominion Bank finally became
operative. He was later to become the Honourable Sir William Mulock, a
chief justice of Ontario, and the holder of other high offices in the public
life of Canada.

The provisional committee that had been set up for the new bank in
1869 had its high hopes dashed by an indifferent public response to its first
offering of shares. With an authorized capitalization of one million dollars,
their special charter required them to secure a minimum subscription of
$400,000 of which $100,000 had to be fully paid up before they could begin
operations. In September of that year, with little progress in sight, the
chastened committee finally decided to place its subscription books in the
hands of the brokerage firm of Pellatt and Osler, which had been formed in
1867, following the collapse of the Bank of Upper Canada. Both Henry
Pellatt (the father of the later Sir Henry Pellatt of *Casa Loma*) and Edmund
Boyd Osler, then aged twenty-four, had been members of the junior staff
of that venerable institution. They cheerfully undertook to secure the required subscriptions for a commission of $2,000 in cash and $2,000 in
stock if successful, and nothing if the full amount was not raised. This arrangement was as unproductive of results as the provisional committee had
been in its earlier, solitary efforts. Clearly, investors were not convinced of
the soundness of the venture, notwithstanding the weight and influence of
the men who had lent their names to the petition for incorporation.

And so, matters had dragged on through 1869 and into the fall of 1870.

Valuable time was consumed in considering the absorption of the dormant Royal Canadian Bank in order to secure the substantial capital interest of that bank's chief stockholders—but those negotiations came to naught. Finally, the energetic James Holden of Whitby, his enthusiasm unimpaired, decided to approach James Austin to enlist his help in getting the new Dominion Bank under way. He was a friend of Austin's, and was aware of the circumstances that had led to his withdrawal from the board of the Canadian Bank of Commerce the previous June.

Austin warily delayed his decision while he assessed the extent of his own enthusiasm for another banking venture. The congenial life of his *Spadina* farmlands was exerting a strong pull in the direction of semi-retirement. Measured in terms of the brilliant success of the Bank of Commerce, the three critical and formative years he had spent with that institution had been intensely satisfying to him. He was now being asked to travel that uncertain road again—although this time the road was even less clearly defined and already marred by pitfalls, detours, and disappointments. When McMaster had invited him in 1867 to join the directorate of the Commerce, he had responded quickly because he was devoted to the idea of building up Toronto's financial strength against the city's threatened domination by the men of Montreal. That battle had not yet been won.

In January 1870, Frank Smith, Austin's lifelong friend and a leading wholesale merchant, had told a Toronto audience that "in a few years Toronto was bound to outstrip in enterprise, and solid commercial progress every other city in Canada as a great trading centre." And the *Montreal Gazette,* taking note of his awful prophecy, grimly warned its readers: "We are satisfied that Montreal must make active exertions to maintain her position as a business centre, or she will be cut out by Toronto which is making vigorous and well-directed efforts to that end."[7]

And it was on this point that Austin's decision finally turned. After conferring with certain of his friends, men like Frank Smith, Joseph H. Mead, and Peleg Howland, whose help he knew would be indispensable to the success of the new bank, he informed a delighted James Holden that he and his associates would throw in their lot with The Dominion Bank.

And so it was that a few of the early provisional directors met again on November 18, 1870, in the law offices of Ross, Lauder, and Mulock. Unlike the gloomy meetings of the past, a new and wholly unfamiliar mood of confidence and excitement quickened their deliberations. It was as if the shutters had been thrown open, allowing the sunlight to come streaming in. A momentous resolution was quickly moved by John Worthington, seconded by the ebullient James Holden, that "Messrs. James Austin, Frank Smith, Peleg Howland, Samuel Nordheimer and J. H. Mead shall be and are hereby declared associates with the Provisional Directors of The Dominion Bank."

The impact of the announcement of the accession of the new group was immediate and far-reaching. The stock books were closed the next day. Over $500,000 was subscribed. The shares, which had been treated by investors with cold indifference the week before, soared to a premium of nine dollars.

Like a seasoned general taking over a new command, James Austin made a rapid assessment of the bank's position. One of the first acts was to secure Robert Henry Bethune of the Quebec Bank as cashier, or general manager, as the office was later called. A banking office had to be obtained in Toronto, and the store of Edwin H. Harris at 40 King Street East was selected at an annual rental of $1,100. And the bank's first string of branches demanded careful attention. Sites were finally chosen in Whitby, Oshawa, Orillia, and Uxbridge. Austin also introduced a concept that was new to Canadian banking practice: he decided to open a branch office in Toronto, on Queen Street West, mainly for the convenience of savings depositors. "You lead, let others follow," was one of Austin's oft-repeated mottoes. The Dominion Bank was the first Canadian bank to open a second branch in the same city—and James Austin became known as the father of the branch banking system of Canada.

By January 10, 1871, the preliminary arrangements for launching the bank had been completed, and on that day, in the Toronto Mechanics' Institute, the final organizational meeting was held. Austin was in the chair, and the tireless William Mulock acted as secretary. James Austin, James Crowther, Peleg Howland, James Holden, Joseph H. Mead, Frank Smith, and John Worthington were elected directors. Samuel Nordheimer, the head of the King Street firm of A. & S. Nordheimer, piano dealers, withdrew at the last moment on the grounds of his frequent absences from town, and because of the pressure of his personal affairs. The Honourable John Ross, one of the early promoters of the bank, and slated to be its vice-president, lay fatally ill in his Dufferin Street home on the Davenport Hill. At a later meeting of the directors that day, James Austin was elected president, and the office of vice-president was filled by Peleg Howland; he was prominent in the milling industry, and was a member of a remarkable family of Quaker origin which had come to Canada from the United States in the 1830's. His brother, Sir William Howland, was president of the Ontario Bank, and another brother, H. S. Howland, was soon to become the first president of the Imperial Bank of Canada.[8]

On February 1, 1871, the new bank opened its doors for business. Once again, William Mulock, the bank's young lawyer, was pressed into service. "Mr. Bethune asked me," he later recalled,

> to go down to the Bank of Toronto with him to draw out the $100,000 and put it in our treasury so that The Dominion Bank might issue its own notes. So we went down in a two-horse cart, a rickety old cart, and I was to stay in it while he went in and brought out the gold. They brought out so many bags that we feared the floor would give way before we got over to our own bank — the roads were bad and rough. At all events I think the gold weighed nearly a fourth of a ton. But we carried it safely and deposited it.[9]

The success of James Austin's new bank, like William McMaster's four years before, seemed assured within a few months of its opening. Of greater importance, perhaps, was the fact that Ontario's confidence in its own financial institutions was now in the process of being restored. The solid, plodding performance of the Bank of Toronto since its inception in 1856, the remarkable success of the Canadian Bank of Commerce since 1867, and now the public's unqualified acceptance of the new Dominion Bank, all were critical elements in the restoration of that confidence. And as a corollary, the emergence at that time of a new, capitalist class in Toronto, tough, shrewd and uncompromising, knelled distantly but with ominous clarity the decline of Montreal as the financial centre of the country.

Chapter 12

A Railroad Saga

When Samuel Nordheimer, who had been nominated as a director of The Dominion Bank, withdrew his name in January 1871, he explained that his frequent absences from town, together with the pressure of his personal affairs, precluded his devoting the time he felt necessary to the business of the new bank. This was entirely true. Nordheimer, then forty-seven, had just become engaged to marry Edith Louise Boulton, a striking woman of twenty-five. He was in the throes of negotiating the purchase of a 25½-acre property on the Davenport Hill, adjoining on the east James Austin's *Spadina* farmlands. Here, on the crest of the hill, he planned to build a magnificent house, and name it *Glenedyth* for his fiancée.[1]

Edith Boulton was the daughter of James Boulton, a Hamilton barrister, who was a son of Judge D'Arcy Boulton. His brother, D'Arcy Boulton, Jr., had built *The Grange* in Toronto in 1817. That ancient citadel of Family Compact days was now occupied by her cousin William Henry Boulton, who, we may assume, was the approving host at a number of carefully arranged receptions in her honour. The engagement of Edith Boulton, a woman of impeccable social credentials, to Nordheimer, a self-made man of means, fitted by almost any measure the Victorian ideal of a desirable marriage.

Samuel Nordheimer, accompanied by his older brother Abraham, had emigrated to New York City in 1839 at the age of fourteen. They had left Memsdorf in Bavaria to seek their fortune together in the New World. After a short period in New York where they became interested in the music trade, they decided to move to Kingston in Canada West, and in the mid-forties finally transferred their business to Toronto. Within a few years the King Street rooms of piano-importers A. & S. Nordheimer had become something of a Toronto landmark.

A musically gifted man of urbane charm, Samuel Nordheimer was quick to recognize the need to create a more buoyant market for his pianos. To accomplish this, he set about the task, almost single-handed, of elevating the musical taste of the entire country. Because of his connections throughout the musical world, he succeeded in persuading a number of celebrated artists, both vocalists and pianists, to visit Toronto long before the city could otherwise have hoped to qualify for inclusion in the concert tours of America. When Jenny Lind, the world-famous singer, appeared in Toronto for a series of concerts in the new St. Lawrence Hall, in October, 1853, it was natural that the ticket sales would be handled through A. & S. Nordheimer's King

Glenedyth, the Victorian mansion of Mr. and Mrs. Samuel Nordheimer, was built on the Davenport Hill in 1871 on the site of Captain A. W. Baldwin's *Russell Hill*. Glenedyth was demolished in the 1920's following the death of Mr. and Mrs. Nordheimer in 1912.

—The Nordheimer Family

Street store. The place was heavily shuttered on that memorable occasion, and was the scene of a near-riot as a great crowd milled round seeking tickets for the "Swedish Nightingale's" performances.

In addition to arranging concerts by musicians from abroad, Nordheimer personally organized local music festivals, and encouraged the development of philharmonic societies. He was president for many years of the Philharmonic Society of Toronto. By the time of his marriage in 1871, his name was a household word throughout the country.

The property on the Davenport Hill that Samuel Nordheimer bought in January 1871, was part of the old 200-acre farm lot (No. 23) that Captain Augustus Warren Baldwin had purchased from Elizabeth Russell in 1817 for £200. The 25½-acre parcel, for which Nordheimer paid $8,100, included the captain's frame house *Russell Hill* which had been built on the crest of the ridge in 1819. The other parties to the Nordheimer transaction were William Augustus Baldwin of *Mashquoteh,* and the heirs of his late brother, the Honourable Robert Baldwin.

Originally part of the Honourable Peter Russell's 900-acre *Petersfield* farm, which stretched from the present Queen Street to Eglinton Avenue, the piece of property purchased by Samuel Nordheimer included the promontory that the receiver general had named the "Sugar Loaf Hill."

Dr. Baldwin's brother had later built his house on a narrow strip of tableland on the top of "Sugar Loaf Hill." And Samuel Nordheimer did the same. He demolished Captain Baldwin's old house and carefully chose a new site for *Glenedyth,* a little to the west of the Captain's dwelling, close to the lot limit that divided the Austin and Nordheimer properties.

Viewed from the south, the Nordheimer parcel was in the shape of an inverted triangle with its apex at the junction of Davenport Road and Poplar Plains Road; its base was formed by a line drawn from a point high on the bank of the ravine, just north of the *Glenedyth* house, across to a point on Poplar Plains Road close to its present intersection with Russell Hill Road. A century later, it was to become popular to refer to the ravine that extends roughly from Bathurst Street to Russell Hill Road as the "Nordheimer Ravine." There is, however, no historical or geographical justification for the use of this term. The Nordheimer estate lay to the south of the ravine proper, and included only a very small part of it at its eastern entrance. In those days, as the Castle Frank stream left its unhurried, easterly course between the steep banks of the glen, it turned south on to the *Glenedyth* property, along the line of the present Boulton Drive. It was in this area, south of the ravine, that Nordheimer created a picturesque waterfall with a duck pond, and installed ornamental bridges and rustic benches.[2] His beautifully maintained property overlooked the eastern entrance to the ravine, but the ownership of the dark and tangled glen that extended to the west lay as it had before, with the three historic estates of *Davenport, Spadina,* and *Russell Hill.* (See pages 24, 25.)

Samuel Nordheimer's marriage to Edith Boulton took place at St. James' Cathedral on the morning of November 15, 1871. A Toronto newspaper concluded its account of the ceremony by noting that the wedding party drove off in their carriages to the "merry chiming of the Cathedral bells. They proceeded to *The Grange* where Mr. Boulton gave a *déjeuner."*

Meanwhile, the construction of *Glenedyth* was proceeding apace. In fact, by the end of the year, Anne and George Arthurs were watching from their neighbouring *Ravenswood* with astonishment and disbelief as Nordheimer's great Victorian house, with its buff brick walls, vaulted verandahs, and commanding towers, soared above them only a hundred feet away. (See opposite page.)

The building of *Glenedyth* was also closely observed that fall from an upstairs window at *Spadina* by Margaret Austin Joice. She had returned home wearily that summer from England, with her small son Charles, safely escorted by her husband Captain Joice. His regiment, the 13th Hussars, was transferred from York to Edinburgh that year, and he had seized the opportunity to obtain leave of absence and bring his little family back to Canada.

The high hopes for her recovery that were held by Margaret's anxious family when she returned to *Spadina* were not destined to be realized. By the following spring it was apparent that her young life was ebbing away— and on the afternoon of April 22, 1872, she died.[3]

During Margaret's illness, young Charles Joice had been kept amused, coddled, and spoiled by his bevy of cousins at *Ravenswood*: Ada, Elma, and Margaret. Upon the death of his mother, the boy, not yet two, was taken into the Arthurs' family where he was a great favourite until his death in 1887 at the age of seventeen. The boy's father retired with the rank of lieutenant-colonel a few years later, and died at Morpeth in the north of England in 1892.

During the summer of 1872, James Holden of Whitby called upon James Austin in his Toronto office to confer with him about the financial plight of the Whitby & Port Perry Railway. Holden owned shares in the line, and had been a director and ardent supporter of it since its beginnings in 1868. The railway was now faced with bankruptcy.

As a railroad, the Whitby & Port Perry enjoyed little distinction. With an authorized capital of $300,000, it was typical of the many locally sponsored lines of that day whose cacophonous locomotives were fretting the quiet farmlands and sleepy villages of southern Ontario. Its trains ran from Port Whitby on Lake Ontario to Port Perry on Lake Scugog, and took an hour to make the trip, including stops at Brooklin, Myrtle, Manchester, and Prince Albert. Originally conceived as the first link in a line to Georgian Bay, the Whitby & Port Perry now looked for its main traffic to the flourishing lumbering and milling centres of Peterborough, Lindsay, and Bobcaygeon. From these points, sawn lumber, square timber, and barrel staves, as well as grain and flour, were barged down the inland lakes to Port Perry for outward shipment via the Whitby & Port Perry to Lake Ontario.[4]

James Holden, an intense man with piercing eyes and a wiry, black beard, had participated proudly in the new railway's sod-turning ceremonies in Whitby in October 1869. His Royal Highness Prince Arthur, Queen Victoria's son, was on hand to do the honours before a vast crowd of 6,000 souls. Among them were the governor-general, Sir John Young, Lieutenant-Governor William P. Howland of Ontario, Sir John A. Macdonald, the Honourable John Sandfield Macdonald, E. H. King, the autocratic ruler of the Bank of Montreal, and Mayor S. B. Harman of Toronto. A silver spade and a bird's-eye maple wheelbarrow were produced by Mr. Bigelow, the president of the Whitby & Port Perry who, with Mr. Dumble the contractor, helped the Prince turn the first sod amidst a wild ovation.

An observer later remarked wryly that "the auspicious proceedings with which the turning of the first sod was inaugurated did not help the road along." His irreverent comment turned out to be a considerable understatement. Before long, the hapless railway was torn by dissension from within and buffeted by criticism from without. Some of the municipalities that had contributed bonuses and subscribed for stock accused the management of bilking the public; and after the line finally became operative in 1871, there was endless trouble with damaged freight and delays in shipment. It was at this point that James Holden turned to James Austin, doubtless encouraged by the success of his approach to Austin two years before when he was struggling to launch The Dominion Bank.

Holden, who was a fellow director of the bank, proposed that James Austin organize a group to take over the troubled line. As in the case of his entry into the affairs of The Dominion Bank, Austin conferred at once with some of his business associates in Toronto. In this instance he approached James Michie and Alexander T. Fulton, who were prominent Toronto importers and wholesale grocers.*

The new group quickly conducted an investigation into the affairs of the Whitby & Port Perry. They concluded the line was worth saving, and

---

*They were the owners of George Michie & Co., and Fulton, Michie & Co. which operated establishments at the corner of Yonge and Front streets, as well as at 7 King Street West, and which were the predecessor firms of the well-known Michie & Company whose specialty grocery business flourished on King Street West until comparatively recent times.

they agreed to buy it. The composition of the management team was then settled, and James Austin became president of the road, James Michie vice-president, and their beleaguered friend James Holden was confirmed as managing director.

The saga of the railroad, including its rescue by Austin's group, was later related by an eyewitness to the event:

> Matters soon changed for the better under the new *régime*. The line was freed from debt, the involved directors relieved from the pecuniary embarrassments which encompassed them, caused by their connection with the undertaking, and the whistle of the locomotive was shortly heard along the line, with trains running regularly, conveying freight and passengers. Whitby took a fresh start on the road to prosperity. Property was enhanced in value, and Port Perry was built up, from an insignificant village at the head of Lake Scugog, to the dimensions of an important town, where quarter-acre lots became as valuable as one hundred acre farms had been a few years before in the same neighbourhood.[5]

By the summer of 1873, the new owners of the Whitby & Port Perry Railway had succeeded in smoothing out the inefficiencies of the line and establishing its operations on a sound, businesslike basis. To publicize the fact, they hit upon the idea of inviting the Board of Trade and a number of other influential businessmen from Toronto to participate in a two-day excursion to Bobcaygeon via the Whitby & Port Perry road. It was their not unreasonable hope that these carefully selected representatives of many different commercial and industrial interests would use the facilities of the line to ship their products into the growing Peterborough-Lindsay-Bobcaygeon triangle. By the same token, it was not unreasonable to expect that a visit to Bobcaygeon and Lindsay by an impressive delegation would strengthen their relations with the important lumbering and milling interests in those centres whose traffic they wanted for the southward haul from Port Perry. A line was already in existence from Port Hope to Beaverton on Lake Simcoe, via Lindsay, called the Midland Railway. The owners of the Whitby & Port Perry sought to draw off some of that road's valuable traffic, the advantage being that Port Whitby on Lake Ontario was closer to the Toronto market than was Port Hope.

And so it was that the Toronto delegation reached Whitby by train early on an August morning, led by the president of the Board of Trade. They were a sombre group, stiffly correct in their manner, attired in the frock-coats and silk hats that were typical of their calling. They were escorted at once to the waiting passenger cars in the station near the harbour. As they made their way down the platform, they passed a gleaming engine snorting like an impatient dragon in anticipation of its full-throttle run to Port Perry. Through the clouds of steam, they could not have failed to notice, under the cab window, the name "James Austin" emblazoned in gold.

The train made the run of less than twenty miles to the Port Perry station on schedule, and the guests, now in a holiday mood, were conducted quickly to the wharf where the steamer *Champion,* gaily decked with flags, was signalling its imminent departure with a series of jarring whistle blasts.

An impressionable reporter from the *Ontario Observer,* published in Port Perry, accompanied the party, and his detailed account of the excursion, in the journalese of the day, appeared in the issue of August 21, 1873.[6]

The voyage from Port Perry to Lindsay was accomplished in about four hours, and at that point the passengers were transferred from the *Champion* to the more elegant *Vanderbilt*, a side-paddle steamer of the Crandell Line, for the final leg of the trip across Sturgeon Lake to Bobcaygeon.

The man from the *Ontario Observer* found Lindsay full of "bustle and stir," and noted that the lumber traffic on the Scugog River was "immense." Austin, Michie, and Holden, who had spent most of the trip strolling round the boat greeting their guests, did not miss the opportunity to draw their attention to the chunky scows that were heading out of Lindsay for Port Perry, and the waiting freight cars of the Whitby & Port Perry Railway.

That evening at 7:30, ninety sturdy Victorians sat down to dinner in the Forest House in Bobcaygeon. They responded, we are told, with great enthusiasm to the toasts that were proposed by James Austin who presided over the proceedings. His toast to the lumberers of the back lakes especially, whose patronage the railway was now seeking, soared to unsuspected heights when he extolled them as "noble pioneers who carry not only prosperity but civilization itself into our back countries and spread the smile of comfort wherever they go." Mr. Mossom Boyd, an influential resident of Sturgeon Lake, scrambled to his feet to respond to the flattering toast. He controlled a substantial part of the lumber business in the Bobcaygeon district, and the directors of the railway must have awaited his remarks with more than passing interest. He began by expressing great hope for the growing lumber trade in his area and ended by proposing, with considerable warmth, a toast to the success of the new railway.

Mr. James Holden spoke finally as managing director, and recalled the long battle he had fought in promoting the cause of the railway. He expressed his satisfaction in now seeing the road completed, and referred to the role played by James Austin and James Michie in helping him realize his dream. "Mr. Austin has been my best friend," he declared with some emotion, "he made me what I am. Some have said that I have rubbed noses with men of wealth, but I am proud to be associated with such men as Mr. Austin, Mr. Michie, Mr. Crowther and others who are the chief men in the land."

The excursionists left Bobcaygeon in high spirits the following morning. They retraced their route to Port Perry where they boarded the familiar passenger cars of the Whitby & Port Perry Railway and headed home.

By the summer of 1876 the road had been extended from Port Perry to Lindsay. It was later amalgamated with its old rival the Midland Railway, and was finally absorbed into the Grand Trunk Railway System. James Austin was undoubtedly right when he addressed the excursionists in the summer of 1873 as they stood patiently on the deck of the *Champion*, "If properly managed," he had said of the railroad, "it can't fail to be profitable to all concerned."

Chapter 13

A Time to Sow

Confidence, the fragile mainspring of prosperity, was tightly wound throughout the summer of 1873. Suddenly, in September, the mechanism was shattered as a major financial panic swept the United States. The New York Stock Exchange, engulfed by heavy selling, was forced to close its doors "for an indefinite period." Jay Cooke, the great innovative banker of the Civil War, who had been thanked by Lincoln personally for his services, was wiped out when he failed to market a huge underwriting of Northern Pacific Railroad bonds. And Jay Gould, the legendary Wall Street speculator, by selling "short," quietly amassed a fortune. The debacle was attributed to the reckless and unsustainable pace of expansion that had occurred in the United States in the final stages of the reconstruction boom that followed the Civil War and the opening of the American West. The railroad builders were identified as the principal culprits. Commodore Cornelius Vanderbilt, himself a railroad owner, summed it up bluntly when he said, "Building railroads from nowhere to nowhere at public expense is not a legitimate undertaking." The collapse of the stock market in New York that September sent tremors round the world. It set in train the severest depression the United States had undergone in its history—and there was to be no respite until 1879.[1]

The effects of the panic in the United States were soon felt in Canada: her export markets for lumber, timber, and grain were sharply curtailed, and there were many casualties among her retailers and wholesalers. "They had stocked up largely and carelessly," one writer put it, "often on credit too eagerly supplied by eagerly competing banks."[2] The severe conditions foreseen by James Austin when he left the board of the Canadian Bank of Commerce in 1870, in protest over McMaster's unwieldy plans for expansion, were now menacing the country. "Bank after bank, particularly in Quebec," wrote Dr. O. D. Skelton, "was forced to cut its capital or close its doors, or at least to draw heavily on its accumulated reserves. . . . The Dominion Bank remained unshaken."[3]

The six-year-long depression that followed the panic of 1873 contained few elements of surprise or novelty for Austin. Having experienced the financial crisis of 1857 at the end of the Russian War, as well as the depression after the Civil War, he had learned the importance of retrenchment in the face of rampant public speculation and extravagance. And on the other side of the coin, he also knew something of the rewards to be won, if the resources were available, through patient investment in times of public concern. It was basic to his thinking that money on hand at the right moment was the *sine qua non* of financial success. "Nothing is cheap," he used to say, "if you can't pay for it." It was for this reason, doubtless, that owls and squirrels were enshrined in the wrought-iron radiator grilles of his *Spadina* house. They stood for the simple virtues of wisdom in the management of one's affairs, and industrious preparation for the onslaught of winter. The years of depression now unfolding were to provide Austin with a host of opportunities to apply his uncomplicated Victorian beliefs.*

As Toronto settled apprehensively into the winter of 1873-74, in the face of the gathering depression, the rector of the Church of the Holy Trinity, Dr. Henry Scadding, published his weighty historical work, *Toronto of Old.* The text ran to 576 closely printed pages. The full title, loosely descriptive of his subject, read: *Toronto of Old: Collections and Recollections Illustrative of the Early Settlement and Social Life of the Capital of Ontario.* The author explained the plan of his book in a section of his preface:

> By inspection it will be seen that the plan pursued was to proceed rather deliberately through the principal thoroughfares, noticing persons and incidents of former days, as suggested by buildings and situations in the order in which they were severally seen. . . . Here and there, brief digressions into adjacent streets were made, when a house or the scene of an incident chanced to draw the supposed pilgrim aside.

While the work by definition was concerned with Toronto's early days, Dr. Scadding frequently introduced material of a later period, especially when an opportunity arose to flavour his text with a flattering reference to a man of prominence in the life of the city of 1870. It is scarcely surprising then, as his "supposed pilgrim" wandered up Yonge Street, to find him touching his cap to the occupants of several large houses of modern vintage along the Davenport Hill:

> Oaklands, Mr. John Mcdonald's residence, of which a short distance back we obtained a passing glimpse far to the west, and Rathnally (sic), Mr. McMaster's palatial abode, beyond, are both modern structures, put up by their respective occupants. Woodlawn, still on the left, the present residence of Mr. Justice Morrison, was previously the home of Chancellor Blake, and was built by him. . . . Summerhill, seen on the high land far to the right . . . was by no means the extensive and handsome place into which it has developed since becoming the property and the abode of Mr. Larratt Smith.

Dr. Scadding knew James Austin well. And yet, paradoxically, in his frequent references to *Spadina* in *Toronto of Old,* he omits any mention of Austin's occupancy and rejuvenation of the old Baldwin property. In one instance Dr. Scadding and his pilgrim viewed *Spadina* from the distant intersection of Queen Street and Spadina Avenue at a time when the southerly extension of that spacious thoroughfare was still called Brock Street (its name was changed to Spadina Avenue in 1884). This is what he wrote:

---

*Another practioner of the same financial strategy at that time was Andrew Carnegie, the American steel magnate. "The man who has money during a panic is the wise and valuable citizen," he once told a Congressional Committee. He built his first steel mill near Pittsburgh during the great depression of the 1870's, and took advantage of subsequent depressions to expand capacity.

> Returning now again to Brock Street, and placing ourselves at the middle point of its great width — immediately before us to the north, on the ridge which bounds the view in the distance, we discern a white object. This is Spadina House, from which the avenue into which Brock Street passes, takes its name. . . . Spadina was the residence of Dr. W. W. Baldwin, to whom reference has already been made.

Dr. Scadding's observation would have been more accurate had he said that the "white object" he and his pilgrim detected in the misty distance marked the site of Dr. Baldwin's earlier house, but was now the modern home of James Austin. The patient reader will recall that Brock Street was not laid out as the southerly extension of Spadina Avenue until after 1837, by which time Dr. Baldwin's original two-storey *Spadina* had been destroyed by fire. It is doubtful if the single-storey structure that replaced it, lying 300 feet back from the crest of the Davenport Hill, could have been seen from the low elevation of Queen Street. The "white object" they discerned, it is more reasonable to conclude, was James Austin's two and a half-storey *Spadina,* which had been a prominent landmark on the hill long before Dr. Scadding completed his *magnum opus.*

James Austin's connection with the Scadding family began in 1844 when he married Susan Bright. Susan's sister Jane, to whom she was devoted, had ten years before married Charles Scadding, Dr. Scadding's older brother. After St. James' Cemetery had been opened at the north end of Parliament Street in 1844, Dr. Scadding, then First Classical Master at Upper Canada College, and the newly appointed rector of Holy Trinity Church, had busied himself helpfully with the arrangements for the reinterment of old Lewis Bright, the father of Jane Scadding and Susan Austin, in the Bright-Scadding plot in the new cemetery.* The plot was jointly owned by Charles Scadding and the Bright family, and Dr. Scadding's mother, Millicent Trigge Scadding, was buried there in 1860.[4]

On June 14, 1857 James and Susan Austin went to Dr. Scadding's church to have their infant son, Albert William, baptized. And when The Dominion Bank opened its office in Orillia in 1871, in an unblushing act of nepotism, James Austin appointed Dr. Scadding's nephew and namesake, Henry Simcoe Scadding, to be its first manager. Young Henry was a son of Charles and Jane Bright Scadding, and his birth was recorded tersely by Dr. Scadding in his diary on November 20, 1836: "My nephew, Henry, born."[5]

All in all, there was a close connection between the Austin and Scadding families through the Brights, and we may be certain that an early copy of Scadding's *Toronto of Old* was scanned critically in 1873 by Susan Bright Austin and her daughter Anne Arthurs.

It is open to us to imagine the effect that Dr. Scadding's studied exclusion of any reference to James Austin's ownership and rehabilitation of the Baldwin property since 1866 must have had on the households of *Spadina* and *Ravenswood.* To the proud Anne Arthurs especially, throughout her long life a zealous upholder of her father's position, Scadding's neglect must have seemed mischievous and perverse. In any event, before a year was out, the

---

*Lewis Bright was reinterred on September 5, 1848.

old Baldwin cemetery, St. Martin's Rood, that lay at the end of Anne
Arthurs' carriage drive overlooking the peaceful glen behind *Ravenswood,*
was whisked away in its entirety to St. James' Cemetery. The mortal remains
of thirty members of the Baldwin family group, including the Honourable
Peter Russell and his sister Elizabeth, were reinterred in a hillside plot
which, like their resting place at *Spadina,* overlooked the Castle Frank
stream as it flowed towards its confluence with the Don. Earlier in 1871,
three years before the mass transfer of the Baldwin graves, Dr. Scadding
had thoughtfully removed the remains of his wife Harriet Baldwin Scadding
from the *Spadina* cemetery for reinterment in his own plot in St. James.

As the depression deepened throughout the country in 1874, James Austin
was elected president of the Consumers' Gas Company of Toronto. The
firm, which manufactured its gas from coal, held the street-lighting contract
for the city, which then boasted a population of nearly 70,000. It also
enjoyed a monopoly in providing illuminating gas to over 2,000 private
users. The company had been established in 1848, and had only 6,000
shares outstanding, each of $100 par value. There were 219 registered
shareholders at the end of 1873.

In the best of times, the lot of a public utility is an uneasy one. The
service it provides, the rates it charges, the profit it makes, are all objects
of unflagging public scrutiny. In the worst of times, public attention can
harden into criticism and controversy. Such was the case in 1874. During
that year, the new president and his board of directors were called upon to
battle an attempted takeover of the company by the Toronto City Council.
They parried the assault by demonstrating that the rates they charged their
customers for illuminating gas were among the lowest on the continent.
Moreover, the company had completed a major programme of expansion
in 1873, doubling capacity, and it now looked forward to a period of rapid
growth. As volume increased, the company argued, its rates would be reduced. It pointed to the fact that in 1863 the consumer had paid $3.00 for
1,000 cubic feet of gas, whereas in 1873 the charge had been lowered to
$2.50. The position the company took in the struggle of 1874 was amply
vindicated in later years: by 1879 the rate had declined to $1.75, in 1893
to $1.05, and at the outbreak of the Great War, to 70 cents.[6]

The fact that the Consumers' Gas Company had seen fit in that troubled
year to restore its dividend rate to its pre-Civil War level had not escaped
the critical eye of the city fathers. In their assessment of the situation, they
weighed the interests of a politically unimportant handful of shareholders
against the greater expediency of distracting the people from their reces-
sionary concerns, and assuring them that the city was doing everything in
is power to alleviate the distress of the times. The expropriation of the
company would be a timely issue, the anxious city fathers had concluded,
and one that was likely to win broad, popular support. The Ontario government thought otherwise. Premier Oliver Mowat's strongly entrenched Reform
Ministry, with Olympian detachment, refused to grant the city the necessary
legislative authority to take the company over. As it turned out, the decision
was in no way politically damaging to Mowat's government, which went
on to enjoy an unbroken tenure of office for more than twenty years.

While the city fathers had grasped easily the idea that the votes of a
few shareholders of a gas company were insignificant in the total electoral
picture, they had underestimated or ignored the strength and influence of

the company's board of directors. A glance at the composition of the group over which James Austin presided in that fretful year is revealing. Its members were: William Cawthra, John Eastwood, William Gooderham, John T. Smith, Isaac C. Gilmour, Samuel Platt, the Honourable William McMaster, Judge Duggan, Thomas H. Lee, A. Lepper, Joseph H. Mead, and Larratt W. Smith, D.C.L., Q.C.

Secure under the umbrella the obliging Premier Mowat had raised over their heads in 1874, the directors of Consumers' Gas were now able to bend their efforts towards building sales and improving efficiency. The results they achieved were impressive. From 1874 to 1879, notwithstanding the depressed times, the company boosted its annual output of gas from nearly 72 million cubic feet to over 135 million. It increased its list of private customers from 2,000 to more than 3,500; and the familiar lamplighters who trudged the streets of Toronto at dusk were tending nearly 2,000 gas lights in the public thoroughfares as compared with only 740 in 1874.

For James Austin, whose maxim it was to buy and build in hard times, a principle he had followed ten years before when he had purchased his *Spadina* property, the hour of opportunity was at hand. Between 1876 and 1878, three institutions with which he was identified embarked upon notable building programs: The Consumers' Gas Company built a new head office building on Toronto Street; the growing Dominion Bank acquired a site at the southwest corner of King and Yonge streets and raised the finest office building of its kind in the city; and the Queen City Fire Insurance Company, of which Austin had been a co-founder with W. H. Howland in 1871, erected an impressive office building on lower Church Street, between Colborne and Wellington streets.

On Toronto Street, the gas company purchased the adjoining City Registry Office in 1876. It was demolished, and the new building raised on the site was numbered 19 Toronto Street. The company wisely retained its old premises next door at 17 Toronto Street (renting most of it for many years. Later, in 1899, the wall was removed between the two structures, a new facade in the Renaissance style was added, and the harmonious whole still exists today as number 19 Toronto Street, the unique head office of a 125-year-old company.

By 1877 The Dominion Bank had outgrown its rented quarters at 40 King Street East where it had opened its main Toronto office in 1871. The growing city was pushing westward, and the intersection of King and Yonge streets was now becoming the business and financial centre of Toronto. William Augustus Baldwin of *Mashquoteh,* James Austin's neighbour on the Davenport Hill, was still the principal owner of the important southwest corner. The parcel comprised a frontage of 57 feet on King Street and 130 feet on Yonge Street. It will be recalled that his father, Dr. William Warren Baldwin, had purchased the corner in 1829 for £750 when the title was transferred to two of his sons as owners, William Augustus and Quetton St. George. Baldwin of *Mashquoteh* was agreeable to renting part of the corner to The Dominion Bank, and a lease was prepared for a term of 999 years covering the King Street frontage and 100 feet on Yonge Street. The document, which called for the payment of an annual rental to the Baldwin family of $4,000, was registered on July 21, 1877, and the following month James Austin advertised for tenders for the project:

Built at a cost of $40,000 in 1878, this head-office building of The Dominion Bank was located at the southwest corner of King and Yonge Streets. A 30-foot section was added to the structure in 1884 which included the elaborate doorway with sculptured figures at the left of the picture. It was demolished in 1913 to make way for a new Dominion Bank head-office building which still stands today.

—The Toronto-Dominion Bank

NOTICE CALLING FOR TENDERS

Toronto, 28th August, 1877.

The Dominion Bank intend erecting a Banking House on the corner of King and Yonge Streets, Toronto at a cost not exceeding $40,000, and are prepared to receive designs for the proposed work.

For information as to the dimensions of the lot and requirements of the Bank, apply to the undersigned.

The Bank shall not be bound to accept or pay for any designs submitted, but if any design is accepted, the author of it will be appointed Architect for the work, on condition that the total allowance for his services until the completion of the work shall not exceed $1,500.

No designs will be received after the 15th October, 1877.

(sgd.) James Austin
President.[7]

Austin's stipulated price of $40,000 for the bank's five-storey premises, embellished with classical pediments and stone ballisters, (see opposite page), provides a striking illustration of the depreciation that was to occur in later times in the worth of a building dollar.

While the Consumers' Gas and Dominion Bank projects were getting underway, Howland and Austin were adding the finishing touches to the new Queen City Fire Insurance Company premises at 24-26 Church Street. It was an elaborate four-storey structure "substantially built of Georgetown and Ohio stone and Italian marble, the three being so blended as to impart to the building a striking and unique front." The façade of the place had a claim to uniqueness for an even better reason: the keystones over the entrance door and the arched first-storey windows were "ornamented with life-like portraits of the directors and managers, excellently carved in stone by a German artist of undoubted taste and talent."[8]

The building on Church Street was demolished long ago, but a memento of the unusual character of its facade still exists at *Spadina* where a plaster head of James Austin, from which the stone effigy for one of the keystones was carved, has long been mounted on a plaque above the doorway that leads to Susan Austin's original parlour (Page 150). The sculptured plaque, undisturbed for nearly a century, bears an inscription in faded red letters which reads: "Presented by the Officials of the Queen City Fire Insurance Co. 1877." Since Austin was vice-president and therefore an official of the company at the time, we must assume that the other "Officials" similarly presented themselves with replicas of their own likenesses. The commemorative gesture of the directors to themselves on the occasion of the opening of their new building, was fairly matched, however, by their generosity to the public. A contemporary writer described the event which caused hundreds of Christmas hearths to blaze more cheerfully that year throughout Victorian Toronto:

> With a thoughtfulness that did them credit the directors, instead of celebrating the opening of their handsome new premises with a champagne dinner, very generously appropriated a sum of money for the relief of the poor at the ensuing Christmas. The money was placed at the disposal of a committee of ladies, consisting of Lady Howland, president; Miss Macdonald, Mrs. James Austin, Mrs. John MacNab, Mrs. James Maclennan, Mrs. W. Thomson, Mrs. Hugh Scott, Mrs. W. H. Howland, Mrs. John Roaf, and Miss Elliot secretary. These ladies worked for a month beforehand compiling a list of families who were in need of charity. The distribution took place at the company's building on Church Street, upwards of 1,500 families, or, at the least calculation, 7,000 individuals, being relieved. An idea of the extent of this charitable

act may be had when it is stated that the committee gave away 8,000 pounds of beef, 4,000 loaves of bread, and 530 pounds of tea, all the provisions being of the best quality.

Many a table that would otherwise have been bare and uninviting was thus supplied with an ample Christmas spread, and many a person still looks back with thankful memory to the noble and generous opening of the Queen City Insurance Company's building.[9]

At the end of the decade of the 1870's, as the depression gradually lifted, James Austin had good reason to be pleased with the progress of his various interests. The Dominion Bank, the Consumers' Gas Company, the Queen City Fire Insurance Co., had all emerged from the depression with strong balance sheets, and were now installed in efficient, new office buildings with the bulk of their costs behind them. The Whitby & Port Perry Railway had extended its profitable line to Lindsay. The North of Scotland Canadian Mortgage Company,[10] of whose Canadian Board of Management Austin was chairman, stood ready, like the others, to savour the economic benefits that were soon to flow from the building of the Canadian Pacific Railway across the limitless lands of the Canadian West.

A plaster head of James Austin on a plaque surmounted by a maple leaf is seen above Susan Bright Austin's old parlour door at *Spadina.* It was presented by the officials of the Queen City Fire Insurance Company of Toronto in 1877, and was used as a model for a stone likeness of Austin that was placed in the keystone of a window overlooking Church Street in the insurance company's new premises. The building was demolished long ago. The sculpture is flanked by a portrait of James Austin.

—Photography by William Robertson

Chapter 14

Manitoba Fever

In the autumn of 1871, a few months after The Dominion Bank had opened its first office in Harris' store on King Street, Albert William Austin, James Austin's youngest son, joined the bank's staff as a junior clerk. He was then fourteen. Having completed his elementary schooling at Upper Canada College, he was, his father had concluded, sufficiently qualified to take his place in the business world, starting, of course, at the bottom. R. H. Bethune, the bank's cashier, needed a junior, and lost no time in setting the president's son to work sweeping out the banking house, filling ink pots, and cleaning pens. He was later given the responsibility of opening the office in the morning. That carried with it the added task of lighting the stoves in the wintertime, and clearing the snow from the plank sidewalk in front of the bank. In order to complete his chores by the required hour, young Austin had to leave *Spadina* on the distant Davenport Hill each morning at daybreak.

In the winter months the boy set out on foot through a wilderness of snow. He made his way down the drifted Aunt Maria's Road, now the carriage drive in front of his sister's *Ravenswood,* then along the Davenport Road to Yorkville. Close to the Red Lion Hotel, just north of Bloor Street, he scrambled aboard a horse-drawn car for the last leg of his journey down Yonge Street. During a heavy snow, the horse-cars were equipped with sleigh runners, and on the coldest days, when the biting wind etched the windows with frost, the boy found a measure of warmth by digging his feet into the straw that was scattered on the floor of the car. By the time he had reclimbed the Davenport Hill at the end of the day, the sun had already fallen behind the dark grove of oaks that lay to the west of the house; the lonely *Spadina* farmlands were held by the complete silence of winter. Only the chimney smoke that hung in the cold air gave promise of the cheerful hearth that awaited his return.

In 1874, having served his three-year novitiate in the formal atmosphere of the banking house, Albert Austin joined the Honourable Frank Smith's flourishing wholesale grocery firm on Toronto's Front Street, as a custom-clerk. He proudly preserved an invoice he wrote up that year covering a wide variety of shipments that were received by F. Smith & Co. through the Port of Toronto. The list, which evokes the musky smell of the grocery store of a bygone age, included ample quantities of black and green tea, boxes of candles, bags of filberts, almonds, walnuts, peanuts, and pimento.

And the young Methodist also resolutely recorded a generous shipment of green gin, rum, Scotch whisky, brandy, and numerous caddies of tobacco. Listed as well were bags of black pepper, barrels of hemp seed and canary seed, currants, arrowroot, many cases of canned goods, and a hundred kegs of bicarbonate of soda.

Young Austin's decision to join F. Smith & Co. was to prove of substantial benefit to him. On grounds of business acumen and amiability, he could not have had a better mentor than Senator Frank Smith.

Like his friend James Austin, Frank Smith had emigrated to Canada from County Armagh in Ireland as a boy. His father had settled on a farm in Etobicoke in 1832 when young Smith was only ten. Five years later, after serving as a government courier in the Mackenzie Rebellion, the boy obtained a clerkship for himself in a general store in Dixie – at a wage of five dollars a month. He later managed several stores in Toronto and other parts of the province, and finally decided in 1849 to establish his own wholesale and grocery business in London, Ontario. He was then just twenty-seven, and his means were limited. He therefore approached Foy and Austin, the rising wholesale house on King Street East, and laid his plans before them. He told them simply that he needed $15,000 to $20,000 to launch his business, and that he had no security to offer. James Austin had earlier formed a high opinion of Smith's character and ability, and without hesitation placed the necessary capital at his disposal.

It was slow going at first. In fact, three years later Smith's indebtedness to the Toronto firm had climbed to $35,000. But by 1853 his prospects had brightened visibly. The great railroad building boom had begun in Canada, and by the end of that year the first locomotive of the Great Western Railway had wheezed into the London station amidst a shower of sparks after making its inaugural run from Hamilton. A few years later the urgent whistle of the Grand Trunk train from Toronto disturbed the silent farmlands around Guelph, Stratford, and London, and in 1856 a twenty-five-mile line was built by local interests that linked London and St. Thomas with Port Stanley on the shores of Lake Erie. In the centre of the construction activity that swirled around the main towns of the province, the merchants who supplied the railroad builders naturally flourished. "So great was the demand for labor, livestock, timber and materials of all kinds by the competition which existed," one writer recalled later, "that prices increased 30, 40 and 50 per cent."[1] Frank Smith's store on London's Dundas Street buzzed with life and profitable activity. After paying off his loan to Foy & Austin, who were adding to their own means with unflagging zeal, he went on to lay the foundation of his own substantial fortune.

By a curious set of circumstances, a further benefit was to accrue to Frank Smith as a result of the railroad boom of the 1850's. His London store had for a considerable time provided supplies on credit to Kiely Bros., who operated a stage coach line between Toronto, Hamilton, and London. The competition from the railway services that spread through the area soon blighted their business, and forced it to close down. The brothers, W. T. and George W. Kiely, had earlier acquired a controlling interest in the Toronto Street Railway, which had been started with a horse-car line on Yonge Street in 1861. Since they were not in a position to liquidate their indebtedness to Smith by a cash settlement, they agreed to assign to him some of their shares in the street railway. Smith later added to his holdings, buying a substantial block of shares from W. T. Kiely, and became the principal shareholder of the company and its president. George W. Kiely retained his interest in the fledgeling transportation system and managed the operation for over twenty years.

After serving a term as mayor of London in 1866, Frank Smith returned to Toronto the following year and established a large wholesale house on Front Street at the foot of Scott Street. He retained his London store, however, as an integral part of a chain of retail outlets that he opened throughout the province. Smith's involvement in municipal politics in London had earlier led him to form a close friendship with John A. Macdonald. Later, on a larger stage, he was to become an important figure in the Conservative Party. As a first step, he was called to the Senate of Canada in 1871 by Lord Lisgar, the governor-general, on the advice of Sir John A. Macdonald. The year before, Smith had been largely responsible for organizing the Ontario Catholic League, an influential group whose support Macdonald was anxious to retain after Smith was appointed to the Senate.

Senator Smith's varied interests provided young Austin with many valuable insights: not only did he see at first hand the development of a great mercantile business, but he also learned something of the operation of a street railway—and the tortuous careers of men in public life. Sir John A. Macdonald, of course, was out of office from 1873 to 1878, during the widespread depression, but by the time of his return to power Albert Austin had decided to strike out on his own. Not surprisingly, as the depression of the 1870's lifted, and the Canadian Pacific Railway project was being revived, he left Toronto in 1880 for Winnipeg, the gateway to the West, and the focal point of a boom that was soon to stir the country.

When young Austin arrived in Winnipeg that summer, after a jolting train ride that carried him through Chicago, St. Paul, and Emerson, he found the town throbbing with excitement. Work on the main line of the transcontinental railroad, which would link Winnipeg with the Pacific, was about to resume, and homesteaders by the hundreds were already pressing into the old fur-trading centre.[2] Winnipeg was like a tightly coiled spring. Its powerful energies were to be released the following April in a frenzy of real estate speculation that was to engulf the town.

On setting out from Toronto, Austin had intended establishing a wholesale grocery business in Winnipeg. His first step was to open an office, and he was fortunate to find space in a clapboard building on Main Street. It was a hive of diverse activities. His office was at the top of a creaking flight of stairs, over the premises occupied by Carruthers & Brock who conducted an insurance and loan business. Above him, on the third floor, Mr. A. Chapman plied his trade as a hardware merchant, and elsewhere in the building Robert R. Keith ran a seed business, and S. & J. Andrew dealt in millinery and fancy goods. And adding a little style to the place, Dr. J. F. Roll's City Pharmacy dispensed relief to the sick from spacious quarters located on the ground floor.

Albert Austin described himself simply as "Agent" when he hung his first sign on his door. But throughout the autumn and winter months of 1880, his mind turned away from the idea of setting himself up as a merchant, and he became absorbed with a different plan. From his window overlooking Main Street, he had pondered the execrable condition of Winnipeg's main thoroughfares. In the hot, dry summer days, when the sun blazed down from the prairie sky and the Assiniboine and Red Rivers turned sluggish in their course, choking clouds of dust swirled along the principal streets forcing pedestrians to seek shelter in the town's stores. And in the late winter months, the grinding wheels of the Red River carts and drays churned the roads into seas of mud. Surely, he reasoned, the town would welcome a street railway system, laid out on stout wooden ties, that could easily be accommodated within the broad limits of Portage Avenue, Broadway Avenue, and Main Street. The time was ripe he concluded, as Winnipeg braced itself for a vast influx of settlers, to launch a public transportation company. Through his association with Senator Frank Smith, he had learned something of the risks inherent in such an undertaking, but he was also keenly aware of the profits that were flowing into the hands of Smith and Kiely from their operation of the Toronto Street Railway.

And so it was, as the speculative boom that was to be called the "Manitoba Fever" gripped the country, that Albert Austin, age twenty-four, was busy laying the groundwork for an offering of shares in the Winnipeg Street Railway Company.

The capitalization was set at $100,000, and one enthusiastic writer later related that the books were closed within an hour. Early in 1882, the Manitoba Legislature was petitioned for the necessary act of incorporation, which was assented to in May. The following July, a further agreement was completed with the city of Winnipeg which included the condition that the first mile of track had to be laid within six months.

Most of the subscribers were men well known in the business life of Winnipeg, like Duncan MacArthur, the local manager of the Merchants' Bank of Canada who served briefly as president of the new company, and R. J. Whitla, a widely respected merchant. Of greater significance, however, was the inclusion in the list of petitioners for incorporation of "James Austin and Edmund B. Osler of the City of Toronto in the County of York and Province of Ontario, Gentlemen."[3]

Edmund Boyd Osler had first caught James Austin's notice when The Dominion Bank was being established in 1871. Osler, it will be recalled, had formed a stockbrokerage firm with Henry Pellatt Sr. in 1867, and during the 1870's James Austin's interests had brought him into steadily closer contact with the young broker and financial agent. Osler's participation in the financing of Albert Austin's street railway was a direct result of the close business relationship that had now grown up between Osler and James Austin.[4]

When Edmund B. Osler withdrew from his partnership with Henry Pellatt Sr. in 1882, his place was filled by Pellatt's son, Henry Mill Pellatt (later Sir Henry), and the firm became known as Pellatt & Pellatt. Osler then formed a new partnership with his friend Herbert Carlyle Hammond, who left his post as cashier of the Bank of Hamilton to join forces with Osler. The firm of Osler & Hammond was destined to play an important role in financing many major projects in the later development of the country. Also in 1882, recognizing the significance of Osler's new brokerage business, James Austin secured his election to the board of directors of The Dominion Bank. Fittingly, the young broker filled the vacancy on the board created by the death that year of Austin's friend of long-standing, the irrepressible James Holden of Whitby.

While the Winnipeg Street Railway Company had been incorporated on May 27, 1882, the City Council was distracted by the collapse of an important bridge over the ice-choked Red River that spring. Meanwhile, Albert Austin fretted over the delay, his anxiety heightened by the shadow it cast over his marriage, which was to take place in Toronto that July. His fiancée was Mary Richmond Kerr, a gifted musician whom he had met in Toronto before he left for the West. Born in Perth, Ontario, in 1860, she was a daughter of Dawson Kerr, then a resident of that town, and Mary Jane (Paul) Kerr of St. Thomas, Ontario. When the Winnipeg City Council finally approved the agreement setting out the conditions under which the street railway was to operate on July 7, Albert Austin, brimming with pride and excitement, sent off a flurry of telegrams to Toronto and followed them himself a week later.

Albert Austin and Mary Kerr were married quietly in Toronto on the evening of July 18. The ceremony, which was arranged on short notice, took place in Dawson Kerr's house on Sherbourne Street. Three bridesmaids attended the bride, and Harvey Smith, a son of Senator Frank Smith, was one of the three groomsmen. The couple left immediately afterwards for the West.

After spending a few days in Chicago, they reached Winnipeg late in July 1882, where the great land boom had crested with the rampaging Red River the previous April. They made their temporary home in a boarding house, and the following year Austin built a substantial house on Carlton Street where they were to live with their growing family until 1894. At the time of their wedding, James Austin had given Mary Austin a Steinway grand piano which was obtained in New York through his neighbour, Samuel Nordheimer. Austin also commissioned J. Colin Forbes, R.C.A., to paint a portrait of his daughter-in-law seated beside it, a roll of music in her hand (Page 182). When the young couple moved into their newly built Winnipeg house in 1883, James Austin's wedding presents were finally uncrated and set out in a room that Albert Austin had planned as a small replica of his father's drawing room at *Spadina*.

On October 20, 1882, the first horse-car of the new Winnipeg Street Railway made its inaugural run along Main Street, well within the time prescribed in the company's agreement with the city. The solemnity of the occasion was marred only by the fact that the first car struck a piece of wood on the track and was derailed. A score of willing hands, encouraged by cheers from the crowd, lifted it back on the rails, and the ceremonial run was completed without further incident. The initial section of the line ran along Main Street from a point close to the site of the old Fort Garry, which had been demolished the previous year, to the new City Hall at William Avenue. At the outset, the company's fleet of street cars was only four in number, and a stable of twenty horses, used in careful rotation, supported the operation. With the first section of the line operating efficiently by the end of 1882, Austin was free to lay his plans for the expansion of his service.

While Albert Austin was busy launching his street railway in Winnipeg, his older brother James Henry was content to remain at home and manage the *Spadina* property. He showed little inclination to involve himself in business affairs. On occasion, he was despatched by his father to Whitby to look into a problem connected with the Whitby & Port Perry Railway, but he reserved his real enthusiasm for the excitement of hunting trips into the region around Lake Scugog. A lover of horses, he not only kept a good stable himself, but he also used his knowledge to buy wisely for his brother's horse-cars in Winnipeg. Some of the horses were bought in Toronto and stabled at *Spadina* while they awaited shipment to the West, but for the

Albert William Austin's Winnipeg Street Railway—a view on Portage Avenue. Some of the horses for his brother's street railway were bought in Toronto by James Henry Austin, stabled at *Spadina*, then shipped out to Winnipeg.

—H. W. Blake

most part they were purchased on his trips to Whitby from the drovers of Ontario County from strains they had sold to the Union Army at a substantial profit during the Civil War.

Jim Austin managed the *Spadina* farm from a small office in the basement of the house. Simply furnished, the room contained a high, sloping desk with a stool where he toiled over his accounts, two stuffed chairs, and a plain table which supported an oil lamp and a rack of pipes. Several well-stocked bookshelves were enclosed on one wall, and his collection of hunting guns was displayed on another. Whenever the work of the farm permitted, he was out happily tramping the *Spadina* fields with his dogs and his gun. As his father's influence in the city grew, and his brother's success in Winnipeg attracted increasingly favourable notice, Jim Austin seemed only to withdraw more deeply into the tranquillity of his unhurried country life.

One of his closest friends at the time, who shared his devotion to the outdoors, was the artist Edward Scrope Shrapnel of Orillia. The two men went duck shooting and deer hunting each fall, and the artist's visits to *Spadina* always provided Jim Austin with a welcome excuse to organize a wild pigeon shoot or some other sporting event for the amusement of his guest and their friends.

Scrope Shrapnel was born in 1845 at Bradford-on-Avon in Wiltshire, England. His father, Henry Needham Scrope Shrapnel, a son of the famous British general who had invented the artillery shell to which he gave his name, had begun his military career as a cornet in the 3rd (The Prince of

A watercolour sketch of James Henry Austin who was a close friend of the artist, E. S. Shrapnel, illustrator of Conant's *Upper Canada Sketches.*

—Private Collection

Wales') Regiment of Dragoon Guards. He subsequently held appointments in India, Ireland, and Bermuda. In 1855, when Scrope Shrapnel was ten years of age, his father was posted to the British fort of Isle aux Noix on the Richelieu River close to its marshy outlet on Lake Champlain. Here, his growing family with him, he held for some years the appointment of Barrack-Master which carried with it the rank of captain. Later, in the 1860's, the captain and his family were stationed in the old walled city of Quebec. At that time, a strong British force was concentrated in the area as a result of the tensions that arose between Britain and the northern states during the American Civil War.

Captain Shrapnel was typical of the host of accomplished British army officers who enriched the social life of the garrison towns of the colonies during the nineteenth century. He was a talented amateur painter, an accomplished musician, and he even tried his hand at composing. We may be sure his tastes brought him and his son Scrope into touch with the celebrated artist Cornelius Krieghoff, who was a familiar figure at that time in Quebec as he strolled the narrow streets of the city in his velvet coat and beaver hat. At the peak of his painting career, Krieghoff was also building a legendary reputation for himself as a *bon vivant* among the officers of the British garrison.

The Shrapnel family finally left Quebec after the end of the Civil War and returned to Salisbury in England, where Henry Shrapnel retired with the rank of major. He then became involved in an unequal struggle with the British government when he attempted to obtain compensation for his father's invention, which had been acknowledged earlier by King William IV and the Duke of Wellington as being of decisive importance to the British army. His petition to the House of Lords in 1868 disclosed that his father, Lieut. Gen. Henry Shrapnel, had spent thousands of pounds from his private purse in developing the shrapnel shell and had died unrecompensed in 1842, a bitterly disappointed man. Major Shrapnel's efforts to obtain satisfaction of his father's claim were wholly unsuccessful. Around 1870 he decided to give up the struggle and return to Canada with his family.

They chose to settle near Lake Couchiching at Orillia, Ontario, and the barrack-like house that he built in 1871 to accommodate his large family still stands. It was there that young Edward Scrope Shrapnel's love of the Canadian outdoors, which had been nurtured in Quebec, was revived, and his desire to become an artist was crystallized. Under his father's guidance he attained a high level of technical proficiency in the use of water colour, his preferred medium throughout his long life.

During the span of his friendship with Shrapnel, Jim Austin acquired a number of examples of the artist's work which still adorn the walls of *Spadina*. They include a portrait of himself seated on his horse (Page 158), a sketch of Austin's hunting dogs posed morosely in front of their kennel, several deer hunting scenes, and an ambitious painting in oil on canvas of an overturned sleigh, its occupants tumbling out on a desolate country road. This latter work, in its vivacity, detail, and dramatic use of colour, undoubtedly owed much to the influence of Cornelius Krieghoff.

Elected to membership in the Ontario Society of Artists in 1876, Shrapnel also obtained an associate membership in the Royal Canadian Academy of Arts when it was formed in 1880. He later held the post of drawing master at the Ontario Ladies College in Whitby. But by the end of the decade, impressed with the reports of artists like Lucius O'Brien, T. Mower Martin, F. M. Bell-Smith and Marmaduke Matthews, all senior Academicians, who had already taken advantage of the completion of the Canadian Pacific Railway to paint the wonders of the West, he left Whitby and settled in British Columbia where he remained until his death in 1920.

While Shrapnel later established a local reputation for himself in Vancouver and Victoria as a competent marine painter and art teacher, he is best remembered as the illustrator of Thomas Conant's *Upper Canada Sketches* for which he provided twenty scenes that were lithographed in brilliant colour.[5] Although he remains a stranger to most anthologies of Canadian art, his views of the rural life of early Ontario provide a unique record of the simple pursuits of the Victorian countryman. Unlike most of his contemporaries, who seemed happiest when they were creating epic landscapes depicting craggy mountains or picturesque waterfalls, Shrapnel's preference lay with less grandiose subjects. Indeed, his work reveals a remarkable freedom from the restraints imposed on composition and style by the arid European conventions of the day against which the Canadian Group of Seven painters were later to rebel.[6]

As the end of the decade of the 1880's approached, James Austin decided to sell off the westerly forty acres of his *Spadina* farmlands. William Reford & Co. of Church Street, Toronto, were appointed agents, and Austin registered his plan of subdivision on July 22, 1889. The subdivision comprised 114 "town and villa" lots, most with a frontage of fifty feet on the four road allowances that were created by the plan. These were Spadina Road (eighty feet), Walmer Road Hill, Walmer Road, and Austin Terrace (each with a width of sixty-six feet). The lands affected by the new plan stretched from Davenport Road to St. Clair Avenue, and were bounded on the east by Spadina Road and on the west by Walmer Road Hill. The most prominent landmarks situated on them today are Sir Henry Pellatt's famous castle on Austin Terrace and his elaborate stables on Walmer Road. Towards St. Clair Avenue, the two Tower Hill apartment buildings of recent construction that stand below that thoroughfare and overlook the Austin Ravine identify the northerly extent of the 1889 subdivision.

James Austin, of course, retained the easterly forty acres of his property, which, lying to the east of Spadina Road, also extended from Davenport Road to St. Clair Avenue. That parcel contained his daughter's *Ravenswood* and his own *Spadina* house and outbuildings; part of it today is occupied by the Sir Winston Churchill Park (St. Clair Reservoir) and the Ardwold Gate subdivision.

When he had purchased the eighty-acre property during the depression of 1866, his friends had admonished him for forsaking his house on Jarvis Street and moving to so remote a location. He had assured them that they would see the day when the city would be knocking at the gates of his new *Spadina*. By 1889, when he was seventy-six, his prophecy had been fulfilled. The city's population had more than doubled in the twenty-three years since he had bought his York Township lands, and new residential areas had nudged forward to Davenport Road between Bathurst and Yonge streets, and were now climbing the Bathurst Street hill as well. There was talk that Upper Canada College would soon vacate its historic premises at King and Simcoe streets and transfer its classrooms and playing fields to the heart of the Baldwins' *Mashquoteh* property north of St. Clair Avenue.[7] Inevitably, new houses would follow the school like iron filings drawn by a magnet. All in all, Austin had concluded, the time seemed opportune to reduce his extensive holdings.

Sales of the *Spadina* lots were brisk. One informed observer later related that Austin, whose crystal ball in such matters was usually clearer than most, had chosen the best possible time to conduct his sales. The prices he realized were not to be seen again for many years. Many of the lots were sold against cash payments with mortgages being given back for the balance of the purchase price. Having paid only $14,200 for the eighty-acre *Spadina* parcel in the dark days of 1866, James Austin had good reason to be pleased with the transaction that yielded him in excess of $200,000 while leaving half his original holding intact.

Of special interest to the student of local history was a revealing condition imposed by James Austin upon the buyers of his land. It appears in the deeds to the new owners as one of eight building restrictions that were attached to their property:

> 8. The said restrictions shall not apply to the old log house now on the said lands known as the Old Baldwin Homestead which may be placed and kept upon any part of the said lands.

There can be little doubt that the "old log house" that Austin was anxious to preserve was the original settler's cabin of William Willcocks' day. It would have been built prior to 1798, when Willcocks received his Crown grant to the property, in order to satisfy the requirements of settlement and occupation. And doubtless it would have resembled the contemporary Scadding Cabin which was removed from its site on the east bank of the Don River in 1879 to its present location overlooking the lake in Toronto's Exhibition Park.

The legal draughtsman of James Austin's deeds, in referring to the cabin as the "Old Baldwin Homestead," was guilty of an excusable error. The long occupation of the *Spadina* property by the Baldwins, reaching back to 1818, naturally led him to conclude too hastily that any ancient cabin on the site would have been of their creation. It will be recalled, however, that Dr. Baldwin's first "homestead" in York was at the corner of Front and Bay Streets—the cottage he prised loose from the Honourable Peter Russell in 1806. His first *Spadina* "homestead" was not a log cabin but the ambitious structure that contained two floors and an attic when it was completed in 1818.

The significance of the building restriction is that it provides a valuable clue as to the location of the first habitation to be built on the historic *Spadina* farmlands. The building restrictions in James Austin's deeds indicate that in 1889 it lay between the present Walmer Road Hill and Spadina Road. It is reasonable to assume that the old log house, which in pioneer days attracted wandering bands of Indians who liked to study their reflection in its glazed windows, was located close to the brow of the hill like Adjutant McGill's *Davenport* just to the west. Since the Willcocks cabin and McGill's *Davenport* were originally constructed in a forbidding and uncleared region far from the infant settlement of York, it would have been natural for the builders to place them close to each other as a matter of mutual security. Moreover, when they were built, the old Indian trail that was to become Davenport Road already led along the foot of the hill, and it would have been convenient for them to have their dwellings as close as possible to the only route that gave them access to York far to the southeast. It is by no means farfetched to conclude that the original settler's cabin on the early Willcocks property of 200 acres was located on or very close to the site upon which Sir Henry Pellatt was later to build his celebrated castle.

While the old log house was the object of James Austin's concern as late as 1889, long after Dr. Baldwin's two *Spadina* houses had disappeared, its fate after that date is unknown. Certainly by 1903, when Lt. Col. Henry Mill Pellatt began to acquire the land for his castle, no trace of the cabin remained in the pleasant fields that stretched north to the Austin Ravine.

Chapter 15

A Bird of Ill Omen

In the summer of 1889, while his father was disposing of part of his *Spadina* farmlands, Albert Austin was badgering the Winnipeg City Council for the right to electrify his street railway system. While his horse-car lines had been extended to meet the needs of the growing city and were now supported by a stable of eighty horses, he was convinced that the new electric trolley-cars then appearing in the United States would quickly make the slow-moving horse-car obsolete. After inspecting different types of electric street-cars, some in the experimental stage, he had come to favour the system that employed an overhead wire with a connecting pole, rather than the alternative methods that drew their power from heavy storage batteries or under-surface collectors running in a slot similar to that used by cable cars. Austin pressed the council to let him at least electrify his important Main Street route. The cautious city fathers, fearful of the danger that might be created by overhead electric wires, declined to tempt Providence. They did, however, grudgingly allow him to experiment with his visionary scheme in the bush south of the Assiniboine River. It was a sparsely settled district, safely removed from the public the new system was intended to serve.

Undaunted, Austin immediately set about clearing and grading the first mile of the proposed line along River Avenue in the Fort Rouge area. He later persuaded the city to let him extend his track south along Osborne Street to the company-owned River Park on the bank of the Red River. Realizing the need to create a major attraction at the end of the line in order to build up passenger traffic, Austin personally purchased for $2,000 an additional 51½ acres of land from the Catholic Church of St. Boniface. It was part of a peninsula formed by a natural loop of the Red River, and lay directly across from the company's River Park. It was a picturesque spot, and Austin named it Elm Park. With the proper recreational facilities established on it, as well as in River Park on the opposite shore, he reasoned, the area would become a popular picnic and amusement centre. Moreover, the novelty of riding on an electric car would be a further inducement to Winnipegers to patronize the new line. But his deepest concern, of course, was his need to convince the city fathers that the electric trolley system was practical and safe. They might then be persuaded to reconsider their earlier decision and allow him to electrify the entire Winnipeg service.

By November 1890, the first electric streetcar to be seen in Winnipeg was delivered, and the following January, in the brittle cold of a prairie winter, limited service on the first mile of track was officially inaugurated.

162

A reporter from the *Manitoba Morning Free Press* was on hand to record his impressions:

> The Street Railway company opened their electric railway on River Avenue last evening. As the manager was not quite certain about everything being in readiness at the hour proposed, no public announcement of the first trip was made; but when the time of starting was definitely fixed at 7:30 o'clock the news soon spread, and at the hour mentioned there were many more passengers waiting than could be accommodated at once. The members of city council were first invited to enter the car, which punctually made its appearance, being drawn over the Main street bridge by horses. After it had been inspected and its appearance and conveniences admired, Acting Mayor Taylor turned on the current. The car was at once brilliantly lighted and the rays of the coal oil lamps which had been doing duty, at once sank into obscurity. By the time the guests had tested the comfortable springs and cushions of the seats, noted the convenient arrangement of buttons for signalling to stop the car and received a word of explanation concerning the invisible source of heat supply, everything was ready for the start. . . . The track was in excellent condition, and of course everybody was ready to vote the car a vast improvement on the horse cars. No doubt when the summer returns and the trip is extended to the park, to which the track has been for some time complete, thousands of people will make frequent excursions to the new and beautiful resort. On the return of the car to the Main street bridge there was another large load of passengers waiting for the second trip. Manager Austin was in the best of spirits, making everybody welcome; and the small boys and girls as well as the prominent citizens were treated to free rides back and forth during the evening. The inauguration of the road was a complete success, the car handling the heavy load of passengers with apparent ease.

With the arrival of summer, Austin's two electric cars with trailers were strained to accommodate the eager crowds, who boarded the gleaming new cars on the south side of the Assiniboine River, just across the Main Street Bridge, after riding as far as the bridge in the horse-cars. The City Council refused to let the old-type cars cross the bridge, so the park-bound passengers either made their way on foot or were carried across in a tally-ho. At the end of the new trolley line, close to the Red River, former Torontonians were astonished to find themselves disembarking at a large, freshly painted station with a familiar name on the sign over the platform: Albert Austin, with a touch of nostalgia, had called it *Spadina.*

A local visitor to Austin's twin parks during the summer of 1891 described the sylvan setting with enthusiasm and pride:

> It was like a fairy land at night to see the different coloured incandescent lights distributed through the parks. On reaching the park the first station is River Park, on the right being the ball grounds and driving park; on the left is Edison Hall, a pretty pavilion where electrical exhibits will be held, as well as summer concerts. The next station is Fern Glen; here is where the campers will camp out and every-day picnic parties get off. It is very nicely situated on the river bank and surrounded by ferns. Passing on to the last station, Spadina, visitors to the park notice a pontoon bridge over the Red River leading to Elm Park, and as a New York gentleman remarked, Central Park was a beautiful place, but all madeup, while Elm Park was the most natural one he had seen, with its large trees and ferns three feet high by the acre.

Another more practical observer, ignoring the botanical delights of Elm

Park, noted that two large buildings had been constructed amidst the trees: a pavilion with a shingled roof of sufficient size to shelter 800 people, with "a strong, smooth floor suitable for dancing," and another structure that contained refreshment stands, tables, and benches for the excursionists.

Austin, naturally, was confident that he had proved his point. A large segment of the city's population, which then numbered 25,000, had accepted his electric trolley-line with unqualified enthusiasm. He had an unblemished safety record behind him, and he had brought distinction to Winnipeg by having pioneered the first commercially operated electric streetcar service in Canada (Toronto did not see its first electric car in regular service until August 15, 1892). With these considerations in mind, Austin again applied to the City Council in August 1891, for the necessary changes in his franchise so that he could proceed with the electrification of the entire Winnipeg system. The city fathers were non-committal.

About this time a bird of ill omen appeared on the Winnipeg scene. His name was George H. Campbell. A jaunty, persuasive man of commanding presence, he had been prominent in Ottawa some years before as a lobbyist for the financially troubled Canadian Pacific Railway. He enjoyed the reputation of being able to deal effectively with politicians at all levels of government. He liked fine cigars and he handed them out freely. He let it be known that he represented important eastern Canadian interests which were anxious to obtain an exclusive franchise for the operation of an electric street railway in Winnipeg. He then submitted a formal proposal to the City Council. He wrote: "I have associated with me a number of gentlemen who are prepared, if the city will grant the necessary franchise, to furnish all the capital necessary to put in a first-class system of electric street railways in this city." According to the City Hall reporter, he did not, however, "gratify public curiosity by mentioning the names of the capitalists whom he represented."

Winnipeg naturally buzzed with rumours, and then it was confirmed that the wealthy James Ross of Montreal, and William Mackenzie of Toronto, former railroad contractors, were the men behind George H. Campbell. The excitement mounted. The suspense was finally broken by a sensational newspaper report. It was headed "Mr. Van Horne In It!" The story read:

> A rumour was current in certain quarters yesterday to the effect that Mr. Van Horne, president of the C.P.R., is interested in the Ross-Mackenzie offer. A reporter called on Mr. G. H. Campbell and asked him if it were true. That gentleman confirmed the report. The impression is that this company will make a stir in Winnipeg the equal of which has not been experienced since boom days, and they possibly will, as the majority of the aldermen regard their offer as far more advantageous to the city than that of Winnipeg Street Railway Company.

It became clearer by the hour to Albert Austin that the ground-swell that Campbell was creating threatened to sweep away his hopes and play havoc with his dreams. He continued to press the city fathers for a decision and attempted to explain the reason why some of his proposals differed from those of the Ross-Mackenzie group. Basically, he sought a longer franchise, he favoured a system with a connecting pole and overhead wires, and he would only commit himself to laying three miles of new track in the city within the first year of the installation of the electric system. Campbell, on the other hand, was conciliatory on all points. Like a fox frisking among a brood of prairie chickens, he quickly established a mastery over the city fathers. He sought a shorter franchise than was customary in other cities; he proposed using a storage battery mode of operation to allay the council's fear of overhead wires;* he promised to lay eight miles of new track by December 1, 1892; and finally, he undertook to carry, free of charge, all uniformed mail carriers, policemen, and firemen.

Enmeshed in a net of its own making, the City Council decided to test the issue of franchise rights, and throw the matter open to all comers. It drew up a formal basis for offers, "To Construct, Own and Operate an Electric Street Railway in the City of Winnipeg."[1] Albert Austin, of course, immediately claimed a prospective infringement of the franchise he had enjoyed since 1882. He contended that all that was needed was to up-date his present agreement to recognize a new form of horsepower.

On February 1, 1892, the battle for the Winnipeg franchise was brought to a head. On that day, a black day from Austin's point of view, the City Council enacted a by-law that awarded the Ross-Mackenzie group the exclusive right to build an electric street railway in Winnipeg. Austin's horse-car franchise, of course, still had fifteen years to run, and he continued to operate his system.

By the following July, the new group placed its first electric car in service on Main Street. It was a gala occasion. The first car, packed with local dignitaries, ran north to Selkirk Avenue, then west to the Exhibition Grounds at Sinclair Street. A member of the press reported, as the car jolted to a stop at the grounds,

> Mayor Macdonald rose to his feet and expressed his complete satisfaction at the successful opening of the road. . . . His Worship then moved a vote of thanks to Mr. Campbell for the energy he had displayed in completing the line in time to accommodate passengers to the exhibition, which was seconded by ex-Ald. Alex. Black, and at the suggestion of his worship three cheers were given for Mr. Campbell. . . . Hearty cheers were then given for the mayor, and the passengers betook themselves to the grounds.

A *Free Press* reporter noted dryly that George H. Campbell, now the manager of the new Company, was prominent in the inaugural proceedings "as he extended the hospitality of the company in a box of luxuriant Havana cigars."

Austin, incensed with the decision of the City Council, immediately launched legal proceedings against the city of Winnipeg and the new Winnipeg Electric Street Railway Company for infringement of his franchise. The mills of Justice grind slowly, however, and while the Supreme Court of Manitoba pondered the issue, Austin continued to run his horse-cars in direct competition with the new electric cars. The four tracks of the two companies paralleled each other on Main Street, and the bizarre result was described by a contemporary writer:

> Horse-cars had the advantage those first winters. They could be put on runners. Electric car axles, brittle in the severe cold, broke easily. One can imagine the derision of the horse-car drivers as they passed stalled electric cars. Bitter rivalry raged between the two Companies. The citizens were partisan and jeers and jibes often led to hectic battles.
> The riding public profited from the competition which led to a price war. Tickets sold at fifty for a dollar. The horse-car Company started it,

---

*The storage battery system was later proved impracticable and was discarded.

the Electric Railway followed suit. There was even talk of a one cent fare.

The cut prices lasted as long as the legal battle for the franchise rights, which didn't end until 1894.[2]

In 1893, two years after Austin had established his successful electric line to River Park on the Red River, and notwithstanding his pioneer role as the founder of the first efficient public transportation system in Winnipeg ten years before, the Manitoba Supreme Court upheld the legality of the City Council's action in granting a competing franchise to the influential Ross-Mackenzie group.

Albert Austin at once decided to appeal the unfavourable decision of the Canadian Court to the Judicial Committee of the Privy Council in England. He retained as his counsel the Honourable S. Hume Blake, Q.C. of Toronto, a brother of the Honourable Edward Blake, Q.C., and in February 1894, they left New York on the Cunard Royal Mail Steamship *Umbria* bound for Liverpool.

Austin's correspondence with his wife, who remained in Winnipeg with their four children, contains an illuminating account of his experiences and impressions while he visited England.

To begin with, the voyage was a nightmare. The ship ploughed through tumultuous seas from the moment it slipped out of the Hudson River until it reached calmer water in the Irish Sea. The steamer tossed and rolled, he related, as if it were a child's toy. He withdrew to his cabin the first day out, and though he managed on occasion to appear on deck, clutching the rail unsteadily, he never entered the dining salon throughout the entire voyage. By the time they reached the Port of Queenstown in southern Ireland, where the *Umbria* paused to unload some mail, he estimated he had lost fully twenty-five pounds as a result of his involuntary fast. Mr. Blake, on the other hand, was a good sailor, as was his wife who accompanied him, and he was able to devote most of the voyage to preparing Austin's case for presentation at Westminster.

The *Umbria* finally docked in Liverpool in a heavy fog, and Austin confessed, "When I put my foot on solid ground I thanked God for my safe arrival." Mr. and Mrs. Blake "had about 20 trunks, valises, etc. which had to be separated, examined and moved dozens of times" before they reached their London destination. At Mr. Blake's insistence the party travelled Third Class (economy) in the special boat train that carried them to London. Austin, who was himself half-starved from his ordeal of seasickness, endeared himself to his fellow-travellers by buying two big lunch baskets at the quayside which were filled with cold chicken, ham, bread, homemade butter, cheese, mustard, and ginger ale. We may be certain that the ginger ale was not chosen as a mix for a more stimulating drink because both Blake and Austin were devout advocates of the cause of Temperance. The party reached London at a late hour, and put up at the Hotel Windsor in Victoria Street, Westminster. Before retiring, Austin luxuriated for a while in a hot foot bath before an open fire. He pondered his deliverance from the perils of the deep, and ended the day reading a few passages from his "mantelpiece Testament."

The following morning, working at a desk in the reading room with Mr. and Mrs. Blake and "others of high rank" around him, the impressionable Westerner reflected upon the hushed and decorous efficiency of his London quarters. Sensitive to an environment that was strangely different to the gusty informality of the hotels he had visited in Chicago, St. Paul, and Winnipeg, like a modern Earl of Chesterfield moralizing on the manners of his time, he noted: "One should never speak in a loud tone to be heard across the room," and upon being introduced to an Englishman, "one should never advance towards him, the arm extended in the expansive American manner, but rather move close to the individual, and then offer a hand."

In that spring of 1894, London seemed very old and venerable; it was a city that dwelt in the fading light of Queen Victoria's seemingly endless reign; but, according to Austin, it was still the centre of the universe.

He was impressed with the rubber-tired hackney carriages that rolled silently through the clean, gas-lit streets of the immense city, but he bemoaned the fact that there were no streetcars in evidence in London, only a horse-drawn omnibus system with "seats on top at a penny a mile." Like travellers of today he wished England would use steam or hot water for heating its hotels. "It is getting so cold in this room," he added, "that I must conclude for the night."

The next day he strolled with Mr. Blake through St. James' Park which was stirring with the first signs of spring. He then called upon Sir Charles Tupper, the Canadian high commissioner, whose wife, it was said, had become so devoted to the glitter of London society that she refused to return to its pale transcript on the Ottawa River.

Voltaire once remarked that the only certain outcome of litigation was its cost — a concern that weighed more heavily on Austin's mind with each passing week as he waited anxiously for his case to be heard. "I do wish I had more money," he wrote to Mary Austin, "to enable me to buy things to take to you, but I must leave this for another time, hoping luck will be in our pathway. I believe I would take half London to you if I had the money for I find myself so often looking at something you would like so much to have."

As things turned out, the luck the homesick traveller hoped to encounter eluded him. He described the frequent meetings that he and Mr. Blake held with their solicitors, Bompas & Co., who thought that Austin had "a good case." And there were further meetings with a junior barrister as a preliminary to their discussions with the eminent counsel Sir John Rigby, who had agreed to appear on their behalf before the Judicial Committee. Rigby, who was also solicitor-general, bore a striking resemblance, Austin irreverently reported to his wife, to Mr. Perrett, the Winnipeg jeweller. "I do hope he has looked at our case since the last interview," Austin commented ominously on one occasion.

The hearing came on finally in mid-March before the highest tribunal in the British Empire. Austin, his thirty-seventh birthday at hand, was mildly optimistic. Sitting as a Committee of the House of Lords, the four elderly gentlemen who comprised the Court, without their customary robes and wigs, ranged themselves informally round a horseshoe table of solid oak. Lord Herschell, the lord chancellor, presided. His colleagues were Lord Watson, who was to write the judgment, Lord Macnaghten, and Sir Richard Couch. The proceedings continued for two days, but at the end it was apparent that their lordships would "humbly advise Her Majesty" that the judgment of the Manitoba Court be affirmed. In their wisdom they decided that the Winnipeg City Council had not granted Austin an exclusive franchise in 1882, and that the council was within its rights in authorizing the Ross-

Mackenzie interests to set themselves up in competition with the existing horse-car system. In a majestic dichotomy, their lordships condoned the simultaneous use of several of the principal streets of Winnipeg by the two competing street railway companies.

Austin, disheartened and dreading the thought of another sea voyage, prepared immediately to return to Canada. He wished he could have travelled overland through the wastes of Siberia rather than expose himself again to the wrath of the Atlantic. He reached Toronto without incident, however, and conferred with his father at *Spadina*. We may be sure that he also sought the advice of his old mentor Senator Frank Smith, who was well informed on street railway matters, as well as that of Edmund B. Osler, who had taken an early financial interest in his project. In any event, he opened negotiations with William Mackenzie, who had recently acquired an important interest in the Toronto Street Railway, with a view to merging the two Winnipeg transportation companies. Mackenzie, impatient with the ticket price-war in Winnipeg, was anxious to see his electric system in that city raise its level of profitability. Agreement was quickly reached in principle that the Ross-Mackenzie group would buy out Austin's street railway company. Matters were left that Mackenzie would proceed to Winnipeg within the week to be on hand for the completion of the transaction.

When Austin returned to Winnipeg early in May, he was interviewed by a reporter from the *Manitoba Morning Free Press*. "Were you satisfied with the counsel who led your case?" he was asked, in reference to Sir John Rigby.

"Not particularly so," Austin answered with the glum candour of an aggrieved litigant. "Had I to go over the ground again I would not employ any of the great English counsel, who are altogether too unapproachable. I should prefer a Canadian counsel, such as Hon. Edward Blake, as senior, with a London junior. The men of high standing in the legal profession in England appear to think that they can master a case if they have it in hand for a few hours before the time of hearing. Our senior counsel was Sir John Rigby, who was also, unfortunately for us, solicitor-general, and much mixed up with the late Gladstone government. Mr. Gladstone having resigned a short time before our trial came on, it was next to impossible to obtain the interviews with him which I considered necessary for the proper presentation of the case."

"Were you much surprised at the attitude of the supreme court?" the *Free Press* reporter continued, referring to the Judicial Committee of the Privy Council.

"I fully expected that the learned judges of the privy council would have taken at least a reasonable view of our case, for I think we fully showed that even if there were any ambiguity in the reading of our charter from the city, yet it was plainly the intention of the council to grant us exclusive rights, and had we not believed this at first, we should never have undertaken to develop a section of country at a large expense only to have our lines paralleled when a return from the outlay was beginning to come in."

A week later William Mackenzie arrived in Winnipeg as planned, and the sale of the Winnipeg Street Railway Company to the Ross-Mackenzie interests was completed against a cash payment of $175,000. The 51½-acre Elm Park property that Albert Austin had bought for $2,000 in 1890 was excluded from the agreement. He decided to retain it as an investment. It was inevitable that the street railway fiasco would leave a residue of bitterness behind it, but by 1907 Austin had good reason to feel better about that episode of his life. In that year he made a cash sale of the Elm Park parcel for $105,000. Time is a great healer, Austin must have reflected on that occasion, but its therapy could not match the benign effect of a well-turned investment.

Following the sale of his company, Austin began immediately to make arrangements for his return to the East. Embittered over the volatile political climate in Winnipeg and concerned with his aged father's declining health, he concluded that the best thing to do in the circumstances was to re-establish himself and his growing family in Toronto. His decision was also influenced by the death of his older brother, James Henry, which had occurred at *Spadina* in December 1891. The affable manager of his father's farmlands had celebrated his thirty-eighth birthday just a few weeks before his end.

Albert and Mary Austin's departure from Winnipeg was not an easy one. They had spent the first twelve years of their married life there; their roots were deep and their friends legion. They had almost come to think of themselves as pioneer residents of the city. They had seen the West ablaze with excitement in the spring of 1885 when troops were rushed through Winnipeg on their way to suppress Riel's insurrection in Saskatchewan. Later that summer, two of Austin's horse-cars had paused to have their photographs taken under a triumphal arch that spanned Main Street. Its banners read: "Welcome Home — Every Man Has Done His Duty — Otter, Middleton, Strange." And in the fall of the same year they had joined the crowds on the railway platform to cheer the departure of a historic train bearing a load of dignitaries to Craigellachie, a mountain clearing in British Columbia, where the bewhiskered Donald A. Smith of the CPR was to tie together two bands of iron, and link Winnipeg with the Pacific and the exotic Orient. Through booms and recessions, floods and droughts, they had watched the city, once a forlorn fur-trading centre, win the accolade of the metropolis of the Canadian West.

Most difficult of all, perhaps, was the sale of their Carlton Street house, which Austin had built when he brought his wife to Winnipeg, at a time the prospects for his street railway seemed as boundless as the western skies, and where their five children had been born.[3]

In Toronto, a pleasant house was rented on Lowther Avenue, a twenty-minute walk from *Spadina,* and by Christmas of 1894 Albert and Mary Austin were gathering together the strands of their earlier life in the city. The faithful Annie Duncan was included in the *entourage* that settled into Lowther Avenue. A pious Scottish woman, she had been recruited in Winnipeg some years before as a nurse for the Austin children. Under her patient hand, her charges made a rapid and untroubled adjustment to their new surroundings. The older children never tired of talking about their Winnipeg days. They never forgot the prolonged, sub-zero temperatures of the prairies; the sound of the telegraph wires singing in the winter night; the scrubby groves of prairie poplar that the Plains Indians called "women's tongues" because their leaves were never still; nor, above all, the flame dance of the aurora-borealis far off in the northern sky.

Chapter 16

The Death of James Austin

Albert Austin had been absent from Toronto for fourteen years. In that time, from 1880 to 1894, the city had undergone a remarkable change. Responding to Sir John A. Macdonald's protective tariff policy, and the completion of the transcontinental railroad, new manufacturing plants had appeared in the city, old businesses had expanded, and Toronto had absorbed half-a-dozen neighbouring municipalities. By the mid-1890's the city's population, which had numbered less than 90,000 in 1880, was now surging towards the 200,000 mark. Toronto's lusty expansion had, however, swirled around and beyond *Spadina,* leaving its rural character wholly undisturbed.

The westerly forty acres of his farmlands that James Austin had sold in 1889 were still vacant land. Towards Bathurst Street, the Wells family held to its ancient *Davenport* house, and next door to *Spadina* on the east, Anne Arthurs, now a widow, continued to occupy *Ravenswood.* Her place had become celebrated for its charity bazaars and garden-fêtes. Overnight, like giant toadstools, marquees sprang up on her lawns, necklaces of Japanese lanterns linked rustic stands that were swathed in brilliant bunting — and a military band was on hand on such occasions to lift the spirits of her guests to levels of impulsive generosity that assured the success of each charitable event.

Just to the east of *Ravenswood,* Samuel Nordheimer's Victorian mansion, *Glenedyth,* still cast the same pale light of elegance across its romantic parklands. Nordheimer, like a Heidelberg fencing master, had affected a flowing, white moustache, and his retinue now boasted a butler in striped trousers and a bumble-bee waistcoat, and a coachman who wore a cockade in his hat by virtue of his master's position as consul in Ontario for the German Empire.[1] *Glenedyth,* like *The Grange* which had been built by Mrs. Nordheimer's uncle, D'Arcy Boulton, Jr., was a house geared to effortless hospitality. A ball or a dinner party could be arranged with little more than a word to a housekeeper. On such occasions, Samuel Nordheimer never tired of leading his guests to his tower room where their gaze could sweep across the panorama of steeples that lay below the Davenport Hill and the blue water that glinted from the lake further south. On a clear day, with the help of a telescope, his guests could discern across Lake Ontario the figures of people moving about on the platform at the top of Brock's Monument on the distant Queenston Heights. And on the southern horizon the pillar of mist that rose perpetually from the great falls of Niagara evoked memories of the ever-popular Clifton House which overlooked the cataract.

In the mid-1890's the residents of the Davenport Hill still encountered endless processions of farm wagons wending their way along the unpaved Davenport Road heading for the St. Lawrence Market. In those days the farmers of King Township entered the city by way of the Vaughan Plank Road, which led from Dufferin Street to Bathurst Street. There was a toll-gate at the top of the Bathurst Street hill and at that point the old toll road cut across the hill in front of the present Hillcrest Hospital. It then descended gradually to Davenport Road in order to avoid the abrupt descent of the often impassable Bathurst Street hill. Traces of the toll road are still visible on that hillside today. The country farmers, perched on top of their hay-wagons, deposited their tolls in a coconut half-shell attached to the end of a pole that was passed up to them by the obliging toll-keeper. Their wagons, often a dozen in number, then resumed their journey down the incline to the Davenport Road. The drivers made little effort to maintain close order in their convoys. The horses attended to that themselves. They plodded contentedly towards the market on Front Street each browsing off the load ahead. When they reached their destination, willing purchasers were on hand to buy the hay by the wagonload, which the farmer then delivered to their stables.

In 1894, James Austin, now in his eighty-first year, was still the active head of The Dominion Bank and The Consumers' Gas Company of Toronto. The *Toronto World* had recently compared him to William Eward Gladstone while that famous British statesman still held the office of prime minister. The article, after commenting upon The Dominion Bank's Annual Meeting of May 31, 1893, went on to say:

> People talk about Mr. Gladstone administering the affairs of England at his advanced years; surely he is doing it no better, if as well, as the venerable but active James Austin, one time a journeyman printer in this town, who presides over the destinies of the Dominion Bank, at the corner of King and Yonge. A bank that still has the same president and cashier (R.H. Bethune) as it had when it began business, and which in the interval has made its rest fund equal to its capital, must be extraordinarily well managed or wonderfully fortunate.[2]

Under Gladstone the Liberal Party in England had reached the pinnacle of its power. No leader approaching his stature was found to succeed him when he withdrew from public life in 1894. In the years ahead, the party in which he had been the dominant figure for decades was to see its influence wither and die. In the case of the leadership of The Dominion Bank, the venerable James Austin took care to set in place a line of succession to himself that was unique in the annals of Canadian banking. His two closest colleagues, Sir Frank Smith and Sir Edmund B. Osler, were to serve successive terms as president until 1924; Sir Augustus Nanton, who had joined the Pellatt & Osler firm as a junior in 1877, later becoming a partner of Osler, Hammond & Nanton in Winnipeg, succeeded Osler as head of the bank in 1924; Nanton died the following year, and Albert Austin then occupied the president's chair until 1933. For more than sixty years of its history, James Austin and the men closely associated with him in his lifetime were the dominant voices in the affairs of The Dominion Bank.

Though often urged by his friends to stand for public office, James Austin

steadfastly refused. His experiences with his old chief William Lyon Mackenzie, which culminated in the epic fiasco of 1837, left him with an intense
distaste for public controversy. He preferred to remain in the background
and lend his support instead to his colleagues, men like Sir Frank Smith and
Sir Edmund Osler who sat in the Dominion Parliament for many years under
the Conservative banner.

Of those two men, Sir Frank Smith's political career was the most remarkable. From 1882 to 1896, as a member of the Senate, he held various
cabinet posts under a succession of prime ministers: Sir John A. Macdonald,
Sir John Abbott, Sir John Thompson, and Sir Charles Tupper. Above all,
however, he is remembered for the decisive role he played in 1885 when he
intervened successfully with Sir John A. Macdonald to obtain a government
loan to aid the financially stricken Canadian Pacific Railway.

It was generally known throughout the business community that during
the railroad's financial crisis of 1885, Senator Frank Smith, the proprietor
of the wholesale grocery firm of F. Smith & Co., was himself seriously extended as a result of having supplied goods on credit to the railroad contractors. Their plight became desperate when the Canadian Pacific ran out
of cash. It was not known, however, that in that critical period, James
Austin and the resources of The Dominion Bank stood solidly behind Frank
Smith, just as Austin and his partner Patrick Foy had backed him in 1849
when he had first set up in business for himself in western Ontario.

The crisis passed, the railroad was completed, and by 1888 James
Austin, addressing a meeting of American and Canadian businessmen in
Toronto, spoke with pride of the Dominion's prosperity, which he attributed
in large measure to the new transcontinental railroad. The occasion was the
16th Annual Meeting of the influential American Gas Light Association.
James Austin and the directors of the Consumers' Gas Company had coaxed
the association to hold its convention in Toronto in the hope that the surrounding publicity would help diminish the threat to gas as an illuminant
that was then being posed by electricity.

While the convention may have strengthened neighbourly ties, however,
it did little to slow the advance of electricity as a competitor of gas. Indeed,
the following year, bowing to the inevitable, James Austin and his board of
directors applied for a franchise to wire the city. They pointed out that under
their system, their elecric wires would be placed underground thus reducing
the forest of poles that was already disfiguring the face of the city. At the
corner of King and Yonge streets, for instance, there were separate pole
installations for the fire alarm and telephone systems, two railway telegraph
services, and the poles and wires of the Toronto Electric Light Company.
Fearing an expansion of its gas monopoly, the city fathers refused to grant
the company an electric lighting franchise. And to make matters worse, the
following year, in 1890, the city blandly asked the gas company to remove
2,300 of its gas lamps from the streets to make way for their arch-rival,
electricity. While some sections of the city retained gas for outdoor lighting,
many of Toronto's familiar lamplighters withdrew that year from its main
thoroughfares and vanished into history.

The company continued to enjoy a strong, competitive edge, however,
insofar as indoor lighting was concerned. Electricity for that purpose still
cost twice as much as gas. The Toronto *Telegram* experimented with an
electric system and switched back to gas. The proprietors of the city's billiard halls, whose critical patrons demanded a clear, steady light for their

game of precision, expressed an emphatic preference for gaslight. And thousands of homeowners throughout Toronto did the same. The gas company officials, however, were keenly aware of the need to diversify their service against the day when the cost of electricity declined. As early as 1880 they had started promoting the use of gas for cooking as well as lighting, and throughout the decade, by establishing special rates, sales of gas and cooking appliances climbed steadily. By the time electricity had become widely accepted as a home illuminant, and the consumption of gas for that purpose had fallen, the public's enthusiastic response to the application of gas for cooking was thrusting the company into a new era of dramatic growth. From 1883 to 1893 the output of gas more than doubled, and the company's meter installations grew from 5,100 to 17,000. By 1903, 32,000 meters were in use, and gas production had doubled again.

In 1896, as James Austin reached the end of an association with the Consumers' Gas Company that had begun with his election to its board in 1859, he had good grounds for confidence about the future. He had even come to accept electricity as a useful partner in sharing the burdens implicit in the operation of a public utility.

By the late summer of that year, his visits to his downtown office were sharply curtailed. Now in his eighty-fourth year, the old Irishman's strength was failing. On a hot afternoon he was at last forced to yield to the cool seclusion of the covered verandah that lay on the east side of *Spadina.* Here, amidst the trailing clematis and hanging flower baskets, he drowsed in his chair, a red silk handkerchief around his neck, his Irish setter panting at his side. The silence was broken by only a shrill-chirping cicada and the oaks and chestnuts as they stirred in the gentle wind.

In his declining years, James Austin used to say that if he could last through March he would be good for another year. In the month of February 1897, it was apparent that he would not. Confined wholly to *Spadina,* it was evident that his life was moving towards its close.

Early in the morning of February 27, Albert Austin was awakened by a knock at the door of his Lowther Avenue house. His father's coachman had driven down from *Spadina* to inform him that James Austin's condition had become critical overnight, and his mother felt he should come at once to his father's bedside.

Albert Austin dressed hastily, entered the waiting carriage, and set out for *Spadina.* The darkness of the interior of the carriage, the black horses, the coachman's sombre livery, all combined to form a premonitory symbol of mourning. A host of unrelated thoughts arose unbidden in his mind. He found himself recalling the fateful silence of a street in London's West End where straw had been laid across the road to dull the sound of the cabs and carriages as they passed a great house whose owner lay dying; he recalled the events of his sister Margaret's return from England, when he was a boy, her death at *Spadina,* and her entombment in the mausoleum that his father had built in St. James' Cemetery before he had bought *Spadina;* and he recalled his father's excitement thirty years ago when they had left their house on Jarvis Street and moved to their hilltop farm; *Spadina* was then a joyous place, especially when his sister and her husband, Anne and George Arthurs, had lived with them briefly while their *Ravenswood* was being built; now George Arthurs was dead, as was his brother Jim Austin; and Charlie Joice, Margaret's son, lay beside his mother in the family vault behind a forbidding door of oak.

The coachman urged his horses up the Old Carriage Drive, now Walmer Road Hill, and *Spadina* came into view, the early morning sun glinting from its buff walls. The coachman pulled up at the end of the covered verandah on the west side of the house and Albert Austin alighted and entered quickly. He made his way up the winding staircase that led to his father's transomed bedroom on the second floor. The doctor in attendance acknowledged his arrival with a nod. After a moment, perhaps intentionally distracting himself, Austin turned and adjusted the gas grate that was hissing in the fireplace. He then looked out across Toronto from his father's window and pondered the absolute stillness of the winter scene before him. Against the background of the motionless lake to the south, the smoke from the city's chimneys looked like taut, white strings tied to a cardboard sky. He finally left the room, and joined his mother and sister, Anne Arthurs, in the parlour at the foot of the stairs. Their vigil that February day was long. The end came just after the sun had fallen behind the great oak woods of *Davenport*.[3]

Susan Bright Austin was eighty-one when her husband died. For a short time she was to be the only occupant of *Spadina*. Her domestic needs were attended to by two hearty Irish girls who had been recruited from the local Protestant Orphanage by her daughter. The girls' bedrooms were located in the cellar, at the foot of the kitchen stairs. Their ground-level windows were fitted with iron bars, a safeguard that was probably designed as much to keep the girls in as it was to keep intruders out. Their duties, which were performed amidst gusts of rollicking laughter, consisted mainly of cooking and cleaning. They were forbidden, however, to menace certain sensitive areas of the house, such as Susan Austin's cherished reception room, drawing-room, and highly polished front staircase, with their brooms and feather dusters. To avoid such predictable disasters as smashed china or scarred woodwork, those sections of *Spadina* were reserved for their mistress's special care, and she guarded them jealously.

In every respect, Susan Austin had been the Victorian housewife *par excellence*. In her attitude towards her children, as towards her servants, she was consistently firm and kind. Her needs for outside diversion were few. A weekly visit in the carriage to the shops on King Street, a boat trip across the lake to Queenston, a brief holiday with her husband at Saratoga Springs, or the Clifton House at Niagara, were the most distant points to which her curiosity carried her. Her real interest lay in running her house. And she did it very well. She did so because she had learned from the early settlers of York to anticipate and respond to the fullness of each season. Like the cottage where her parents, Lewis and Margaret Bright, had lived on Lot Street, *Spadina* was always attuned to the rhythms of the year. In the springtime the house was filled with the fragrance of lilacs and lily-of-the-valley; in the fall a rich aroma issued from the preserving kettles of the *Spadina* kitchen; and in the wintertime the comfortable scent of home-made bayberry candles and blazing pine logs hung heavily around the place. The finale of domestic preparation was always reached at Christmas because of the tradition in the Bright family of celebrating that day with greater than customary warmth: Lewis Bright, the founder of the family in York in 1802, had been born in Gloucestershire, England on Christmas Day, 1747.

Susan Austin was by no means a matronly recluse. Like any energetic housewife, she delighted in testing the efficiency of her domestic arrangements against the demands of evening entertainment. The ample and varied fare of her table was legend. A handwritten note in the margin of an old copy of Dr. Scadding's *Toronto of Old,* inscribed by her niece Sophia Scadding beside a reference to *Spadina,* reads: "I can never forget the rich cream and butter pats and Aunt Susan's cellar." Sophia, of course, was the daughter of Jane Bright Scadding.

In the tradition of those Victorian times, when each member of a social gathering was expected to take a turn with a musical instrument, or even break into tremulous song, Susan Austin's forte was recitation. Her voice was resonant, her memory good, her ear for dialect keen. While her repertoire included verses from Sir Walter Scott and Longfellow, it was generally agreed that she achieved her best effect with the Irish ballads she rendered in her husband's Ulster speech.

The question of the future occupancy of *Spadina* was quickly settled. After having been the mistress of the house for over thirty years, Susan Austin, in a selfless gesture of concern, insisted upon removing herself and her servants to the nearby cottage library that the Honourable Robert Baldwin had built when he retired to *Spadina.* She wished the big house to be available in its entirety to Albert and Mary Austin and their five children.

Perhaps James Austin was partly responsible for her decision. In 1892, five years before his death, he had divided the remaining forty acres of his *Spadina* farmlands between his two children, Albert Austin and Anne Arthurs. By deed that year, the *Spadina* house with 20 acres of land around it, extending from the Davenport Road to St. Clair Avenue, was transferred to Albert Austin while he was still in Winnipeg wrestling with the problems of electrifying his street railway. The easterly twenty acres, upon which the Arthurs' *Ravenswood* was located, were transferred at the same time to Edmund B. Osler, a director of The Dominion Bank, and Robert H. Bethune, the bank's general manager, to be held in trust for Anne Arthurs and her three children. Among the assets of the trust were mortgages covering over forty of the lots included in James Austin's subdivision of 1889, when he had sold off the westerly forty acres of his original *Spadina* property. Curiously, the Arthurs' trust also included a lease to part of the St. Lawrence Hall on King Street East. The origin of the lease is of particular interest because of the recent restoration of that famous landmark as part of Toronto's celebration of the Centennial of the Dominion.

James Austin's leasehold interest in the St. Lawrence Hall had arisen as a result of the Great King Street Fire of April 1849, when he and his partner Patrick Foy were carrying on their wholesale business in premises on the north side of King Street East, close to Church Street. The holocaust that destroyed the old Town Hall and Market Place on the south side of King Street, as well as St. James' Cathedral on the north, also gutted the offices of Foy and Austin. It has been said that while the Great Fire of London was still smoldering, Sir Christopher Wren began laying his plans for the new St. Paul's that was to rise on the site of the old. In Toronto, while the acrid smell of destruction still filled the air over King Street, the idea of building a new centre on the site of the old Town Hall–Market Place was born. William Thomas was appointed architect of the project by the city, and tenders for construction were called in August 1849. The following October 15, before any serious work could begin on the site, Patrick Foy and James Austin obtained from the city a lease of the desirable northeast corner of the proposed new hall. Their ground floor space occupied a frontage of twenty-five feet on King Street, and extended south along what was then called East Market Place (now Jarvis Street) for a distance of seventy-five feet. A year later, on October 30, 1850, the city of Toronto announced that it would hold a public auction to dispose of the leases of the new shops in the St. Lawrence Arcade as well as the cellars underneath. The Foy and Austin lease, of course, was not affected by that sale when it occurred a few days later. While they may have originally intended to re-establish their business in the hall when it opened, the city directories of the period indicate that they found new offices elsewhere. We may conclude, therefore, that after the St. Lawrence Hall was formally opened with a glittering St. Andrew's Society ball in December 1850, the partners decided instead to retain their leasehold interest simply as an investment and rent the corner premises to other tenants.

In 1888, James Austin took over his former partner's interest in the lease, and in 1892 it was assigned to Osler and Bethune as trustees of the Anne J. Arthurs Trust. The Dominion Bank, which opened a Market Branch on the site in 1885, paid a rental as sub-tenant to Anne Arthurs for many years. Subsequently, it took the lease over itself. The present St. Lawrence Hall branch of the Toronto-Dominion Bank, therefore, occupies a site with which it has had an unbroken, though tenuous connection, through James Austin, since 1849. As has been shown, the bank's present leasehold interest is older by a year than the St. Lawrence Hall itself, and antedates as well the founding of both the Bank of Toronto (1856) and The Dominion Bank (1871).

During the summer of 1897, while the loyal citizens of Toronto were enjoying the dazzling celebrations that marked Queen Victoria's Diamond Jubilee, and Albert Austin and his mother pondered the alterations that seemed necessary to the two houses at *Spadina*, Anne Arthurs at *Ravenswood* was preparing for the marriage that November of her oldest daughter, Ada Austin Arthurs. Her fiancé was Henry Victor Holton Cawthra, the only son of Mr. and Mrs. Henry Cawthra of *Yeadon Hall*, Toronto. The wedding reception was to take place at *Ravenswood*. For the practiced and energetic Anne Arthurs, who was happiest when she was staging some highly original entertainment in her mid-Victorian house, the undertaking that lay ahead was to provide a stern test of her organizational skills. It was not that arranging a wedding reception was a novel experience for her. She had managed that to perfection early in the summer of 1894 when her daughter, Margaret, had been married to Sydney Anson Clifford Greene, a young Toronto lawyer. It was simply that a November wedding precluded the use of her picturesque grounds, and meant that the hundreds of guests who had been invited would have to be accommodated one way or the other inside the house.

The Arthurs-Cawthra wedding took place in St. Thomas' Anglican Church in Toronto on the afternoon of Wednesday, November 24, 1897. The church was packed and a vast throng repaired to *Ravenswood* for the reception afterwards. That the event occurred on a Wednesday should not lead to the conclusion that life in those Victorian times was so casual and unhurried, so indifferent to the demands of business, that the populace betook itself at will to such affairs. It must be remembered that seventy-five years ago the five-day week did not exist. Saturday was a business day. It mattered little, therefore, which day was chosen for a marriage ceremony, although a Victorian factory owner was more sympathetic to a request for the day off from a worker who wished to be married on a Saturday than if he had chosen some other day. Presumably, the day of rest afforded by the intervening Sabbath ensured the groom's return to work on Monday in reasonably effective condition. In modern times, in atonement for the abridged, forty-hour week, society has conceded that its weddings should take place only during non-business hours, that is, in the evening or on Saturday. And so, a rite whose importance was unchallenged and immutable in Victorian times, has settled comfortably today into the category of leisure-time activity.

Following the service at St. Thomas' Church, where the decorations according to one newspaper account "presented a picture of such beauty that has never been surpassed by any wedding in Toronto," a procession of victorias, phaetons, and landaus, gleaming with fresh lacquer, set out for the Davenport Hill. As the carriages mounted the steep drive that led from the Davenport Road to *Ravenswood* above, few of the guests would have been aware that they were traversing Aunt Maria's Road of the Baldwins' day, the old carriage drive that linked Dr. Baldwin's *Spadina* house with the Davenport Road, and Yonge Street, three-quarters of a century before.

"It was like entering a fairy palace," the *Toronto Sunday World* exclaimed, describing Anne Arthur's house, "where great globes of light, shaded in pink, hung like stars below the ceiling and flowers bloomed in endless profusion."

The list of guests included people from almost every branch of life, like Professor James Mavor, an academic of international reputation, F. H. Torrington who was extending his musical influence in the city as director of the Toronto Philharmonic Society and organist and choirmaster of the Metropolitan Methodist Church, Madame Lillian Nordika, the celebrated operatic singer, Lt. Col. William D. Otter (later General Sir William Otter, K.C.B., C.V.O.), Major Henry M. Pellatt, The Right Reverend Arthur Sweatman, Anglican Bishop of Toronto, and of course Edmund B. Osler, vice-president of The Dominion Bank.

As was the custom in those days, the newspaper accounts of the wedding did their best to gratify their readers' curiosity on all important points. They described in detail not only what the guests wore, but what they gave. Mr. Henry Cawthra, the groom's father, presented his son, we are told, with the deed to a property on St. George Street where a house was in course of construction, and he gave the bride "a beautiful set of stone marten furs." The bride's mother, Anne Arthurs, also combining the practical with the aesthetic, presented the couple with a cheque and "a beautiful jubilee chair" with the royal coat-of-arms embroidered on a white panel. Outlined in gilt, the chair commemorated Queen Victoria's Diamond Jubilee that year. Sir Frank Smith, the president of The Dominion Bank, recognizing the bride's devotion to music (she had studied opera abroad), made her a gift of an upright piano. Mr. and Mrs. Duncan Coulson provided "a Dresden clock, mounted in gold, with candelabra to match." Mr. Coulson at the time was general manager of the Bank of Toronto, a position in The Dominion Bank that was to be filled a few years later by Mr. Clarence Bogert who was one of the ushers. The Honourable and Mrs. William Mulock gave "a lovely statue," and Mr. George Beardmore "an exquisite china lamp." Mr. W. G. Gooderham, who like Henry Cawthra was a director of the Bank of Toronto, presented the couple with a cut-glass fruit bowl, and Mr. and Mrs. Samuel Nordheimer of *Glenedyth* next door were reported as having given "a case of costly silver."

Susan Bright Austin's *Spadina* parlour was converted into a dining room by her son Albert Austin in 1898. The swinging curtain conceals the pantry from the viewer's gaze, and the epergne on the sideboard, depicting a seated Arab with his camel under a lofty palm tree, was presented to James Austin in Aberdeen on New Year's Day, 1880, by the North of Scotland Canadian Mortgage Company.

—Photography by William Robertson

Following their wedding trip, Victor and Ada Cawthra returned to Mr. and Mrs. Henry Cawthra's *Yeadon Hall,* an imposing house of dignified calm which then graced the south side of College Street at the foot of St. George Street. Early the following year, in 1898, they moved happily into their new house, which still stands today at 163 St. George Street.[4]

Meanwhile at neighbouring *Spadina* it had been decided that before the main *Spadina* house was in a position to accommodate Albert Austin's family of seven comfortably, and the old Baldwin cottage library could absorb Susan Austin and her retinue, both houses would require extensive alterations. Accordingly, plans were developed during the fall of 1897 that led to the construction early the following spring of a two-storey addition to *Spadina,* and a substantial remodelling of the interior of the cottage.

As a result, in the first of the three major renovations that were to be undertaken by Albert Austin, *Spadina* was extended north by over thirty feet. The old kitchen on the east side of the house was demolished and a billiard room measuring over thirty-five feet in length was built in its place.

The billiard room as it is today at *Spadina*. It was built in 1898 by Albert William Austin when he extended the house north by 30 feet. It replaced the old *Spadina* kitchens. The "art nouveau" frieze was an important decorator's accessory at that time.

—Photography by William Robertson

A new kitchen and pantry were added on the west side of the house, adjoining Susan Austin's old parlour, which became the new dining room. The former dining room on the east side was converted into a library which gave access to the billiard room on one side and opened on to the old, ivy-embowered verandah to the south. These structural changes resulted in Dr. Baldwin's ancient front door, with its sidelights and elliptical transom, being moved to the end of the longer back hall that emerged from the new design, separating the billiard room from the kitchen area. Above these ground floor extensions, five new bedrooms were added, two of which were for the use of servants who otherwise would have been consigned to their habitual quarters in the basement.

The masons and carpenters finished their work late in the summer of 1898, and Albert Austin's family immediately moved into the refurbished *Spadina* from their rented house on Lowther Avenue. Susan Austin, after gathering together the furnishings she needed, likewise moved into her new abode. The renovated cottage now lay only about fifteen feet to the north

of the enlarged *Spadina,* overlooked by two great plate glass windows that had been set into the north wall of the new billiard room (Page 179). The cottage was a well-built, clapboard structure, as we have seen earlier, with a deep cellar and stone foundation. The old iron bell that the Honourable Robert Baldwin had installed in a cupola on the roof, with a thick rope descending to the side of the building, was still in place. A covered verandah faced the east, and through a screen of lilacs the aging Susan Austin looked out upon a small rock garden that she liked to tend herself. Beyond it a pleasing parterre of iris, peonies, day lilies, hollyhocks, and sunflowers provided her with a summer-long vista that she found entirely satisfying.

As Albert and Mary Austin settled into *Spadina,* we are reminded of the feeling of exhilaration that touched Dr. Baldwin and his children eighty years before when they had moved from the confining *Russell Abbey* to the freedom of their new *Spadina.* We are reminded as well of the excitement of James Austin and his family when they removed themselves from their Jarvis Street house in 1866 to occupy their new *Spadina.* Like the children of Dr. Baldwin and James Austin, Albert and Mary Austin's five children, with the faithful Annie Duncan in attendance, never tired of exploring the cool fastnesses of the glen behind their house. And they soon found that the lawns of *Spadina* yielded ample space for a tennis court, a croquet lawn, and a putting green.

Albert Austin had become intensely interested in golf. The game was attracting a growing following throughout the city. Before the turn of the century, he laid out several fairways and greens on his father's former property, which was still vacant land, on the west side of Spadina Road. The first hole, in fact, was in the centre of the land now occupied by *Casa Loma,* and the driving tee was located in the present Spadina Road Park just to the east. A few other holes were laid out on the west side of Spadina Road as far north as St. Clair Avenue. The make-shift course was used only by Austin, a few of his friends, and his oldest children.

The idea grew in popularity, however, and a larger group of enthusiasts was recruited, mainly from men living below the hill in the district now known as the Annex. Under Albert Austin's leadership, a club was set up which became known as the Spadina Golf Club. At that point, the layout was moved farther north, and a farmhouse was rented close to the northeast corner of Spadina Road and St. Clair Avenue. A clapboard structure, it stood in the midst of a bountiful apple orchard, which offered an unusual nineteenth hole diversion to the members who took their ease after a round on the "links," sampling the crop around them.

Mr. James E. Landon, today a resident of Willowdale, was employed as a caddy on the Spadina Golf Club course when he was a boy living on Howland Avenue, and I am indebted to him for a description of the club's design. The first driving tee, he relates, was at the southwest corner of Spadina Road and St. Clair Avenue. The golfers drove from that point across St. Clair Avenue, which was then a dirt road, to a green at the northwest corner of

---

Albert William Austin (1857-1934). This portrait, showing the terrace balustrade and the lawn to the south, was painted by J. Colin Forbes, R.C.A. It was commissioned by Anne Arthurs and presented to her brother in 1915, on his birthday.

—Private Collection

the intersection. A two-plank sidewalk ran along the north side of St. Clair Avenue at that time, and many balls were lost by duffers who plowed their shots into the cavernous recesses beneath it. The small boys in the district spent many productive hours searching for golf balls in that well-known trap. The course then meandered up the west side of Spadina Road as far as Old Forest Hill Road, just south of Eglinton Avenue. Only two fairways existed on the east side of Spadina Road: one extended east and lay above the present Lonsdale Road, the players returning to Spadina Road on another fairway which lay just to the south. As Mr. Landon recalls it, the course operated with a minimum of nine holes, and the most difficult obstacle was the deep gully that stretched from the west of Spadina Road to the ravine behind the Holy Rosary Church. Today, the gully has been filled in, and is now a small park bordered on the north by Strathearn Boulevard.

A pewter cup on the mantelpiece of the *Spadina* billiard room recalls the heroics that must have been performed on that early course. The inscription reads: "SPADINA GOLF CLUB—Handicap—Won by A. W. Austin— Sep. 6th—1902." It is also evocative of the familiar sight on a summer weekend, at the end of Queen Victoria's long reign, of golfers climbing the creaking, wooden steps in the Spadina Road Park as they made their way north to the club house. They wore peak caps, Norfolk jackets, knickerbockers and thick-ribbed socks, and carried their varnished "golf-sticks" in canvas bags over their shoulder. Some used the old *Spadina* driving shed that lay close to the road as a changing room, and all paused for a moment, if the day was hot, to refresh themselves at the pump at the back of the house.

When the Spadina Golf Club had been formed, the owners of the farmlands north of St. Clair Avenue (part of the present Forest Hill Village) had permitted the members to use their fields as fairways for a nominal rental. Early in 1902, recognizing that the farmers would soon be tempted to dispose of their lands to developers, the members decided to seek a more permanent location. They had also become exasperated with the students of neighbouring Upper Canada College. There had been instances when the boys had filched golf balls from the fairways, and it was suspected that they were also the culprits responsible for the mysterious disappearance of the flags from the greens at night. In any event, it was generally conceded by the discouraged members of the Spadina Golf Club that the college pupils tested their tempers more sorely than did any of the natural obstacles on the course itself.

As they developed their plans for a new golf club, the Spadina members finally concluded that they would have to broaden their membership in order to raise the necessary capital to cover the cost of buying their own land and building and equipping their own club house. Their search for a low-cost

Mary Richmond Kerr Austin (1860-1942), the wife of Albert William Austin. The portrait, which was painted by J. Colin Forbes, R.C.A., was commissioned by James Austin as a wedding present for Mary Austin in 1882. The artist placed his subject in front of a piano, also a wedding gift from James Austin, which was obtained in New York through Austin's neighbour, Samuel Nordheimer.

—Private Collection

The Lambton Golf and Country Club, established in 1902, grew out of the Spadina Golf Club. This view of the members taking their ease on the verandah was taken in 1904 at the time of an Invitation Tournament. The band of the 48th Highlanders is seen to the left. (Below)—Dr. A. H. Young's four-in-hand in front of the new Lambton Club House in 1903, since demolished (1961).

—Private Collection

property led them to Lambton Mills in the western outskirts of the city. In that district they were fortunate to obtain an option on a 150-acre parcel. It lay on Scarlett Road, just south of the town of Weston, and a line of the CPR linked the property to Toronto's Union Station. With their land option in hand, the organizers then solicited support for the as yet unnamed club from a wide group of enthusiastic golfers throughout the city who, like themselves, were members of clubs whose facilities at that time were held under tenuous arrangements with local farmers. Their announcement read:

The Proposed
GOLF and COUNTRY CLUB

A large number of the members of the Rosedale, Spadina, High Park and Highlands Golf Clubs have determined that the time has arrived, when it has become necessary in the interests of the game, that they should purchase a property, suitable for a country club and golf links, capable of accommodating a sufficient number of members.

An option for the purchase of 150 acres of land beautifully situated on the Humber River in close proximity to Lambton station and easy of access by the street cars has been secured at a reasonable figure.

At a meeting of representative members of the above mentioned clubs, held on the 22nd instant, a committee was appointed to arrange for the organization of a company to purchase the said lands being the westerly portions of Lots 7 and 8 on the Scarlett Road and the River Humber.

The property has been thoroughly examined by many of the most experienced golf players in Toronto, all of whom pronounce it capable of being, at small expense, converted into the best golf course in Canada. It has also been approved of as an ideal spot for a country club.

The committee has decided to offer the shares of the company for subscription to the golf players and others interested to whom this notice is sent, in the hope that they will be able to secure the land before the option expires.

It is intended to organize the proposed new club early next season, the necessary club house and other buildings being erected this fall.

A special feature of the club will be that a course will be laid out for ladies, on which they will be entitled to play every day.

It is estimated that $30,000 will pay the purchase money for the property, erect a club house and other buildings and put the grounds and links in first class condition.

The capital stock of the company will consist of 300 shares of $100 each, 50 per cent. of which shall be payable on or before the 7th day of May, 1902, and the balance within one year thereafter. A cheque for the 50 per cent. must accompany each application. . . .

The following are the names of the Provisional Committee:— Messrs. M. McLaughlin, G. S. Lyon, C. H. Stanley Clarke, John Dick, A. E. W. Peterson, R. H. Coleman, Geo. J. Webster, A. W. Austin and J. E. Robertson.

Intending subscribers are requested to make their cheques payable to Albert W. Austin, Esq., or M. McLaughlin, Esq., as trustees, and send the same to J. E. Robertson, 18 Toronto Street, the provisional secretary.

Dated at Toronto the 24th day of April, 1902.

A few months later, encouraged by the response to their circular, the Lambton Golf and Country Club, Limited was formed, and Albert Austin was elected president. The first golf club in the Toronto area to be organized with share capital, its early affairs were conducted from his office in the Confederation Life Building on Richmond Street East.

The first annual meeting of the shareholders was held in a large, ground-floor room in that building on March 14, 1903. *The Toronto Sunday World* covered the event at length. It noted that the membership of the new club was already close to the "400 mark," and that the course was expected to be open for play after April 1. While the president's announcement that a telephone had been installed in the new club house and was "already in working order" was roundly applauded by the shareholders, the response was more enthusiastic when he informed them that "an ice-house had been built, adjoining the club house, in which about 100 tons of Lake Simcoe ice are now stored." They were also told that Willie Dunn of New York had laid out the two courses, one of eighteen holes and another of nine holes for the ladies, and that the arrival of a steam-roller was expected daily to complete work on the fairways.

By Saturday, June 13, 1903, all was in readiness for the official opening of the Lambton Golf and Country Club. The ceremonies that afternoon were marred by a driving downpour. As the members and their guests approached the porte-cochère in their carriages, they took note of the ample proportions of the club house, and, peering out through the sheets of rain, were also struck with the resemblance of its two-tier verandahs to the decks of a Mississippi river boat. A reporter from the *Toronto Daily Star* recorded his impressions of the opening day:

> That one thousand people should have gone five miles out into the country in a pouring rain on Saturday, proved the popularity of the new Country and Golf Club at Lambton, and the curiosity also to see, every man for himself, how the idea had been worked out. In the throng all cliques of society were represented, and nearly every one present was a member of one, two, three, or half a dozen clubs of all sorts. Nevertheless, a man might belong to twenty clubs, and even yet not attain anything but a small portion of the many delightful and various interests combined in this last one of all, which is also the most ideal, the most complete. President Austin and his fellow governors may congratulate themselves upon having provided and established, after nine months' effort, a country club which will rank with the best things of the sort in America. The golf links, grandly picturesque, covering 120 acres in extent, and 6,000 yards in length, take in the Humber River and Black Creek, which are crossed nine times in the course of 18 holes. The scene from the club house, which is most commodious, and supplies every need imaginable, but is unpretentious exteriorly, is one of great pastoral beauty. No other part of Canada could have supplied a scene of such picturesqueness.

With the new golf club launched, Albert Austin remained watchful of opportunities to enhance its reputation as a leading centre of golfing activity in Canada. In Winnipeg, ten years before, he had successfully promoted the use of his street railway's electric line by arranging unusual events of interest in his two Red River parks; in Toronto, he was now to apply the same techniques in vigorously promoting the Lambton Golf Club. In October 1903, for example, he travelled to Philadelphia where Miss Rhona Adair, the reigning woman golf champion of Great Britain, was playing in an invitation tournament. He persuaded her to visit Toronto at the end of her match and compete in a special ladies' tournament that was planned for Lambton in November. Her appearance in Canada created something of a sensation. "Miss Adair is of the typical style of Irish beauty," one reporter observed, "with fair hair, blue eyes and a complexion like a rose."

Rhona Adair, whose home club was in Portrush, Ireland, was matched in the Lambton tournament against Miss Florence L. Harvey of Hamilton,

Ontario, the Canadian woman champion. It was an unequal contest. The British player turned in a score of 94, against bogey of 83 for the Lambton course (the word 'par' was not then in use), while Miss Harvey took 119 strokes to complete her round. Both contestants, naturally, were subject to the limitations imposed on their play by contemporary Edwardian fashion, as well as by the imperfect equipment then in use. They toured the course in full skirts, long-sleeved blouses, and wide-brimmed hats, their golf clubs had heavy, wooden shafts, and the golf balls they used had little in common with those of today.

Rhona Adair and her sister stayed at *Spadina* during their visit to Toronto—an event that was marred only by the grim discovery by Annie Duncan, the children's devout Scottish nurse, that the Irish ladies were smoking cigarettes in their bedrooms at night. After the Lambton tournament, Albert and Mary Austin conducted them to the Chateau Frontenac in Quebec City where, before embarking for Ireland, the British champion was again the object of public attention.

The following year, in September 1904, the Lambton Golf Club attained international renown when its captain, George S. Lyon, won the World Championship at St. Louis where he defeated the U.S. Amateur Champion, H. Chandler Egan. On his return to Toronto, accompanied by Albert Austin, the CPR express paused long enough at the Lambton station to permit a convivial delegation from the Lambton Golf Club to clamber aboard and accompany Lyon on the run to the Union Station where a further welcome awaited him.

In 1907, Albert Austin was elected president of the Royal Canadian Golf Association, succeeding George H. Perley of Ottawa. The following year, satisfied that his work was done, he retired as president of the Lambton Golf Club, and became its honorary president.

Chapter 17

Pomp and Circumstance

On the afternoon of Sunday, September 4, 1904, had Samuel Nordheimer been studying the view from his *Glenedyth* tower room, he would have been astonished if he had brought his telescope to bear on a group of men who were strolling across the neighbouring lawns of *Ravenswood* and *Spadina*. He would have certainly recognized the Right Reverend Arthur Sweatman, the Anglican Bishop of Toronto, Edmund B. Osler, and Albert Austin, but identification of the other two figures, in silk hats and frock-coats, would have required a longer and steadier application of his glass. Only then would he have been certain that he was observing the Archbishop of Canterbury, the Primate of All England, and J. Pierpont Morgan of New York.

His Grace, the Most Reverend Thomas Randall Davidson, D.D., the Archbishop of Canterbury, was visiting Toronto for a few days before going on to the United States where, as Morgan's guest, he was to attend an important Episcopalian conference in Boston. The great financier had joined him in Quebec, and following the archbishop's sojourn in Toronto, was to conduct him to New York in his private train.

As soon as word had reached Toronto that the Primate of All England intended visiting the city, the Bishop of Toronto had moved quickly to arrange an exhausting program for the fifty-six-year-old prelate. He planned a luncheon at the University of Toronto on the Saturday of his arrival, and it was to be followed by a special convocation at which an honorary degree was to be conferred; later in the afternoon a reception was to be held at Trinity College on Queen Street, and after that a dinner party at Government House. He also arranged for the archbishop to preach two sermons on Sunday and to tour the city the following day, stopping briefly at such points of interest as Havergal College, Bishop Strachan School, and the Toronto Industrial Exhibition.

In the flurry of excitement that greeted the news of his grace's proposed visit, the Toronto press reported that Professor Goldwin Smith had rushed off a letter to the archbishop in England urging him to stay at *The Grange*. It was then announced that Edmund B. Osler, M.P., had also invited the primate to visit him at *Craigleigh,* his Rosedale estate. The celebrity sweepstake was on. While over the years Goldwin Smith had entertained a number of well-known people as house guests in his ten-acre park, including such English writers as Matthew Arnold and John Morley, Osler's thirteen-acre *Craigleigh* had welcomed an equally impressive list of visitors. Shortly after the Boer War, for instance, young Winston Churchill, while lecturing in Toronto, had been a guest at Osler's mansion. While that visit hadn't been particularly successful from Osler's personal point of view, it had created a considerable stir in the city. Churchill had grumbled about the pillows in his room, and found fault with other things as well. After Osler had informed him that it was not their custom to dress for Sunday supper, Churchill had replied, "I do"—and he did. The owner of *Craigleigh* never forgot his guest's less than adequate manners, and in later years, when Churchill had attained cabinet rank, his former host continued to refer to him as "that young pup."[1] On balance, informed observers in Toronto were inclined to give Osler the edge in the sweepstake—and they turned out to be right. We have no way of knowing the point upon which the archbishop's decision finally turned, nor to whose advice he responded, but he did in fact end up staying at Osler's spacious park.

The special CPR train that carried the Archbishop of Canterbury and J. Pierpont Morgan from Montreal to Toronto, pulled into the old Union Station at the foot of York and Simcoe streets at 8:15 on Saturday morning, September 3. As they entered the city, the two men observed the gutted buildings in the downtown area which still marked the path of the great fire that had occurred the previous April. The lingering scenes of destruction must have reminded Morgan of the ruined cities he had seen in the South at the time of the Civil War. A number of carriages were drawn up at the station door, and the party divided itself into two groups: the archbishop's retinue, led by Edmund B. Osler, set out for *Craigleigh,* while Morgan and his servant were driven to the new King Edward Hotel where a suite of rooms had been reserved. They weren't ready, of course, and the great man had to cool his heels in "a private parlour" elsewhere in the hotel while his suite was being made up.

Morgan wielded vast financial power in the United States. His public actions were viewed with awe and reverence by millions of Americans. He maintained a sleek, black, ocean-going steam yacht, the *Corsair,* in a berth on the Hudson River, and his houses were the last word in opulent splendour. He was the most notable art collector of his day, and like the Medicis, he liked to surround himself with beautiful things.

Unmindful of J. Pierpont Morgan's deep interest in the affairs of the American Episcopal Church, which had led him to Canada to meet the Archbishop of Canterbury, the Toronto newspapers immediately linked his appearance in the city with a major investment transaction that was rumoured to be imminent. They were aware that he had visited France earlier that year, as was his custom, and that he had picked up a few incomparable art treasures for himself as well as the assets of the New Panama Canal Company for the U.S. Government. Perhaps the weight of his influence was about to be felt in Toronto. *The Evening Telegram* sent a man to the King Edward Hotel to find out. After the magnate had breakfasted, read the papers, and examined his mail, the reporter was ushered into his presence. He was startled to find the great man simply playing solitaire and thoughtfully puffing on a cigar. His first reaction was that Morgan appeared "kindly and affable." Questioned about the rumour that his visit was connected with a large financial transaction, Morgan denied that there was any truth to the story. "This is my first visit here," he explained patiently to the reporter, "and I know very little of the city, but from what I have seen of the country and the city, I am much impressed. I have heard nothing of any anticipated commercial venture." As the interview wore on, and it became evident that the financier had no intention of being lured off the safe ground of generalities, the disheartened reporter revised his earlier impression of Morgan and withdrew. He ended his report by likening him to a stoic and an oyster.[2]

The Bishop of Toronto had arranged for the Archbishop of Canterbury to preach to the congregation of St. James' Cathedral on the Sunday morning of his visit, and to the 400 members of the unfinished St. Alban's Cathedral on Howland Avenue that evening. Since Anne Arthurs was active in the affairs of nearby St. Alban's, and Osler the trustee of her family trust, it was not surprising that *Ravenswood* was chosen as the setting for the archbishop's high tea before the evening service. Afterwards, the gentlemen had withdrawn for a stroll on the lawns of *Ravenswood* and *Spadina* where the primate pondered the remarks he would make to the parishioners of St. Alban's, and Morgan, contemplating the view from the hill, enjoyed a fine cigar. The sound of the evensong church bells drifting up from the city finally summoned Anne Arthurs' guests to their carriages, and the party departed for the waiting cathedral.

In a sense, J. Pierpont Morgan's visit to the Davenport Hill that September afternoon was portentous. Just a few hundred feet away from where he had strolled, Sir Henry Pellatt was in the process of buying the land upon which he was to raise his storybook castle. The builder of *Casa Loma* was a man in whose mind the princely style of J. Pierpont Morgan had already struck a deep and abiding echo.

On April 7, 1903, Edwin Henry Kertland and Thomas Taylor Rolph, both of Toronto, sold twenty-five "town and villa" lots on the top of the Davenport Hill to Mary Pellatt, the wife of Lt.-Col. Henry Mill Pellatt. The lots, which had not been built on, were part of the forty-acre tract of land that James Austin had subdivided and sold in 1889. As a result of the transaction, Lt.-Col. Pellatt, who was knighted the following year, obtained the block of land upon which he was later to build his celebrated *Casa Loma.* He also acquired most, but not all, of the property he needed to construct his stable and greenhouse complex on the west side of Walmer Road. The purchase from Kertland and Rolph included as well a good part, but again not all, of the land that he was to develop into a garden and deer park on the north side of Austin Terrace directly across the road from his castle.

The price Pellatt paid for the twenty-five lots was not disclosed in the deed. The document, which was short and straightforward, did reveal, however, that the property was already known as *Casa Loma,* a name that was later accepted as the romantic invention of Lady Pellatt. The relevant part of the Kertland-Rolph grant to Mary Pellatt, which encompasses the site of the now-historic castle, reads:

> They the said Grantors DO grant unto the said Grantee in fee simple ALL those certain parcels of land situate in the Township of York in the County of York called *Casa Loma* and composed of Lots numbers One Two Three and Four on Davenport Road Five Six Seven and Eight and the private road between lots numbers Five and Six and the private road between lots numbers Seven and Eight on the south side of Austin Terrace . . . according to registered plan number 930.

It is probable that the name *Casa Loma,* which in Spanish means a "house on a hill," was originated by the two owners of the twenty-five lots

BUILDING PERMIT

No. 18643

Plan No._____

Lot No._____

Toronto,_____ DEC 16 1909 ____19____

Permit granted to

Mr. *Col Sir H M Pellatt Traders Bank Bg*

To erect a *Foundation for dwelling*

_____ *near Walmer Rd.*

on *Davenport Rd.*

Architect *E. J. Lennox*

Builder *E Gearing*

Cost of Building, $ *30,000*

Plans and Specifications approved by_____

No. of Block Plan_____ *M.S.*

Limit_____ *out* Water, $_____

This Permit does not include any openings in sidewalks or encroachment past line of street

A copy of the building permit for *Casa Loma* dated December 16, 1909.

—Toronto City Hall Records

simply to identify the small, semi-private area they intended developing, like the nearby Wychwood Park, for the enjoyment of a few owners. They could scarcely have imagined that a single purchaser would relieve them of their valuable land and incorporate it into a baronial estate of nearly twenty acres. They must have been flattered that Sir Henry retained their name.

On the same day as the Kertland-Rolph sale, Pellatt also purchased from Albert Austin the lot at the northeast corner of Walmer Road and Austin Terrace. He thus rounded out the land he needed for his garden and deer park. Curiously, Austin held on to a critical fifty-foot lot that lay in the heart of Sir Henry's proposed stable complex on the west side of Walmer Road, and did not sell it to him until September 1, 1905. Immediately after that transaction, work started on the palatial *Casa Loma* stables.

They were designed to include a large heating plant to serve the stables as well as the intended castle by means of a connecting tunnel, and for that reason, together with the fact that Sir Henry was anxious to provide a home at the earliest possible moment for the magnificent horses he already owned, the stable complex was constructed first. It was completed, along with its

A view from the tower of the newly built *Casa Loma* stables taken around 1908. Sir Henry Pellatt's vegetable garden and deer park occupy the foreground, but construction of the castle in the open field to the right, overlooking the city, was not to start until 1910. In the distance, at the end of the tree-lined carriage drive (now

Austin Terrace), *Spadina* drowses in the summer sun of an Edwardian afternoon. The driving shed at the edge of Spadina Road was removed in 1912, and in the same year a third floor was added to the house.

—Casa Loma Archives

adjoining greenhouses and staff houses, in 1907 just as a financial panic rocked Wall Street and led to a period of depressed stock prices in Canada. As a stockbroker, Sir Henry was accustomed to seeing his fortunes spin like a weather vane, so he simply deferred construction of the castle for the time being, and sat back to await the end of that particular period of financial attrition. He didn't have long to wait. With the opening up of the Porcupine mining camp in northern Ontario, in which he had a substantial stake, he was soon in a position to proceed with his castle-building plans. On December 16, 1909, he applied to the city of Toronto for a building permit "to erect a foundation for dwelling" on Davenport Road, near Walmer Road. The cost of the project was shown as $30,000, and the architect was Edward J. Lennox who had designed Toronto's new City Hall on Queen Street. E. Gearing was recorded as the builder. (See page 191.) With that formality in hand, construction of the famous castle began the following year.

In choosing the hilltop site for his house, Sir Henry Pellatt was influenced by a number of considerations. No single factor was paramount in his mind. All blended inevitably, even logically, into the spectacular result that was to be *Casa Loma*. Sir William Mulock wrote of Sir Henry, "He was big in everything he undertook." His castle was simply a reflection of that spacious style. As a boy, it is said, he was fascinated with castles: he liked to draw them and dream about them. As commanding officer of the Queen's Own Rifles of Canada, he thrilled to the heel-clicking precision of military parades and the pomp and pageantry of royal processions. It was natural for him on two occasions to take formations at his own expense to England, the heart of Empire, where moated castles abounded. And when he heard that the property on the top of the Davenport Hill was available, motivated partly by a feeling of nostalgia, he decided to buy it. As a young officer he had camped on it, when the area was popular with local units for military training. Writing from *Ravenswood* in 1893 to her sister-in-law, Mary Austin, Anne Arthurs testified to this fact when she observed, "The Gov Gen's Body Guard are encamped on the hill," adding perceptively, "so the domestics have a nice time." She referred, of course, to the lands that stretched north to the Austin Ravine from the site of Sir Henry Pellatt's later castle.

The question naturally arises as to why Sir Henry laid out his *Casa Loma* estate in the manner he did when at the outset it must have been obvious to him his place would suffer from the defect of having its three integral sections separated from each other by public thoroughfares. A stroll in his private garden thus required him to cross Austin Terrace. To visit his greenhouses and stables, he had to traverse Walmer Road, unless he chose to saunter through the connecting tunnel. Wherever he moved on his multi-million dollar property, he was exposed to the gaze of a fascinated public.

The explanation of this serious defect in the layout of the castle grounds lies in the fact that at an early stage in their development Sir Henry was led to believe that the township of York, within whose jurisdiction his property then lay, would grant him permission to close off the offending sections of Spadina Road, Austin Terrace, and Walmer Road, thus permitting him to consolidate his *Casa Loma* lands into a wholly private estate. To accomplish this, his plan was to extend Walmer Road Hill north beyond Austin Terrace, passing just behind his stables and, at a point a little beyond them, to swing the road east and join it to Spadina Road. Such a realignment of the local road system, of course, would have sealed off the main entrance of Albert Austin's *Spadina* at the head of Austin Terrace. While Sir

Sir Henry Pellatt's palatial *Casa Loma* stables on Walmer Road await their gleaming yellow-tile roofs, gates, and iron fences. This view was taken from the vegetable garden in the fall of 1906. In 1929 the garden became the site of a number of duplexes, and the present Castleview Avenue was laid out to the left of Sir Henry's gravel walk.

—Casa Loma Archives

Henry undoubtedly would have entered into an agreement with Austin, giving him the right to use the *Casa Loma* driveways, it is doubtful if the owner of *Spadina* would have accepted the arrangement with either enthusiasm or equanimity. To Pellatt's intense disappointment, and Austin's immense relief, the city of Toronto in 1909 absorbed the township lands that Sir Henry was seeking to reorganize, and the first thing the city fathers did was refuse him the right of closure of the three public roads in question. At that point, with the stable complex already completed, only two alternatives were available to Sir Henry: either abandon the project entirely, or proceed with construction of the castle notwithstanding the limitations that the fragmented character of the property would impose upon his enjoyment of his estate. He chose to build his castle.

To provide himself with a little more elbow-room, Sir Henry next attempted to take over the present Spadina Road Park which today adjoins the castle property on the east. He argued that since he had already given up part of his land on the west in order to expand Walmer Road Hill from a narrow carriage drive into a broad boulevard, it would be equitable if he were allowed to acquire from the city a comparable parcel on the east. The city fathers were cool to that idea as well—and for the same reason. A favourable decision would have resulted in the closure of a public road allowance and its conversion to private use. Moreover, it would have denied the public the right-of-way it had enjoyed for decades as it made its way to the open land at the top of the hill by way of the wooden steps that led from Davenport Road.

An indignant letter to the editor of the *Toronto Star,* which appeared in its issue of June 12, 1911, gave strong expression to the views of at least one writer on the subject of Sir Henry's proposed appropriation, and may have played a part in influencing the City Council against his proposal:

> Editor of The Star:
> I read with something like consternation that Sir Henry Pellatt proposes to annex to his already cumbersome estate one of the beauty spots of Toronto. It would take the pen of Mr. S. H. Blake to express what should be said of this proposal. No terms of mine would be sufficiently denunciatory. The crest of the hill at the head of Spadina Road is unquestionably one of the finest locations in Toronto, and by a piece of extraordinary good luck it has been preserved to the city. Yet it is this valuable property that Sir Henry M. Pellatt proposes to appropriate. I have a very clear recollection of another of our streets that was dealt with, at first in much the same way. A mild request was made by Sir William Mackenzie to the City Council to be allowed to annex Edward Street to his property, and most of us will recall that the same mild request was ultimately backed up with physical force. Let the citizens see to it that history does not repeat itself, and let the City Council take immediate steps to have the spot beautified and the whole neighborhood made more accessible even though the improvement does encroach somewhat on the Seats of the Mighty. And let the Guild of Civic Art also get busy.
>
> A LOVER OF JUSTICE

It will be recalled that S. Hume Blake, Q.C., referred to above, was Albert Austin's counsel before the Judicial Committee of the Privy Council in England in 1894 when Austin appealed the Canadian court decision which had confirmed the granting of the electric street railway franchise in Winnipeg to the Mackenzie-Ross interests. The citing of Sir William MacKenzie in the letter, along with S. H. Blake, leaves the identity of "A Lover of Justice" open to a good deal of conjecture.

At that time, as today, the so-called Spadina Road Park was in fact an "untravelled road allowance." In the present scheme of Toronto's parks it is an anomaly. Its unusual status dates back to 1889 when James Austin registered his plan of subdivision and dedicated a road allowance having a width of eighty feet for the northerly extension of Spadina Road from the foot of the Davenport Hill to St. Clair Avenue. The steepness of the grade of the hill at that point naturally discouraged development of the land for a road. In 1910, after the city had taken over the road allowance, and Sir Henry was first eyeing it with interest, an attempt was made to have the unused land formally dedicated as a public park. The proposal never reached the city council for determination.

Subsequently, in 1912, when John Chambers was the head of the City Parks Department, the "untravelled road allowance" was transformed, as if by magic, into a beauty spot on the crest of the hill. Quite unofficially, the old wooden steps were replaced with concrete, a rustic drinking fountain was installed at their summit, benches were set out, and pleasant gardens were added between the new, field-stone walls of the adjoining owners— Pellatt and Austin. The park was maintained for years by the same gardener. Aloof and mysterious, he rarely conversed with anyone. He rode to his job on a bicycle, a cap pulled low on his head, and his toolshed was carefully concealed in a clump of lilacs in the shadow of Sir Henry Pellatt's wall.[3]

In the light of the frustrations and disappointments he encountered in laying out his castle estate, it is of interest to consider a different interpretation of Sir Henry's real estate activities on the Davenport Hill, if only because it holds promise of becoming woven into the fabric of Toronto folklore.

Shortly after Sir Henry Pellatt's death in 1939, Frederick Griffin, a Toronto newspaperman, wrote a monograph on the life and career of the deceased knight. The book, which sold for fifty cents, carried a brief foreword by Sir William Mulock, and the proceeds of sale were devoted to a war-time charity. Notwithstanding the difficulty encountered by the late owner of *Casa Loma* in trying to fit his castle into a suitable setting, like an eagle squeezing into a sparrow's nest, Griffin began his chapter entitled "The Builder" as follows:

> Now we come to one of Sir Henry's most successful real estate operations, and the fulfilment of a dream, the building of Casa Loma. Sensing the northward extension of the city, he purchased several hundred acres of land at farm prices on what was then known as Wells Hill, the site being to the north of the city limits, and he subdivided this land for sale. The public was apathetic and sales were slow. He then and there decided to build Casa Loma in order to awaken interest in his subdivision and as a suitable site for his dream castle. In 1906 the magnificent stables were first completed and popular attention was awakened. Sales in the district were brisk and, by the time the walls of Casa Loma were up, the subdivision had been disposed of at a profit said to be some one million dollars over and above the cost of the castle itself.[4]

The first point of departure from recognizable terrain in Griffin's statement is the reference to Pellatt having purchased several hundred acres of land at farm prices on what was then known as Wells Hill, before he had acquired his *Casa Loma* property. The Wells Hill district, it is to be noted, comprises only eighty acres; it is bounded by Davenport Road, St. Clair Avenue, Walmer Road Hill (extended north), and Bathurst Street.[5] While *Casa Loma* is often referred to as being located on the Wells Hill, the castle in fact lies to the east of that historic district.

Insofar as the Wells Hill area itself is concerned, it was not until 1908, after the *Casa Loma* stables were completed, that Sir Henry bought a parcel of land in the shape of a rectangle at the southeast corner of St. Clair Avenue and Bathurst Street. Doubtless it was this isolated transaction that was to give rise to the legend that Pellatt made millions of dollars speculating in hilltop real estate. He paid $40,000 for the land, scarcely a farm price, and in 1911 registered a plan which subdivided the property into sixty-eight lots. Most had a width of fifty feet. The land covered by his plan extended south from St. Clair Avenue along the east side of Bathurst Street to Nina Avenue, then east 124 feet to a point beyond Hilton Avenue, and north again to St. Clair Avenue. Pellatt began selling off his lots in 1911, and two fifty-foot parcels on the east side of Bathurst Street, just below St. Clair

Avenue brought him $2,000 for each. Applying that yardstick of value to the subdivision as a whole, it is evident that the entire transaction, after deducting the necessary legal costs and commissions, couldn't have yielded Sir Henry much more than the expense he incurred in building the battlemented tower in his stable.[6]

In the vicinity of *Casa Loma* itself, where he had purchased his first land in 1903-5, Sir Henry bought a private house on the east side of Walmer Road in May 1913. It still exists today as number 371. That transaction, however, was innocent of any speculative motive because he lived in the house briefly while he added the finishing touches to the castle. He sold it in June 1914, shortly after he had taken up his residence in *Casa Loma*.

Supporting the conclusion that Sir Henry Pellatt did not speculate wildly in real estate in the district surrounding the castle, nor blanket the area with purchases, is the further evidence that may be gleaned from two transfers which occurred across the road from *Casa Loma*, in the Wells Hill district. In 1905, Edward J. Lennox, the architect of the *Casa Loma* project, purchased for $18,000 a large lot at the corner of Walmer Road Hill and Austin Terrace, and extending south to Davenport Road. Lennox built himself an impressive house on the site which he occupied until his death in 1933. The house is still extant. The seller of that lot was not Sir Henry Pellatt as suggested by the Griffin legend, but a John Edwards of Toronto. And four years later, in 1909, Albert Austin bought a similar hilltop lot adjoining the Lennox property on the west. He paid $17,000 for it. It also extended from Austin Terrace to Davenport Road. Again the seller was the John Edwards' estate, not Pellatt. Clearly, had Sir Henry been sensitive to the speculative opportunities that were being presented in the area, those desirable lots would hardly have escaped his notice. They lay right under his nose. On the other hand, Austin's purpose in buying the lot next to the Lennox property was entirely speculative. In the atmosphere of excitement that surrounded the near-completion of the castle in 1913, Austin sold his holding for $60,000 to Stephen Haas of Toronto. Haas carried the property through World War I, and finally disposed of it in 1922 to Lt. Col. John B. Maclean, the publisher of *The Financial Post* and *Maclean's Magazine*, who built a house on the property which is still known as 7 Austin Terrace.

There is little doubt that the development of Sir Henry Pellatt's hilltop lands, beginning with the building of his remarkable stables and greenhouses and the laying out of his beautiful garden across the road, created intense interest throughout the city. Indeed, during 1912 and 1913, one of the most popular diversions in Toronto on a Sunday afternoon—and there were few —was for the citizenry to stroll up to "the hill" to observe the progress of Sir Henry's castle. As its battlements and towers climbed higher, their curiosity and astonishment increased. Even before it was finished, Toronto had taken Sir Henry's castle to its heart.

Chapter 18

Only Yesterday

Late in the summer of 1906, as Sir Henry Pellatt's great stable tower was rising over the former *Spadina* farmlands, Anne Arthurs called at the Baldwin cottage at *Spadina* to pick up her mother, Susan Bright Austin. It had been arranged that they would drive in the Arthurs' victoria that afternoon to the Exhibition on the lakefront. As Spadbrow, the coachman, helped the ninety-year-old lady into the carriage, she firmly asked her daughter if she would proceed by way of Yonge Street so that they could pass the site of the old Bright house on Queen Street. It had been demolished long ago. The Eaton store and the then new City Hall dominated the block which once was given over to the cottages and gardens she had known as a girl. Recovering quickly from her astonishment at her mother's request—in the normal course their route would have led them down Dufferin Street to the Exhibition grounds—Anne Arthurs confirmed the change of direction to the coachman, and dismissed the thought that there was perhaps something premonitory in her mother's request. When they finally reached the Exhibition, they lingered longer than usual at the Indian display which was always an object of intense interest to Susan Austin. It evoked the familiar sight of her childhood when the country Indians roamed the streets of the town of York, hawking the boxes and baskets they had fashioned from birchbark, quills, and sweetgrass. On that afternoon, she filled the victoria with Indian handicrafts to take home as presents for her grandchildren. As they drove back to *Spadina*, Anne Arthurs noticed that her mother had fallen into a fitful sleep, lulled by the motion of the carriage and the pervasive scent of sweetgrass. As the carriage climbed the Walmer Road Hill, she roused herself, and observing the lofty Pellatt stable tower, shook her head in disbelief. With a flash of her familiar, ironic humour, she remarked softly to her daughter, "I wonder how many horses Pellatt thinks he can stable in that tower." A few days later, Susan Austin suffered a stroke, and she was moved from the Baldwin cottage to *Ravenswood* so that Anne Arthurs could better tend her needs. She languished throughout most of the winter, and died peacefully in her daughter's house on February 21, 1907.

In the fall of that year, Anne Arthurs rented her house, and with her daughter Margaret Greene, who was now a widow, and her granddaughter Doris Margaret Greene (Betty), she set out for a Grand Tour of the Mediterranean countries and Europe.[1] Her travels abroad removed her from the country for nearly two years, and when she finally returned to *Ravenswood*

James Austin and his colleagues, Sir Frank Smith and Sir Edmund B. Osler, who guided The Dominion Bank through the first fifty years of its growth. Osler was president of the bank from 1901 until his death in 1924. This layout was used by The Dominion Bank at the time of its 50th Anniversary, in 1921.

—The Toronto-Dominion Bank

in 1909 it was for the purpose of clearing out the house which had been her home for over forty years. While she was absent, her brother, Albert Austin, had negotiated the sale of the *Ravenswood* property on her instructions to John Craig Eaton (later Sir John).

When James Austin died in 1897, his son Albert had been elected to the board of directors of The Dominion Bank and at the same time his father's colleagues, Sir Frank Smith and Edmund B. Osler, had become president and vice-president respectively. Two years later, in 1899, Timothy Eaton, the "pioneer and foremost practitioner in Canadian merchandising," as Dr. O. D. Skelton has put it, was elected a director of The Dominion Bank to fill a vacancy that had occurred on the board. On Timothy Eaton's death in 1907, John Craig Eaton succeeded his father as a director of the bank, as well as in the presidency of the great merchandising organization his father had founded. At the time of the sale of the *Ravenswood* property, therefore, Austin and Eaton were fellow-directors of The Dominion Bank.

The parcel of land that Eaton agreed to purchase from Anne Arthurs in 1908 extended from the Davenport Road to the glen behind her *Ravenswood* house, including the Castle Frank stream. She retained her interest in the property lying north of the ravine, which stretched to St. Clair Avenue (now the Sir Winston Churchill Park). Eaton also agreed to purchase from Albert Austin a small corridor of land lying to the north of Austin's *Spadina* house which gave the new owner an entrance to his property on Spadina Road. That corridor also extended to the foot of the ravine, and included the Castle Frank stream. As had his sister, Austin retained his half interest in the land to the north that was bounded by St. Clair Avenue.[2]

John Craig Eaton and his wife Flora McCrea, after their marriage in 1901, had lived on Walmer Road, a short distance north of Bloor Street. With his accession to the presidency of the T. Eaton Company, Eaton had concluded that he needed a larger house than the one he then occupied, not only for the round of entertaining that would be expected of him as head of the country's largest retail store, but to accommodate his growing family as well. As a boy, he had come to know the glen behind *Spadina* and *Ravenswood* well. Wandering up Spadina Road from his father's house at the corner of Lowther Avenue, young Eaton and his friends joined forces with the Spradbrow children who lived in the picturesque coachman's cottage on the *Ravenswood* estate, close to the south bank of the ravine. The children spent long hours prowling the heavily forested glen together. When Eaton heard that Anne Arthurs was prepared to dispose of the hilltop portion of her property, he quickly made up his mind to buy it. Not only did it hold a happy association for him that reached back to his boyhood, but it lay in the heart of the district that was then the object of widespread public attention because of Sir Henry Pellatt's castle-building plans.

The Eaton purchase was completed in Albert Austin's office in the Confederation Life Building on January 22, 1909. John Craig Eaton, jaunty and affable, arrived with his lawyer at the appointed hour. Eaton was carrying a black valise. It contained $100,000 in banknotes, secured by elastic bands, the price he had agreed to pay Anne Arthurs and Albert Austin for their properties. While the amount involved in the transaction was not recorded in the deed, the parties were anxious the purchase price remain a matter of secrecy. By making his payment in cash, therefore, Eaton eliminated the need for his cheques to be cleared through the bank of which both men were directors.

The general satisfaction of those concerned with the sale was soon clouded by an unexpected development. A real estate agent, Sherman T. Sutton by name, demanded a commission of $5,000 from Albert Austin for his alleged part in influencing Eaton to buy the property. Beyond a perfunctory telephone conversation with Sutton, Eaton denied that the agent had affected his decision to buy the property in any way. Sutton threatened legal action. By doing so, he must have reasoned, a favourable out-of-court settlement might have been expected because Austin and Eaton would be loathe to expose themselves to the publicity that court proceedings would inevitably attract. Finding both men indifferent to such a possibility, he launched his action. It was finally disposed of in the Supreme Court of Ontario in 1915 where Sir John Eaton appeared to give his evidence in support of his neighbour's position. The Toronto *Mail & Empire,* in its issue of December 10, 1915, tersely reported the outcome of Sutton's suit:

Sir John's Properties
Real Estate Man's Action for Commission Dismissed

"I was asked to believe the unsupported testimony of the plaintiff against that of Sir John Eaton and the defendant," said Chief Justice R. M. Meredith yesterday when he dismissed the action brought by Sherman T. Sutton, a real estate agent, against Albert W. Austin for $5,000.

The suit arose over the sale of the Arthurs and Austin properties in 1908 to Sir John Eaton. Sutton claimed that he had been promised a liberal commission by Austin if he interested Sir John Eaton, and a sale resulted. In the witness box Sir John Eaton stated that Sutton had called him up on the telephone, but that he had in no way influenced him in purchasing the property.

For Anne Arthurs it was an unhappy task removing her possessions from *Ravenswood,* particularly in the knowledge that her house was about to be demolished to make way for John Craig Eaton's new *Ardwold.** While she was glad to be relieved of the burden of maintaining a ten-acre estate, and looked forward to establishing herself in a more manageable property in the Annex below the Davenport Hill, the memories of her forty-year sojourn at *Ravenswood* stirred deeply in her mind. Widowed at an early age, she had directed her boundless energies towards the support of all manner of charitable organizations throughout the city. "When the history of charitable entertainment in Toronto comes to be written," the Toronto *News* observed in its issue of April 3, 1909, "the name of Mrs. George Allan Arthurs will surely loom up larger than all the rest."

Anne Arthurs was always quick to recognize and encourage artistic talent in the young. In one extravaganza she staged at Massey Hall, a young girl who later found fame in Hollywood as Irene Dunne was given a prominent part. A talented amateur artist herself, Anne Arthurs also lent her support to a number of young painters who were struggling to gain recognition. Among them was the artist-naturalist Ernest Thompson Seton who was a familiar visitor at *Ravenswood* in the closing years of the nineteenth century. At that time, in order to calm his mother who had grown concerned that his change of name was having a divisive effect upon her large family, he had reverted temporarily to his given name, Ernest Evan Thompson.[3] He usually approached *Ravenswood* along the private drive that curved across the *Spadina* lawn from the west, and was always recognized by his swinging gait and the mass of black hair that curled beneath

---

*The name Ardwold is an Irish word signifying a high, green hill.

Sir John Eaton's *Ardwold* shown here lies close to Samuel Nordheimer's *Glenedyth* which may be seen through the trees to the right. *Glenedyth* was demolished in the 1920's, and *Ardwold* in 1936.

—Eaton Archives

his broad-brimmed hat. Attracted by the flight or call of a bird, he would often check his stride, and standing motionless, observe it with prolonged concentration. Anne Arthurs purchased from Seton a faithful copy in oil of Sir Edwin Landseer's *Stag at Bay* that he had made as a student in England. She presented it one Christmas to her brother, Albert Austin, and it was placed on a wall in the dining room of *Spadina* where it has remained for over three-quarters of a century.

When Anne Arthurs moved from *Ravenswood* in 1909, and shortly later bought a house at the northwest corner of Admiral Road and Bernard Avenue (the present 78 Admiral Road), a number of the musical activities of which her house had long been the centre, shifted to Albert and Mary Austin's *Spadina*. Mary Austin, who was fifteen years younger than her sister-in-law, was herself an accomplished musician.

An early pupil of Dr. F. H. Torrington, the dominant musical personality

The lawn south of *Ravenswood*, looking towards the crest of the Davenport Hill. The old carriage drive called Aunt Maria's Road descends the hill through the declivity shown in the middle distance. The figures on the lawn, from left to right, are Anne Arthurs and her two daughters, Mrs. Sydney Greene and Mrs. Victor Cawthra with her daughter Isobel. The photograph was taken around 1905.

—Private Collection

in Toronto of his time, she had been appointed pianist for his Toronto Philharmonic Society in 1877 when she was only seventeen. On her return to the city from Winnipeg in 1894, her musical talents led her to a long and active connection with the Chamber Music Association and the later Chamber Music Society. Both groups, as their principal object, arranged concerts in Toronto by the leading string quartettes from Europe and the United States. The present Toronto Symphony Orchestra, of which Mary Austin was vice-president at its inception, was the result of those earlier groups which had worked to raise the level of musical appreciation throughout the city. From 1904 to 1907 she was Dr. Torrington's substitute organist and choirmaster at the Metropolitan Methodist Church on Queen Street when its cathedral setting won acclaim as the leading centre of religious music in Canada. A few years later, from 1910 to 1913, she held the

Sir John Eaton transformed the setting described opposite when he laid out his *Ardwold* in 1910-11. Using as a reference point the oak tree in the distance with its near-horizontal limb, which appears in both scenes, a striking comparison is revealed between Sir John's classical Italian garden and the rustic simplicity of Anne Arthurs' *Ravenswood.*

—Eaton Archives

office of president of the Toronto Women's Musical Club. And so it was, with Anne Arthurs' withdrawal from *Ravenswood,* the drawing room of *Spadina* became the focal point of a growing number of musical gatherings and entertainments.

After Mr. and Mrs. John Craig Eaton had occupied their new *Ardwold* in 1911, they were frequent guests at Mary Austin's musical parties at *Spadina.* Lady Eaton has left a record of her impressions of those post-Edwardian receptions:

Mr. and Mrs. Albert Austin, neighbours on our west, were friendly, open-handed hosts, of the type who would never let any disparity in age stand in the way of friendship. The only fence between their place and *Ardwold* was an attractive grape arbour which bounded their vege-table garden. . . . Mrs. Austin was one of the leading hostesses in

Toronto's music circles, and very frequently Jack and I were among the guests when she entertained visiting artists. Just before Christmas she always gave a party for the young people of their connection and acquaintance. For every social occasion, and indeed at any time, the Austins' rooms were filled with quantities of flowering plants from their greenhouses and conservatory.[4]

In 1907, Albert Austin took a second step in the renovation of his forty-year-old house. Having just sold his Elm Park property in Winnipeg at a gratifying profit, and with Sir Henry Pellatt's elaborate stable complex nearing completion close by, he had concluded that his own mid-Victorian house was in need of further rejuvenation. Accordingly, he conferred with Carière and Hastings, a New York firm of architects who were responsible for the design of the great New York Public Library and the neo-classical Bank of Toronto head office building at King and Bay Streets in Toronto. As a result, plans were prepared for the construction of a porte-cochère in wrought iron and glass at the main entrance of *Spadina,* as well as a conservatory and terraces on the south side of the house. His father's verandah, which overlooked Austin Terrace, was demolished, and a circular driveway with a ring of flowerbeds was laid out as the formal approach to the new entrance.

The balustered terraces of the renovated *Spadina,* surmounted by stone flower-urns, afforded a matchless setting for the outdoor entertainments that were popular in the Edwardian era. To the south, a sweeping lawn carried the eye to the crest of the oak-lined Davenport Hill and, beyond it, to the blue expanse of Lake Ontario. Tables with colourful cloths and chairs were set round on the terraces at strawberry time, for example, and the guests feasted on an ample tea whose central theme was the fleshy *Spadina* strawberry. Those occasions were particularly popular among the young friends of Adèle and Bertie Austin, two of Albert and Mary Austin's five children. On one spring afternoon, when the chestnut trees were heavy with blossoms, the youngest Austin girls, Kathleen and Margaret, observed the proceedings stealthily from a second-storey window overlooking the terrace. The guests, they were to recall, included the young Vincent Massey and his close friend Harold Tovell. Massey was a frequent visitor at *Spadina* in those days, and later attained the distinction of becoming Canada's first native-born governor-general. Lawren Harris, who had already embarked upon a career as an artist which was to win him national renown, was also in attendance with his later fiancée, Beatrice (Trixie) Phillips of Queen's Park. Harris at the time liked painting scenes which weren't always accepted as "artistic." Eschewing the fussy and romantic, he ranged round the city, often through Cabbagetown, and sketched in his own distinctive style subjects that were often in stark contrast to the pretentious dwellings in the neighbouring districts. In 1909, struck with the elaborate nature of Sir Henry Pellatt's hilltop estate, he recorded his impression of a more sombre part of that region, and called his sketch "Top of Hill, Spadina Avenue, Toronto, 1909." (See opposite page.)

In those Edwardian times, the loneliness of the hilltop lands around *Spadina* was even more pronounced during the winter months. After sundown it was unusual to see a sleigh or even a solitary wayfarer on the unlit roads around the place. Occasionally, evening parties of snowshoers from the Annex assembled in the present Spadina Road Park at the top of the steps that lead from Davenport Road and, breaking the winter stillness with laughter, trudged north to the trails through the ravine.

This sketch in oil, entitled "Top of Hill, Spadina Ave., Toronto, 1909" was painted by Lawren Harris, a guiding light of the Group of Seven Painters. A frequent visitor at *Spadina*, his eye caught and recorded the contrast that existed between the motley collection of buildings depicted here and the spacious houses nearby.
—Howard K. Harris

Such rural and romantic scenes, however, were destined soon to disappear. By 1912, the construction of *Casa Loma* had been carried to the point where the large conservatory on the east side of the building had been roofed in, and the castle walls and towers were climbing above it. Houses were being built on neighbouring Walmer Road as well as throughout the Wells Hill district. The new E. J. Lennox house on Austin Terrace had mellowed in its setting of well-kept lawns and gardens, and the glinting tile roof and new, yellow brick of John Craig Eaton's *Ardwold* was beginning to acquire the appearance of weathered permanence. Next door to the Eaton property, in 1912, both Samuel Nordheimer and his wife Edith Boulton Nordheimer died within a few months of each other at *Glenedyth,* the mid-

Spadina after its 1907 renovation when a porte-cochère in wrought iron and glass was added to a new front entrance which replaced the covered verandah of 1866. A ground floor sunroom and an encircling terrace with balustrades and urns were also added at that time. The house did not receive its third-floor addition until 1912.

—Private Collection

Victorian mansion they had occupied since their marriage in 1871. Their house was to be maintained by their family until the early twenties, when it was demolished.

Meanwhile, at *Spadina,* responding to the castle-building activity that was going on next door, to say nothing of John Craig Eaton's impressive new layout to the east with its terraces, greenhouses and indoor swimming pool, Albert Austin was busy further developing his own property. By 1912 he had demolished the old Baldwin cottage and incorporated the field-stones from its cellar into a picturesque pergola which screened the service area at the rear of his house. He had also built a two-section greenhouse, and the old coach house with a stable attached was converted into a gardener's cottage. The stable, which is still extant, was used until the late twenties to house a Jersey cow which was pastured on the Davenport Road hillside. Finally, acknowledging the arrival of the age of the automobile, Austin demolished his driving sheds and constructed a three-car garage in stone which contained as well a chauffeur's residence. Since watermains had now reached the district, the year 1912 also witnessed the removal of the old windmill at the rear of the house. Shorn of its vanes, it was transferred to the top of the hill near the "battery" or lookout, and converted into a flag-pole. (The structure later became unsafe, and was demolished.) And in the same year, the fate of the Spadina Road Park having at last been settled, Austin completed the field-stone wall, embellished with flower-urns, which still marks the western boundary of the *Spadina* property.

In terms of the architectural development of the house, however, the year 1912 was perhaps more significant because of the addition of a massive third storey that was begun in the early summer of that year. It was to be the last renovation of James Austin's 1866 *Spadina*. The new addition contained two large bedrooms with adjoining sitting rooms that overlooked the city, and a separate servants' quarters which included three bedrooms and a sitting room. The work dragged on through the fall and winter of 1912, and when Austin's daughter, Kathleen, was married to Stanley Seton Thompson that October, the reception following the service at the Metropolitan Methodist Church had to be held at the new York Club at the corner of St. George and Bloor Street, *Spadina* then being in total disarray. Kathleen's husband was the son of John Enoch Thompson of St. Vincent Street, Toronto, the oldest brother of the artist-naturalist Ernest Thompson Seton.

During 1912, while Albert Austin was pressing forward with his improvements to *Spadina,* he was elected president of The Consumers' Gas Company of Toronto upon whose board he had sat as a director since 1900; and as a director of The Dominion Bank, he was also deeply involved along with Sir Edmund Osler, the bank's president, in preparing plans for a new head office building which the bank was about to construct on its site at the corner of King and Yonge Streets.

The existing bank building, it will be recalled, had been built in 1878 by James Austin on land that was leased from the Baldwins of *Mashquoteh*. The structure was subsequently enlarged by him in 1884. In 1905, The Dominion Bank succeeded in buying the site from the Baldwin family for $350,000—the same property that had been purchased in the names of two of his sons by Dr. William Warren Baldwin in 1829 for £750. In 1912, The Dominion Bank was also able to buy the balance of the land it needed to extend its proposed new building south to Melinda Street, and the following year its old head office was demolished. Like its predecessor, the new structure, which still stands today, was erected in an atmosphere of financial gloom, when costs were low and labour in abundant supply. "The year 1913," Sir Edmund Osler told the shareholders at their annual meeting in January 1914, "was one of general financial and commercial depression throughout the world, which conditions became more accentuated during the closing months of the year." He added that he looked forward "with some anxiety to the year 1914," and went on to identify the causes of Canada's economic malaise, causes that had fretted the country into depressions before, and would do so again: "We have had a set-back, and in a measure we have deserved it because of the wild speculation which has taken place, especially in real estate, and this is bound to have its effect and be reflected in the general business of the country."[5] In November, 1914, a few months after the outbreak of the Great War, the bank moved into its new premises. Osler's earlier expression of "anxiety" over the outlook for 1914 had already been fully and grimly vindicated.

Earlier in 1914, work on the interior of *Casa Loma* had reached the point where Sir Henry and Lady Pellatt were able to occupy it. Many of the upper rooms were still unfinished, and the grand staircase which was to lead from the main hall to the second floor had not yet arrived from Europe. The outbreak of war that summer prevented the shipment, and a makeshift replacement was installed later. Downstairs, however, where Sir Henry's receptions and entertainments took place, the spacious halls and rooms had been completed and lavishly furnished. On one occasion during the war, Lady Eaton was taken on a tour of the castle by its proud owner. As they ghosted down a long corridor together, Sir Henry startled her by exclaiming, "I wish I had another million dollars. What do you think I would do with it?" Without waiting for a reply, he continued, "I'd finish this house —and then I'd die happy."[6]

The "house" was never finished. The soaring costs of maintenance and wartime taxation imposed an insupportable burden upon Sir Henry to which the depression after the Great War added its toll. In the spring of 1923, his city real estate taxes in arrears, Pellatt began selling off his garden and deer park on the north side of Austin Terrace, and the following year, after the death of Lady Pellatt, he abandoned the castle entirely. Since Lady Pellatt had been the legal owner of *Casa Loma* and its contents, his final act, as the executor of her estate, was to organize an auction sale of the furnishings of his fabulous house. Jenkins Art Galleries were placed in charge of the sale, and it took them five days, beginning on Monday, June 23, 1924, to liquidate the collection. For the delectation of the crowds that surged through the place, the auctioneers arranged with the catering service of Hunt's Limited to provide buffet luncheons for the week of the sale. The first session was held in the conservatory, and each day thereafter at a different location in the castle: the dining room, the library, the Napoleon drawing room, and the main hall.[7] Sir Henry attended some of the proceedings himself, and on one occasion rose to point out morosely that a piece of furniture which had just fallen under the hammer had brought less than the amount he had paid to have it refinished a few months before. The proceeds of the auction sale undoubtedly would have been applied against Pellatt's substantial indebtedness, incurred in his wife's name, to The Home Bank of Canada. That institution had collapsed amidst a storm of scandal in August 1923. As a result of the Jenkins sale, the contents of the celebrated house were diffused throughout the country. One piece, however, a heavily ornamented Dresden mirror with candelabra, was bought by Mary Austin and removed to *Spadina*. A furnishing of Lady Pellatt's boudoir, it was said to have come from some great house in Germany.

In the late spring of 1925, gazing out from a third floor window of *Spadina*, Albert Austin reflected upon the transientness of the scene around him—on the Davenport Hill and in his business life as well. His friend and neighbour Sir John Eaton had died suddenly in 1922. Though *Ardwold* was still occupied by his widow and children, Austin missed the vigour and warmth of Sir John's personality. He often recalled the hot summer day in 1919 when both of them had stood bareheaded outside the gates of *Spadina* waiting for the young Prince of Wales to drive by on his triumphal tour of the city. His Royal Highness had played a round of golf at the Lambton Golf Club earlier in the day, and his motorcade was scheduled to pause for a moment at the entrance to *Spadina* for a word of welcome from Eaton and Austin. As soon as the open limousine had stopped, Sir John, who had prepared himself with a big bouquet of roses from his garden, darted forward and thrust them into the surprised prince's arms. He then invited the heir-apparent to visit *Ardwold* for refreshment. An anxious equerry broke in to explain that their schedule could not be disrupted, and after a brief exchange of pleasantries, the royal procession continued on its way to St. Clair Avenue.[8]

To the west of *Spadina*, Austin contemplated *Casa Loma* and its overgrown gardens, now largely stripped of their exotic plants and shrubs. The lights that had blazed from the castle's hundred windows were out; only bleakness and gloom remained. Shortly after the end of the Great War, when Austin drove his Russell automobile downtown each morning, he often paused at the castle to give Sir Henry Pellatt a lift. Pellatt's usual route took him on foot through the Spadina Road Park to Dupont Street where he boarded a streetcar. The Dominion Bank held a mortgage on *Casa Loma* at that time for $200,000.[9] Consequently, on the occasions when Sir Henry shared the front seat with him, Austin's driving style, habitually confident, was transformed into one of hyper-caution. He descended the Walmer Road Hill at a snail's pace, and only when he reached the safety of Davenport Road did he allow the car to gather momentum.

Insofar as The Dominion Bank was concerned, by the late spring of 1925, its links with its earliest days were being rapidly severed. Sir Edmund Osler, who had had a hand in placing the bank's original stock, and who had been appointed a director by James Austin in 1882, had died at *Craigleigh,* his Rosedale house, in August 1924. A towering figure in the financial life of Canada, his death was like the falling of a great tree, rending the forest and intensifying its silence. He was succeeded as president of the bank by Sir Augustus Nanton of Winnipeg, an early partner of Osler, Hammond, and Nanton. Sir Augustus had barely moved to Toronto before he too fell ill, and died in April 1925. Albert Austin, then sixty-nine, had been called upon to fill in for Osler and Nanton during the periods of illness which preceded their deaths. A vice-president of the bank since 1919, the board of directors elected him president in May 1925, to succeed Sir Augustus Nanton.

Following Sir Edmund Osler's death, the presidency of the Canada North-West Land Company (Limited), which Osler had been mainly instrumental in forming in 1893, also devolved upon Albert Austin. The company had been organized to buy nearly 200,000 acres of prairie land from the English holders who had acquired them earlier from the CPR. When it was incorporated, the composition of the company's provisional board of directors offered strong proof that the ancient animosities that divided the financial interests of Toronto and Montreal had at last been overcome.* During Albert Austin's tenure of office as president, the com-

---

*The directors named were: Sir William Van Horne, Sir Donald A. Smith (later Lord Strathcona), Richard B. Angus, Thomas G. Shaughnessy, and James Burnett, all of Montreal, Edmund B. Osler, R. H. Bethune (General Manager of The Dominion Bank), and Osler's partner, Herbert C. Hammond, all of Toronto, William Hendrie of Hamilton, and Thomas Skinner of London, England.

pany's principal activity, as in the past, was the liquidation of its land portfolio. In later years, as exploration for oil and gas intensified throughout the prairie provinces, the mineral rights to many of its lands, which the company had wisely reserved to itself, were to launch the Canada North-West Land Company into the unforeseen role of an explorer and developer of energy resources.

When the shareholders of The Dominion Bank met in January 1926, they were informed by the officers of the bank that the new year was beginning under favourable auspices. "Undue optimism is not justified," C. A. Bogert the general manager cautioned, "but there is certainly a better feeling in the air." The pace of recovery from the post-war depression quickened, and the following year, in January 1927, Albert Austin was able to report to the bank's shareholders that the statement for 1926 was "one of the best that we have ever issued." The profit that year, in fact, was second highest in the bank's history.

Uncertain of the duration of the business recovery that was gaining momentum throughout 1926, Albert Austin and Anne Arthurs accepted an offer from the City of Toronto for the vacant land they owned equally which stretched north from the Castle Frank stream to St. Clair Avenue, between Spadina Road and Russell Hill Road. The property, which was later to be named the Sir Winston Churchill Park, was needed by the city for a reservoir to serve the growing needs of the district. Austin and his sister received $205,000 for the land, and the new reservoir was completed by 1929.[10] Keenly aware that the transaction represented the sale of the last portion of the eighty-acre farm his father had bought in 1866, other than his *Spadina* estate of nearly six acres, Austin used his part of the money from the sale to purchase shares of The Consumers' Gas Company of which he was then president. He distributed them to his family the following Christmas, explaining quietly that they were in effect a gift from their grandfather. "Put money ahead, put worry behind," he used to tell them in a fervent response to his own Victorian upbringing.

In the late twenties, ominous clouds were again forming on the business horizon, though few in the financial community could or wished to recognize them. While from his public utterances there is little evidence that Austin foresaw the severity of the debacle of 1929, his natural caution in the face of rampant public speculation, inculcated in him by his father, had led him largely to consolidate his affairs before the storm broke. Also in 1929, the lights had come on again briefly in *Casa Loma* where an American syndicate, seeking to capitalize on the mood of the hour, offered its guests residential accommodation in an authentic castle. A new orchestra, formed for the dances that were held there, turned out to be the only successful result of the short-lived undertaking: it later attained fame throughout America as Glen Gray's Casa Loma Orchestra.

As the tempo of life accelerated towards the end of the decade, Albert Austin found a measure of tranquillity at his fruit farm at Port Dalhousie, across the lake from Toronto. He had bought the property in 1910; it comprised nearly 80 acres, and extended along the lakefront immediately east of the turning basin which served the old Welland Canal. His eldest son, James Percival, who had been severely shell-shocked while serving overseas during the Great War, managed the farm for a number of years. To reach the place, Austin simply boarded the lakeship *Northumberland* or the *Dalhousie City* at the Toronto Docks, and after a pleasant sail across

Lake Ontario disembarked at "the Port" and arrived at his farm house after a few minutes' walk. It stood on a hill overlooking Port Dalhousie. In the fall of 1930, after the farm house had been closed for the winter, an unexplained fire broke out and gutted the dwelling. It was never rebuilt.

By 1933, crippled with arthritis, Austin was confined to his house in Toronto. On July 5, 1934, in the midst of the Great Depression and as the city bravely celebrated the 100th anniversary of its incorporation, Albert Austin died at *Spadina*.

Early in 1936, Lady Eaton announced her decision to sell *Ardwold* and move to the country near King. The house she had occupied for twenty-five years was demolished, and the eleven-acre property was divided into residential lots through which a new road, Ardwold Gate, was laid out. In a scene that was reminiscent of the famous auction sale at neighbouring *Casa Loma* in 1924, as the house was being wrecked its fixtures were disposed of: the organ was bought by a church; the flooring, panelling, and bookcases of the library were removed by a purchaser and reassembled in his new house in the city; and the bronze and silver chandeliers, even the eavestroughs that were decorated with owls cast in bronze, were sold.[11] By the end of 1936, Sir John Eaton's proud villa, built in the golden age of the great houses on the Davenport Hill, had vanished.

With an empty tract on one side and an abandoned castle on the other, something of the loneliness of the hilltop lands that *Spadina* had known in Confederation times had unexpectedly returned. When James Austin had built the place in 1866, he confidently told his friends that they would see the day when the city would grow to his gates. Like a stubborn matriarch, *Spadina* was destined to witness a good deal more than he had prophesied. After two World Wars, it was to find itself engulfed by a metropolis of over two million people. Once on the remote periphery of the City of Toronto, it came finally to lie at its heart.

Chapter 9

1. This account of the Austin family's arrival in York in 1829 is contained in a memorandum written by James Austin around 1877 which is still extant. Nicholas Flood Davin used it as a basis for his discussion of Austin's career in *The Irishman in Canada* (1877).
2. From James Austin's memorandum, *ibid.*
3. The Consumers' Gas Company had commenced business in Toronto in 1848. Charles Berczy, the postmaster of Toronto, was the first president. See *75 Years, 1848-1923, a History of The Consumers' Gas Company of Toronto,* wherein the names of the directors and their term of office are recorded.
4. Joseph Schull, *100 Years of Banking in Canada, A History of The Toronto-Dominion Bank* (Toronto: Copp Clark Publishing Co. Limited, 1958), p. 43.
5. The Toronto *Saturday Night,* in its issue of January 9, 1915, told the story of *Spadina* in an extensive, illustrated article. Albert W. Austin, who was frequently quoted, discussed the auction and the competing bidders.

Chapter 10

1. J. L. H. Henderson, *John Strachan* (Toronto: University of Toronto Press, 1969), p. 98.
2. The deed of *Spadina* to James Austin was dated February 19, 1866, and was registered on March 16, 1866, as No. 89051, Township of York. The grantors were William Gordon and Stephen Richards, who held earlier mortgages on the property, and William W. Baldwin and his wife. The purchase price was recorded as £3,550.0.0.
3. The Toronto *Saturday Night,* January 9, 1915. Albert W. Austin described the wild pigeons around *Spadina* in his boyhood.
4. A description of the gate-keeper's lodge and the long carriage drive lined with chestnut trees is contained in the Toronto *Saturday Night* article of January 9, 1915.
5. Anne and George Arthurs now had three daughters: Ada Austin (1864), Elma Helen (1866), and Margaret Georgina (1869), who was born a month after her namesake's wedding at *Spadina*—Anne Arthurs and her girls, with their governess, are included in the family group pictured on the *Spadina* lawn around 1873. (See page 113.)

Chapter 11

1. In Victor Ross, *History of the Canadian Bank of Commerce* (Toronto: Oxford University Press, 1920-21), it is stated that James Austin was elected a director of the Commerce in May *1869,* on the withdrawal of Mr. John Macdonald, M.P.P. from the Board. Elsewhere it is stated that Macdonald was a founding director who "Three weeks after his election . . . resigned over some difference of opinion with the Hon. Wm. McMaster, and the directors selected Mr. James Austin to fill the vacant place." The earlier reference to 1869 is an obvious printer's error. Austin did in fact become a director of the Commerce in 1867.
2. McMaster's plan to increase the capitalization of the Canadian Bank of Commerce was pushed through, and the fears of his dissident shareholders were proved groundless as the bank's affairs prospered.
3. Donald Creighton, *Canada's First Century* (Toronto: Macmillan of Canada, 1970), p. 6.
4. Nicholas Flood Davin, *The Irishman in Canada* (1877).
5. See Joseph Schull, *100 Years of Banking in Canada, The Toronto-Dominion*

Bank (Toronto: Copp Clark Publishing Co. Limited, 1958) for a full discussion of the problems besetting the Ontario banks at the time of Confederation.

6. See Dr. O. D. Skelton, *Fifty Years of Banking Service, 1871-1921, The Dominion Bank* (Toronto: Privately printed, 1922) for an informative discussion of the establishment of that bank.

7. See D. C. Masters *Toronto vs. Montreal*, The Canadian Historical Review, 1941.

8. Henry Stark Howland (1824-1902) served as vice-president of the Canadian Bank of Commerce from its inception until, like James Austin, he left and assisted in founding the Imperial Bank of Canada in 1875. He was its first president, holding that office until his death. He was also for many years head of the wholesale hardware firm of H. S. Howland, Sons and Company, Toronto.

9. The incident of Mulock and the bank's gold is recounted in Joseph Schull, *100 Years of Banking in Canada.*

Chapter 12

1. Samuel Nordheimer, however, did accept the presidency of the new Federal Bank of Canada a short time later. It opened its head office in Toronto in 1874. Its affairs became involved in 1887, and it went into voluntary liquidation the following year, after meeting its liabilities in full.

2. William French, *A Most Unlikely Village,* The Corporation of the Village of Forest Hill. Speaking of Nordheimer's *Glenedyth,* L. W. Archer, first clerk and treasurer of Forest Hill when it was formed in 1923, recalled " a very nice falls on the west side of Poplar Plains Road, just opposite the city waterworks pumping station."

3. Perhaps it was a coincidence, or a mark of respect, but James Austin's Dominion Bank closed its books the same afternoon, April 22, 1872, and ended its first fiscal period. Thereafter, its year-end was December 31.

4. J. M. & E. Trout, *The Railways of Canada* (1871) and G. R. Stevens, *Canadian National Railways* (Toronto: Clarke, Irwin & Company Limited, 1960).

5. W. H. Higgins, *The Life and Times of Joseph Gould* (Toronto: 1887), p. 221.

6. A copy of the August 21, 1873 issue of the Port Perry *Ontario Observer* is on file in the Ontario Provincial Archives.

Chapter 13

1. Robert Sobel, *Panic on Wall Street, A History of America's Financial Disasters* (London: The Macmillan Company, 1968).

2. Joseph Schull, *100 Years of Banking in Canada* (Toronto: Copp Clark, 1958).

3. Dr. O. D. Skelton, *Fifty Years of Banking Service, 1871-1921,* (The Dominion Bank, 1922).

4. The Bright-Scadding relationship was drawn closer by the marriage on September 29, 1840, of William Bright to Charlotte Trigge. Bright was an older brother of Jane Bright Scadding. Charlotte died in 1850 and was buried in the Bright-Scadding plot. The unusual name "Trigge" would suggest that Charlotte must have been related to old Mrs. John Scadding, née Millicent Trigge, or "Melicent Triges" as her name appears in T. A. Reed's monograph on the Scaddings (see earlier reference). It is also of interest to note that the St. James' Cemetery records show that the remains of a William Trigge were removed from St. James' Churchyard (no date given) and were reinterred in the Bright-Scadding plot between 1850 and 1855.

The York Directory lists a William "Trigg" as living at George 4th Inn, 10 Market Lane, in 1833-34. He too must have been a relation of old Mrs. Scadding who was given away by Governor Simcoe at her marriage to John Scadding in Dunkeswell Church in Devon, and feted afterwards at a banquet at the Simcoes' *Wolford.*

5. T. A. Reed, *The Scaddings, A Pioneer Family in York,* Papers and Records of the O.H.S., Vol. XXXVI (Toronto, 1944).
6. *75 Years, 1848-1923, A History of the Consumers' Gas Company of Toronto.* (Toronto: Privately printed, 1923).
7. Skelton, *op. cit.*
8. C. Pelham Mulvany, M.A., M.D., *Toronto Past and Present until 1882* (Toronto: 1884).
9. *Ibid.*
10. The North of Scotland Canadian Mortgage Company, Ltd., was organized in Scotland in 1875, primarily to lend money on mortgages in Canada. Its head office was at Canada House, Aberdeen, Scotland, and it maintained offices in Toronto and Winnipeg as well. Along with James Austin, Edmund B. Osler (later Sir Edmund), and R. H. Bethune of The Dominion Bank were active in the early management of the company's Canadian affairs. Augustus M. Nanton (later Sir Augustus) of Osler, Hammond, and Nanton of Winnipeg succeeded them.

Chapter 14

1. J. M. & Edw. Trout, *The Railways of Canada* (1871).
2. While the C.P.R. line had earlier been extended west of Winnipeg a distance of over 100 miles, it awaited its connecting link with Ontario, around the head of Lake Superior, and the laying of steel to the Pacific Coast.
3. The First Annual Statement of The Winnipeg Street Railway Company, dated October 20, 1883, listed the following shareholders whose investment was $1,000 or more:
Duncan MacArthur ($10,750), H. Archibald ($1,000),
A. W. Austin ($8,750), James Austin ($12,750),
E. B. Osler ($10,000), W. J. Baynes ($1,750),
G. B. Spencer ($1,000), R. J. Whitla ($1,000),
T. G. Phillips ($1,000), Hon. A. Boyd ($1,000),
James Henry Austin ($1,000).
4. An episode involving the Pellatt & Osler firm during the "Manitoba Fever" was recalled by the *Toronto Evening Telegram* in its issue of August 5, 1924: ". . . in the early eighties . . . a mob crammed the office of Pellatt & Osler in their eager rush to buy shares in the Qu'Appelle Land Co., promoted by this firm to dispose of about 30 square miles of land that had been purchased from the C.P.R. at $3 an acre; the windows of the office were smashed and other damage done to the furnishings in the scramble that took place for allotments. Oldtimers who recall that scene laugh heartily at the recollection. Clergymen as well as laymen, were in the "crush." One of the former was Rev. Mr. Baldwin of All Saints Church [Arthur Henry Baldwin (1840-1908), a son of Dr. Baldwin's brother, John Spread Baldwin]. He had a most uncomfortable time, having got jammed up against a hot coil and being unable to extricate himself."
5. Thomas Conant, *Upper Canada Sketches,* William Briggs (Toronto, 1898)
6. The writer is indebted to Mr. and Mrs. Ivor E. Brown, Orillia, Ontario, for biographical material relating to the Shrapnel family.
7. Margaret Fry Baldwin (1834-1904) the widow and second wife of William Augustus Baldwin of *Mashquoteh,* entered into an agreement with H. M. The Queen in the right of the Province of Ontario, dated July 2, 1888, which provided that within a year from that date the Ontario Government

would begin to erect the buildings required for the uses and purposes of Upper Canada College. They were to be completed within three years of the date of the agreement at a cost of not less than $100,000.

A deed, covering thirty acres, giving effect to the agreement, was signed by Mrs. Baldwin on April 4, 1889, and the school opened on its new site in 1891.

Subsequently, in 1901, Mrs. Baldwin sold 22½ additional acres to Upper Canada College in its own right. They lay to the west of the lands covered by the earlier sale.

Chapter 15

1. Herbert W. Blake, *The Era of Streetcars in Winnipeg, 1881 to 1955* (Winnipeg: Privately printed 1971).
2. Walter E. Bradley, *A History of Transportation in Winnipeg* (Winnipeg: Privately printed).
3. The five children of Albert and Mary Austin were: James Percival, born in 1885, died unmarried at *Spadina* in 1954; Adèle Mary, born in 1886, died at Toronto a widow (Mrs. Reginald D. Warwick), without issue, in 1968; Albert Edison, born in 1888, died unmarried in Cairo, Egypt in 1913; Anna Kathleen, born in 1892 (married Stanley Seton Thompson in 1912 and their three children are: Patricia Mary Seton (Evans), Esmé Kathleen Seton (Pepall) and Austin Seton Thompson); Constance Margaret, born in 1894, died unmarried at *Spadina* in 1966, a few days after the 100th anniversary of the purchase of *Spadina* by her grandfather, James Austin.

   By the turn of the century the Carlton Street house had been converted into a school, called Havergal Women's College, and a wing had been added. Later, to avoid confusion with the school of the same name in Toronto, it was called Rupertsland. During the Second World War, the enlarged house which by then included a gymnasium, was taken over by the Royal Canadian Air Force. Today, the building with its additions has been demolished, and the property converted into a municipal parking lot.

Chapter 16

1. The right of Nordheimer's coachman to wear a cockade was a matter of whispered dispute. Strict protocolists insisted that the privilege was reserved exclusively for the livery of representatives of the British Crown.
2. William Ewart Gladstone, born in 1809, was actually three years older than James Austin. Moreover, the great statesman outlived him by more than a year, dying at Hawarden, England, on May 19, 1898.
3. A private funeral service was held at *Spadina* for James Austin the following Tuesday morning, March 2, 1897, which was conducted by the Reverend Dr. John Potts and the Reverend James Allen, pastor of the Metropolitan Methodist Church. The entombment service which followed at the family vault at St. James' Cemetery was conducted by the Reverend A. U. DePencier who was then occupying *Davenport,* the old Wells' house near *Spadina.*
4. Isobel Muriel Victoria (Mrs. Holgar Johnson) of Greenwich, Connecticut, was the only child of Ada and Victor Cawthra. Born in 1904, she married Herbert Latham Burns (1906-1936) of Toronto in 1928, and of that marriage, Latham Cawthra Burns (b. 1930) of Toronto is the only child. Mrs. Johnson died at her home in Greenwich on December 18, 1974.

Chapter 17

1. The incident of Winston Churchill's visit to *Craigleigh* is recounted in Anne Wilkinson, *Lions in the Way, A Discursive History of the Oslers* (Toronto, Macmillan Company of Canada Limited, 1956).

2. The Toronto *Evening Telegram,* September 3, 1904.
3. The city of Toronto maintained the "park" until 1953, when responsibility for its care was transferred to the Roads and Traffic Department of Metro Toronto.
4. Frederick Griffin *Major-General Sir Henry Mill Pellatt, C.V.O., D.C.L., V.D. A Gentleman of Toronto 1859-1939.* With a foreword by Rt. Hon. Sir William Mulock, K.C.M.G., P.C., L.L.D., K.C. (Toronto: The Ontario Publishing Company Limited, 1940) See also Bruce West, *Toronto* (Toronto: Doubleday Canada Limited, 1967), p. 180, where the Griffin version is enthusiastically repeated, and see also Katherine Hale, *Toronto, Romance of a Great City* (Toronto: Cassell & Company Limited, 1956), p. 190, for an even more romantic view. She wrote, speaking of Pellatt, "he bought the entire section known as Wells Hill and by the time the castle was ready for occupation he had sold all the vacant land at a profit above what he had spent on the buildings."
5. Lt.-Col. Wells, it will be recalled, purchased the McGill farm lot of 200 acres in 1821, extending from the present Bloor Street to St. Clair Avenue. The term "Wells Hill" has always implied the hilltop portion of his estate.
6. Plan D.1325 was registered by Sir Henry Pellatt on February 23, 1911, in the Registry Office for the Registry Division of West Toronto. Elsewhere in the Wells Hill district proper, in 1916, Pellatt purchased a good-sized lot behind his stables, not for speculation, but for use as an exercise ring for his horses.

Chapter 18

1. Doris Margaret Greene (1896-1961) was married to Major Clifford Sifton, D.S.O., of Toronto, in 1920. Of their marriage there were three children: Elizabeth Ann Jane (Mrs. Llewellyn G. Smith) born 1922, Margaret June (1925-1947), and Michael Clifford (b. 1931).
2. The Arthurs deed to John C. Eaton was dated January 22, 1909, and was registered the next day as No. 61157. The A. W. Austin deed, bearing the same dates, was registered as No. 61158.
3. "Thompson" was an assumed name taken by Alan Cameron, Ernest's ancestor, to conceal his identity when he fled to England after the battle of Culloden. He was a brother or cousin of the famous Evan Cameron of Lochiel who helped raise the clans in the Stuart cause. The "Thompsons" later married into the Seton family which had held the honours of the Earldom of Winton. Though lineally a Cameron, Ernest correctly asserted his right to the surname Seton. See Seton's *Trail of an Artist Naturalist* (Scribner's, New York: 1941).
4. *Memory's Wall, The Autobiography of Flora McCrea Eaton* (Toronto: Clarke, Irwin & Company Limited, 1956).
5. Proceedings of the Forty-third Annual General Meeting of the shareholders of The Dominion Bank, held on January 28, 1914.
6. *Memory's Wall,* op. cit.
7. *Catalogue of the Valuable Contents of Casa Loma,* published by The Jenkins Art Galleries, Toronto and Montreal, covering the sale from June 23 to June 27, inclusive, 1924. Mr. Charles M. Henderson conducted the auction.
8. The Toronto *Globe,* August 28, 1919.
9. The mortgage was discharged in 1922.
10. The Arthurs deed to the city of Toronto was dated May 27, 1926, and was registered on June 1, 1926 as No. 5413. E. M. and A. W. Austin's deed bears the same dates and was registered as No. 5414.
11. *Toronto Daily Star,* September 14, 1936.

INDEX

Adair, Miss Rhona 186
Aikens, Hon. J. C. 133
Aitkin, Alexander 22
Allan, William 72, 74
Allcock, Henry, Chief Justice 41, 49
Ardwold 202, 207, 211, 213
Ardwold Gate 115, 160, 213
Arthur, Professor Eric 84
Arthur, Sir George 88, 90
Arthurs, Ada Austin 176
Arthurs, Anne Jane 118, 125, 145, 170
    176-177, 199, 202, 212
Arthurs, George Allan 118, 125
Arthurs, Margaret Georgina 176, 199
Aunt Maria's Road 82, 115, 125
Austin, Albert William 118
    baptized by Dr. Scadding 145
    junior in The Dominion Bank 152
    joins F. Smith & Co. 153
    goes West 154
    establishes Winnipeg Street Railway
      Company 155
    efforts to electrify his horse-car
      system rejected 162
    trouble with Ross-Mackenzie
      interests 164
    his lawsuit 165-168
    sells Winnipeg Street Railway Co. .. 168
    returns to Toronto 169
    organizes Lambton Golf and
      Country Club 185
    sells property to Sir Henry Pellatt .. 191
    speculates in hilltop real estate 198
    negotiates sale to Sir John
      Eaton 201, 202
    President, Consumers' Gas
      Company 209
    President, The Dominion Bank 211
    President, Canada North-West
      Land Co. 211
    negotiates sale of Sir Winston
      Churchill Park 212
    his farm at Port Dalhousie 212
    his death 213
Austin, James, apprenticed to
    William Lyon Mackenzie 108
    in partnership with Patrick Foy 108
    buys interest in Consumers' Gas
      Company 108
    buys *Spadina* at public auction 111
    builds a new *Spadina* 115

a director of the Canadian Bank of
    Commerce 128
his resignation 133
launches The Dominion Bank 135
buys interest in the Whitby and
    Port Perry Railway 140
his financial beliefs 143
President of Consumers' Gas
    Company 146
co-founder, Queen City Fire
    Insurance Co. 147
builds The Dominion Bank office
    building 147
Chairman, The North of Scotland
    Canadian Mortgage Company 151
interest in Winnipeg Street Railway
    Company 155
sells 40 acres of *Spadina* farm 159
compared to W. E. Gladstone 171
his death 173
Austin, James Henry .. 118, 122, 156, 169
Austin, John Marks 107
Austin, Margaret Louisa 118, 126, 133
    139
Austin, Mary Richmond 156, 167, 187
    203-204
Austin, Susan Bright 117, 118, 174-175
    179, 199
Austin Terrace 115, 125, 159, 194

Baby, James 22, 42
Badajoz 68
Baldwin, Alice 77
Baldwin, Augusta Elizabeth, (wife of
    Hon. Robert Baldwin) 84, 96
Baldwin, Augusta Elizabeth, (daughter
    of Hon. Robert Baldwin) 95, 96
Baldwin, Captain Augustus Warren .. 70
    75, 78, 92, 96, 110, 119
Baldwin, John Spread 39, 46, 76
Baldwin, Margaret Phoebe 83, 91, 92
Baldwin, Mary Warren 72
Baldwin, Phoebe Maria 96
Baldwin, Quetton St. George 54, 82, 83
Baldwin, Robert the Emigrant, arrives
    in York 39
    settles in Clarke Township 40, 42
    proposes marriage to Elizabeth
      Russell 60
    in walk to Baron de Hoen's 72
    his death 75

219

Baldwin, Hon. Robert .. 50, 53, 76, 83, 86
　　　　　　88, 89, 92, 95-98, 115
Baldwin, Robert (son of Hon.
　Robert) 81, 96
Baldwin, William Augustus 54, 76, 83
　　　　　　91, 93, 96, 147
Baldwin, Dr. William Warren, arrives
　in York 39
　settles with his father in Clarke
　　Township 40
　visits *Russell Abbey* 43
　opens school in York 45
　qualifies himself as a lawyer 49
　marries Phoebe Willcocks 50
　buys house from Peter Russell 52
　obtains office of master in Chancery 55
　supports Judge Thorpe 55
　appointed registrar of Court of
　　Probate 60
　the famous will of Elizabeth Russell 63
　Dr. Baldwin as executor and
　　trustee 64
　fights duel 67
　invasion of York 71
　inherits *Spadina* property 68
　anxiety in York 74
　his law office in *Russell Abbey* 77
　builds *Spadina* 77-80
　his dynastic dream 81
　Maria Willcocks' executor 83
　builds new family residence 84
　meets Lord Durham 88
　idea of responsible government 90
　named to Legislative Council 90
　his death and funeral 90
　his will 91
　his *Spadina* door retained by
　　James Austin 115
Baldwin, William Willcocks 69, 98, 110
　　　　　　112, 125
Bank of Montreal 41, 130
Bank of Toronto 109, 136
Bank of Upper Canada 129, 134
Beardmore, George 177
Berczy, William von Moll 33
Bethune, R. H. 135, 171, 175, 211
Bishop Strachan School 188
Blake, S. Hume, Q.C. 166-167, 196
Bobcaygeon 141, 142
Bogert, Clarence A. 177
Bompas & Co. 167
Bonnycastle, Capt. Richard H. 80
Boulton, D'Arcy 62, 66, 68, 70
Boulton, D'Arcy Jr. 79, 137
Boulton, Edith Louise 137-139
Boulton, H. J. 84
Boulton, James 137
Boulton, William Henry 137, 139
Boyd, Mossom 142
Bright, Lewis 48, 118, 145, 174
Brock, Major-General Sir Isaac 71
Brock, Sir Isaac (frigate) 71-72
Brock Street 80, 144

Cameron, Duncan 67
Campbell, Chief Justice Sir William .. 66
Campbell, George H. 164-165
Canada North-West Land Company
　(Limited) 211
Canadian Bank of Commerce 128, 133
　　　　　　136

Canadian Pacific Railway 164, 169
Carnegie, Andrew 144
Cartwright, Richard 46
Casa Loma .. 115, 181, 190-198, 210, 212
Castle Frank 38, 68
Cawthra, Henry 176-177
Cawthra, Henry Victor Holton .. 176, 178
Cawthra, Joseph 69
Cawthra, William 112, 147
Cayley, Hon. William 96
Chambers, John 196
Charivariing explained 49
Chauncey, Commodore 72, 74
Chewett, William 38, 72
Churchill, Winston 189
Clarence Square 80
Clifton House (Niagara Falls) 88, 171
Commercial Bank of Canada 129
Conant, Thomas (*Upper Canada
　Sketches*) 159
Consumers' Gas Company of
　Toronto 108, 128, 146-147, 171-173
　　　　　　209
Cook, Capt. James 21
Coulson, Duncan 177
Craigleigh 188-189, 211
Crawford, John, M.P. 133, 134
Crowther, James 133, 142

Danforth, Asa 38
Davenport 36, 50, 77, 161
Davenport Road 27
Davidson, His Grace, the Most
　Reverend Thomas Randall, D.D.,
　Archbishop of Canterbury 188-190
Dearborn, General 72
Denison, John, manager of *Petersfield*
　　　　　　37, 64, 68
Detlor, John 62
Dominion Bank, The 133, 134-136, 143
　　　　147-148, 155, 171, 176, 201, 211
Dunne, Irene 202
Durham, Earl of 86-89

Eaton, Sir John Craig 201-202, 210-211
Lady Eaton (née Flora McCrea) .. 201, 213
Eaton, Timothy 201
Edwards, John 198
Edward, Prince of Wales 211
Elm Park (Winnipeg) 162-163, 169
Elmsley, John, Chief Justice 35

Farm lots, Township of York 26
Fenians 112, 116
Firth, William 66
Fitzgibbon, Colonel James 86
Forbes, J. Colin, R.C.A. 156
Forbes, Kenneth 121
Fort Niagara 73
Fort Rouillé 71
Fort York 22, 67, 72, 112
Fothergill, Charles 102
Fougères, Capt. Augustin Boiton de .. 48
Foy, Patrick 108, 153, 175
Fulton, Alexander T. 140

Gallows Hill 86
Gearing, E. 194
Gladstone, William Ewart, ... 168, 171
Glenedyth 139, 170, 188, 207

Gooderham, William 109, 147
Gooderham, W. G. 177
Gooderham & Worts 109
Gore, Francis 55, 60, 71
Gould, Joseph 133, 134
Governor-General's Body Guard 194
Grand Trunk Railway 142
The Grange 79, 137, 139, 188
Grant, Alexander 22, 55
Grasett, Rev. H. J. 91, 98, 118
Gray, John 29, 41
Gray, Robert Isaac Dey 36
Greene, Sydney Anson Clifford 176
Griffin, Frederick 197

Haas, Stephen 198
Hagarty, Sir John H. 96
Hamilton, Robert 46, 52, 70
Hammond, Herbert Carlyle 155
Harris, Edwin H. 136
Harris, Lawren, L.L.D. 206
Harvey, Miss Florence L. 186
Havergal College 188
Head, Francis Bond, Sir 80, 86
Heward, Stephen 60
Heyden, Lawrence 93
Hoen, Frederick, Baron de 72-73
Holden, James 133, 135, 139-142, 155
Holy Trinity Church 145
Howland, Henry Stark 136
Howland, Peleg 135, 136
Howland Plains 122
Howland, Sir William 136
Howland, W. H. 147
Hunter, Peter, Lieutenant-General 38
                                    47, 57

Jackson, John Mills 70
Jacques & Hay 121
Jarvis, William 35, 47
Jenkins Art Galleries 210
Joice, Capt. William Hamilton ... 126, 133
                                      139
Judicial Committee of The Privy
   Council (England) 166-168

Kerr, Dawson 156
Kertland, Edwin Henry 190
Kiely, George W. 153
Kiely, W. T. 153
King, E. H. 130-131, 140
King Edward Hotel 189
Krieghoff, Cornelius 158

LaFontaine, Louis H. 90, 92
Lambton Golf and Country Club .. 185-187
                                      211
Larchmere 40, 69
Large, John 70, 84
Law Society of Upper Canada .. 66, 91, 98
                                      126
Lee, Walter Sutherland 133
Lennox, Edward J. 194, 198, 207
Loring, Robert Roberts 50
Lovekin, Richard 39
Lind, Jenny 96, 137
Littlehales, Edward Baker, Brigade
   Major and secretary 21
Lyon, George S. 185, 187

MacArthur, Duncan 155

Macdonald, Sir John A. .. 95-96, 154, 172
Macdonald, John (Merchant Prince)
                                 109, 133
Macdonnell, John 66-68
Mackenzie, Sir William .. 164, 168, 196
Mackenzie, William Lyon .. 29, 69, 85, 108
Maclean, Lt. Col. John B. 198
MacNab, Allan Napier 86
Macaulay, Judge James B. 84
Maitland, Sir Peregrine 54
Marther, Samuel 30
Mashquoteh 91-92, 160
Massey, Vincent 206
Mavor, Professor James 177
McGill, John, Ensign and Adjutant 27
                                  35, 36, 50
McMaster, Hon. William 128, 131, 147
Mead, Joseph H. 128, 147
Melbourne, Lord 86, 88
Metcalfe, Sir Charles 90
Metropolitan Methodist Church .. 177, 204
                                      209
Michie & Company 140
Michie, James 140
Midland Railway 141-142
Millbrook 40, 69, 84
Moore, Thomas 75
Morgan, J. Pierpont 188-190
Mountain, Bishop Jacob 46, 71
Mowat, Sir Oliver 146
Mulock, Hon. Sir William .. 134-136, 177
                                  194, 197

Nanton, Sir Augustus 171, 211
Newark (Niagara-on-the-Lake) .. 22, 29-30
Nordheimer, Samuel 135, 137-139, 156
                          170, 177, 188, 207
Nordika, Madame Lillian 177
North of Scotland Canadian
   Mortgage Co. 151

Oaklands 109
Ontario Ladies College, Whitby 159
Orphans Home 96
Osgoode, William, Chief Justice of
   Upper Canada and member of
   Executive Council 22, 27
Osler, Sir Edmund 134, 155, 171, 175
                          188-190, 209, 211
Osler and Hammond 155
Otter, Lt. Col. William D. 177

Papineau, Louis-Joseph 86
Park lots, Township of York 23
Pellatt and Pellatt 155
Pellatt, Henry Sr. 134, 155
Pellatt, Sir Henry Mill .. 161, 177, 190-198
                                  210-211
Pellatt, Lady Mary 210
Perley, George H. 187
Petersfield farm 36-38
Pike, General Zebulon 72
Playter, Ely 48
Playter, George 27
Poplar Plains Road 38
Port Dalhousie 212
Powell, Dr. Grant 74
Powell, Judge William Dummer 84
Puisaye, Comte de 39

Queen City Fire Insurance Company
147, 149-150
Queen's Own Rifles of Canada 116, 194
Queen's Rangers 22

Rathnelly 129
Ravenswood 125, 170, 176-177, 201, 202
Ridout, Samuel 60, 62
Ridout, Thomas 27, 60, 62, 71
Riel's Rebellion 169
Rigby, Sir John 167-168
Robertson, William 22
Robinson, Christopher, father of
    John Beverley Robinson 23, 30
Robinson, John Beverley 23, 47, 70, 71
Robinson, Dr. Percy J., (author of
    *Toronto During the French
    Régime*) 81
Rolph, Dr. John 86
Rolph, Thomas Taylor 190
Ross, Aaron 133-134
Ross, James 164
Ross, Hon. John 95, 109, 133, 136
Ross, Lauder, and Mulock 133
Royal Canadian Bank 128, 135
Royal Canadian Volunteer Regiment .. 47
Russell Abbey 33, 39, 77, 82
Russell, Elizabeth, settles at Newark .. 29
    moves to York 33
    describes Dr. Baldwin's visit to
        Adjutant McGill's 50
    intervenes between Willcocks and
        St. George 52
    her opinion of Phoebe Willcocks .. 54
    inherits her brother's estate 60
    her illness 61
    she makes her will 62
    flees *Russell Abbey* 72
    her dejection 74
    sells lot *(Russell Hill)* to Capt.
        A. W. Baldwin 75
    her death 80
Russell Hill 76, 78, 119
Russell, Peter, member Executive
    Council 22
    his personal land grants 26
    letter to John Gray, his career 29
    settles at Newark 29
    buys Christopher Robinson's house
        in York 30
    moves to York and writes to
        Simcoe 33
    Russell Abbey described 33
    his administration 59
    his Crown grants 36
    letter to Osgoode 37
    builds roads 37
    seeks appointment as lieutenant-
        governor 38
    entertains the Baldwins 39
    expands his property in *Spadina*
        enclave 42
    sells house to Dr. Baldwin 53
    letter to Charles Willcocks 56
    his death 59
    his will 60
St. Alban's Cathedral 190
St. George, Laurent Quetton de .. 45, 72, 74
St. George Street 46
St. James' Cemetery 145, 146

St. James' Church (Cathedral) 59, 90
    107, 118, 126, 190
St. Lawrence Hall .. 96, 107, 137, 175-176
St. Martin's Rood Cemetery 59, 63, 82
    84, 96, 146
Sampson, Theophilus 83
Scadding, Jane Bright 145
Scadding, John, father of Rev. Henry
    Scadding 23
Scadding, Reverend Henry, D.D. 23, 54
    56, 57, 63, 65, 144-146
Scadding, Henry Simcoe 145
Scadding, Millicent Trigge 145
Scadding, Sophia 175
Selkirk, Thomas Douglas, Earl of 51
Seton, Ernest Thompson 202-203
Shank, Capt. David 27, 49
Shaw, Capt. Aeneas 27
Sheaffe, Major General Roger 72
Sherwood, Judge L. P. 84
Shrapnel, E. S., A.R.C.A. 157-159
Simcoe, Francis 68
Simcoe, John Graves, establishes
    York 21
    his settlement instruction 26
    leaves York 33
    appointment as governor-general
        rumoured 38
    his death 54
Sir Winston Churchill Park 160, 212
Smith, David William 35, 38
Smith, Hon. Sir Frank .. 128, 135, 152-154
    171, 172, 177
Smith, Professor Goldwin 188
Smith, Larratt W. 144, 147
Spadina Avenue 80, 144
Spadina Golf Club 181, 183
Spadina Road Park 181, 195-197, 209
    211
Strachan, Rev. John 46, 51, 55, 67, 70
    73-74, 79, 84, 86, 112
Stuart, Rev. Okill 71
Sugar Loaf Hill 43, 75, 138
Sullivan, Barbara 76
Sullivan, Daniel, Jr. 77
Sweatman, The Right Reverend
    Arthur, Anglican Bishop of
    Toronto 177, 188
Sydenham, Lord 89

Tandragee, County Armagh 107
Taylor, Lieut. Thomas 67
Thorpe, Judge Robert 55
Toronto Philharmonic Society 138, 177
    204
Toronto Street Railway 153
Toronto Symphony Orchestra 204
Torrington, Dr. F. H. 177, 203
Tovell, Harold 206
Tupper, Sir Charles 167

University of Toronto 95, 188
Upper Canada College 75, 91, 116, 122
    160, 183
Vanderbilt, Cornelius 143
Van Horne, Sir William 164, 211
Victoria Square 80

Wakefield, Coate & Company 107
    109-111
Wellington, Duke of 87, 90, 159

Wells Hill 197
Wells, Lt. Col. Joseph 50, 68, 93
Whitby and Port Perry Railway .. 140-142
                                                          151
White, John 30, 41
Whitla, R. J. 155
Widmer, Dr. Christopher 83
Willcocks, Charles 23, 35, 36, 56, 69
Willcocks, Eugenia 35, 48
Willcocks, Margaret Phoebe 35, 69
Willcocks, Maria 35, 54, 68, 69, 77, 80
                                                          83
Willcocks, Phoebe 35, 54
Willcocks, William, provisionally
   granted the later *Spadina* property .. 23
   builds house in York 35
   appointed magistrate and post-
      master 35

grant of *Spadina* property confirmed 35
his settler's cabin 36, 160
supports Judge Henry Allcock 41
resigns from postmastership 42
his daughter Eugenia marries 48
his windows broken 49
supports Judge Thorpe 55
proposes marriage to Elizabeth
   Russell 55
his will 68
his death 70
Winnipeg Electric Street Railway
   Company 165
Winnipeg Street Railway Company
                                       155-156, 162-166
Women's Musical Club of Toronto 205
Worthington, John 133
Yeadon Hall 176, 178